HIPPOCRENE CONCISE DICTIONARY

BEMBA
BEMBA-ENGLISH/ENGLISH-BEMBA

D1571799

HIPPOCRENE CONCISE DICTIONARY

BEMBA
BEMBA-ENGLISH/ENGLISH-BEMBA

Rev. E. Hoch

HIPPOCRENE BOOKS, INC.
New York

© E. Hoch, 1960
Hippocrene Books Paperback Edition, 1998

For information, address:
HIPPOCRENE BOOKS
171 Madison Avenue
New York, NY 10016

ISBN 0-7818-0630-5

Cataloging-in-Publication Data available from the Library of Congress.

Printed in the United States of America.

PREFACE

This pocket dictionary has been compiled to help Bemba-speaking people to study English and English-speaking people to study Bemba. In order to simplify this study, only words in every day use have been included.

The English-Bemba part of the dictionary has been illustrated by many phrases. The aim of these phrases is: (1) to help beginners to pick up some colloquial expressions, (2) to explain the difference in meaning — if there is any — of several Bemba words given' to an English word.

I am greatly indebted to the following for their kind assistance:-

Rev. E. Brencher, W.F. — correction of English.

Rev. F. Tanguy, W.F., O.B.E. — correction of Bemba.

L. D. E. F. Vesey-FitzGerald, Esq., Principal Scientific Officer, International Red Locust Control Service. — Lists in the appendix containing names of trees, birds and snakes.

G. H. Wilson, Esq., M.B.E., Director of the Publications Bureau, Lusaka, and his staff. — a great deal of most useful advice.

CONTENTS

PRELIMINARY NOTES

1. The Bemba Alphabet:

- The letters: r, q, v, x, z, do not exist.
- The letters: d, g, j, exist only in connection with 'n', e.g.: nda; nga; njelwa.
- b   in connection with 'm' is pronounced as in the English word 'tumbler'; otherwise it is a soft 'w'.
- c   is always pronounced as 'ch' in the English word 'church'.
- ch is only maintained in proper nouns; e.g. Chitimukulu; Chinsali.
- h   is only used in combination with the letter 's', as 'sh' and is pronounced as the English 'sh', but there is always a slight i-sound in it; e.g. shani is pronounced as shyani.
- ŋ   is a letter which is special to Bemba. It is pronounced as 'ng' in the English word 'singing'.
- The vowels are the cardinal vowels a, e, i, o, u.
   The English vowels more or less corresponding to the Bemba vowels are:
      a as in far, father
      e as in the first sound of the diphthong "ei" in **mate**
      i as in see (but without diphthong)
      o as in molest
      u as in boot
- There are three diphthongs in Bemba: ai, au, ay, They are pronounced like the separate vowels.

2. Notes for the use of the dictionary:

- The prefix of the plural of the Bemba noun is given in brackets after the nouns; e.g. muntu (ba), i.e. bantu.
   Some nouns form the plural by adding a prefix to the unchanged singular. This is shown in the dictionary by a dash added to the plural prefix; e.g. cibusa (ba–), i.e. bacibusa.
   Nouns which are not followed by a prefix are generally used either in the singular or in the plural only; e.g. 'buci' which is used in singular only, or 'male' which is used in plural only.
- Nouns, adjectives and the inf. of all verbs can have preprefixed the vowel of their prefix, e.g. 'umuntu' instead of 'muntu'. These preprefixes have been

ommitted in the dictionary for the sake of a clearer classifying of the words.

- All adjectives are shown with three dots in front, which indicate the missing prefix.
- A list of the prefixes according to the different classes of nouns is given in the appendix in TABLE I.
- All verbs are shown with a dash in front; e.g. –cita This is the stem of the verb.
- The modified stem is always given between brackets after the verb, e.g. (citile).
- The Bemba verb can be extended in many ways. The principal extended forms are: the applicative, causative, completive, frequentative, intensive, passive, reciprocal, reflexive, reversive, stative, etc., etc. It is not in the scope of a pocket dictionary to give all the extended forms of each verb. They are given only of those verbs which either have a different meaning from that of the simple verb or are among those others which do not follow the general rules for making extended forms as laid down in the grammars, but which are of frequent use.
- Different meanings of one word are numbered. Different expressions of the same meaning of a word are separated by a semicolon.

SIGNS

Three dots in front of a word make the word known as an adjective.

A dash in front of a word makes it known as a verb.

A dash standing alone means that the previous word is to be repeated.

A circumflex on top of a vowel makes the vowel long.

/ between two words means 'or'.

A colon indicates that an example is given.

+ in front of a noun indicates that the noun belongs to the 'li–' class, (see Appendices T. I, VII).

ABBREVIATIONS

abbr.	abbreviation
adj.	adjective
adv.	adverb
adv. adj.	adverbial adjective
aux. v.	auxiliary verb
cf.	see, compare
cj.	conjunction
dim.	diminutive form
e.g.	for instance
etc.	and so on
fig.	figurative
i.e.	that is
imp.	imperative
inf.	infinitive
int.	intensive
inter. pr.	interrogative pronoun
interj.	interjection
lit.	literally
math.	mathematics
n.	noun
neg.	negative
num.	numeral
pers. pr.	personal pronoun
pg.	page
pr.	pronoun (demonstrative)
prep.	preposition
rel. pr.	relative pronoun
s.	singular
subj.	subjunctive
T.	TABLE
v. appl.	applicative extension of the verb
v. caus.	Causative extension of the verb
v.i.	intransitive verb
v. rec.	reciprocal extension of the verb
v. red.	reduplicated extension
v. refl.	reflexive extension of the verb
v. rev.	reversive extension of the verb
v. stat.	stative extension of the verb
v.t.	transitive verb

Part I

BEMBA — ENGLISH

— A —

A–, he, she, it, cf. T. II, 2.
aba, these, cf. T. III.
–abika (abike), soak; put under water.
abo, 1. those, cf. T. III. 2. whom, cf. T. IV.
...abo, their (referring to nouns of class "mu/ba").
–abuka (abwike), cross water. –abuka panshi, wade across. –abuka pa bulalo, cross over a bridge.
–abula (abwile), take out of water after soaking.
–abusha (abwishe), carry or ferry across.
abwe, interj. of impatience: "nonsense"; "stop"; etc.
adeleshi (ma–), address.
–afwa (afwile), help; aid; assist; support; do a favour.
–afya (afishe), 1. v.t. annoy; bother; molest. 2. v.i. be difficult; ...afya, trouble-some.
–afyanya (afyenye), 1. v. rec. of –afya. 2. v.t. dispute; quarrel.
aka, this, cf. T. III.
–aka (akile), blaze; take fire.
–akana (akene), v. rec. divide; share.
–akanya (akenye), v.t. distribute; portion out.
ako, that, cf. T. III.
...akwe, his; hers; its.
ala, 1. interj. of surprise: "is it so!" 2. interj. of impatience: "stop"; etc.
alai, interj. of strong negation; "not at all!"
–alasha (aleshe), make known; publish.

ale, pl. alêni or alwêni, interj. "come on"; "go on!"
alufu (ba–), thousand.
–aluka (alwike), v.i. become different; alter; vary; change; turn.
–alula (alwile), v.t. change; alter; vary; translate; interpret. –alule mbuto, make crop rotation; graft.
–amba (ambile), 1. v.t. slander; backbite; speak ill of. 2. v.i. begin; start; commence.
–ambakala (ambakele), look in vain for.
–ambukila (ambukile), contaminate; infect; be contagious.
–ambukisha (ambukishe), pass on or spread (a disease); infect.
–ambula (ambwile), take from; ambulo bulwêle, catch a disease.
–ambulula (ambulwile), skim (cream, etc.).
–amfula (amfwile), creep; crawl (like a child).
–amina (amine), protect crops from birds or animals.
–ampa mu mulandu (ampele), interfere or involve in a case. –ampo mulandu umbi, interrupt.
–ampana (ampêne), 1. v.t. help one another. 2. v.i. be very friendly/intimate.
–ampanya bantu (ampenye), reconcile people.
–ampula (ampwile), same as –ampa. –ampula mu milandu ya bêne,. intrude in other one's matters.
...anakashi, female (of human being).
–ananya (anenye), divulge;

broadcast.
...andi, my; mine.
–andike mfuti (andike), aim a gun at.
–andula (andwile), take away; remove.
–anga (angile), dance for joy.
–angala (angêle), play; amuse oneself. –angale fyabipa, fornicate.
–angalila (angalile), supervise; watch over.
–angasha (angeshe), play with something; amuse.
–angufyanya (angufyenye), v.i. hurry up; make haste; hasten; accelerate; be quick.
–anguka (angwike), 1. same as –angufyanya. 2. be light in weight; thin; fine (of cloth); be easy; active.
–angusha (angwishe), make light, easy, quick; facilitate.
–angula (angwile), trim.
ani, pl. bâni, who? whom? –anika (anike), spread out to dry or air.
–anka (ankile), catch something thrown.
–ankula (ankwile), answer back; join in a song.
–ansa (anshile), spread out. –anse tebulo, lay the table. –anso busanshi, make the bed.
–ansha (anshishe), overcome; defeat; be beyond one's power/imposible.
–ansula (answile), roll up.
–anuna (anwine), take away things spread out; remove.
apa, here.
apa pêne, just here.
apabula, without.
apakalamba, very much;

greatly.
apatali, from afar.
apo, 1. cj. whereas; whenever. 2. pr. there, cf. T. III. 3. adv. as much as.
apo pêne, 1. cj. at once; suddenly; immediately; straight away; already; 2. pr. just there.
–asama (aseme), gape; open the mouth.
–asasa (asashile), pant.
–ashima (ashime), borrow; lend; hire.
–asuka (aswike), answer; reply.
–asukila (asukile), v. appl. of –âsuka.
ata, interj. of disapproval; "leave it"; "stop", etc. ata sê, int. of ata.
atemwa, or; otherwise; else; lest. atemwa ... atemwa, either ... or.
ati or atini, interj. of asking approval: "is it not so?"
–aula (awile), hail, welcome. –aulo tupundu, utter shrill cries of welcome. –aulo mwau, yawn.
...aume, male (of human being).
awe, interj. of refusal: "no".
awi, same as awe, of contempt.
aya, these, cf. T. III.
ayo, 1. those, cf. T. III. 2. which; what, cf. T. IV.

— B —

Ba, 1. they, them. cf. T. III. 2. of, cf. T. I.
–ba, be.
–baba (babile), itch; singe;

roast (groundnuts).
–**babatala** (babatéle), be
level; flat; stoop.
–**babilile cipinda** (babilile),
make a fireguard.
bafa (ma), bath.
–**baka** (bakile), care for
something.
–**ba ku** (or kuli), depend
on.
–**bala** (balile), first. *pa kubala,* at first.
–**balala** (balele), be spotted;
be of different colours.
–**balâlika** (balalike), paint
in different colours; spot.
–**balika** (balike), shine as
sun or stars.
–**balikila** (balikile), bless.
balo (ba–), thy husband.
–**balula** (balwile), blossom.
balya, those yonder, cf. T.
III.
–**bamba** (bambile), 1. kill
game. 2. –*bambe ŋoma,* fix
a skin on a drum.
bambeni, greeting, cf. T.
VII.
–**ba na,** be bound to; must;
have.
–**ba nga,** be as if; look as if;
seem; to be like.
–**banga** (bangile), tie poles
of a wall together.
–**bangilila** (bangilile), start
early; do first; begin with;
anticipate.
–**bangula** (bangwile), extract; pull out (thorns,
etc.).
bâni, pl. of ani, who?
whom?
bantu, pl. of muntu; people.
baomba, pl. of muomba,
choir.
–**bâsa** (bâshile), plane;
carve.
bati or batini, pl. of ati.

–**batisha** (batishe), baptize.
–**beya** mushishi (beyele), cut
hair. –*beyo lukuso,* cut all
hair. –*beyo mwefu,* shave.
–**bêbêta** (bëbête), peer at.
–**beka** (bëkele), shine;
glitter; be bright.
–**bêla** (bêlele), 1. obey;
observe; fit; suit. 2. be
situated.
–**belama** (belëme), v.i. hide;
conceal oneself.
–**belamika** (belamike), v.t.
hide; conceal.
–**belebensa** (belebensele), be
queer; mischievous; un-
manageable; peculiar;
strange.
–**beleka** (beleke), give birth
to the firstborn.
–**belela** (belele), be accustomed; tame. –*belela ne
calo,* be accustomed to a
country. –*belelo luse,* forgive; have mercy; excuse
somebody.
–**belêlela** (belêlele), be
everlasting, perpetual, immortal; remain for ever.
–**belenga** (belengele), read;
check.
–**belesha** (beleshe), v.t.
adapt; tame; accustom;
make familiar.
bemba (ba–), lake; sea.
bemba mukalamba, ocean.
–**bembuka** (bembwike),
commit adultery.
bena, pl. of mwina, people
of.
–**benda** (bendele), talk incorrectly; make mistakes
in talking.
–**bendêla** (ba– or mendêla),
flag; banner.
–**bendêla** (bendële), creep
like a hunter.
benye (ba–), relic of a

deceased chief.

–bepa (bepele), cheat; deceive. *–bepo bufi,* lie; tell a falsehood.

–bepesha (bepeshe), blame falsely; calumniate; belie.

beseni (ma–), basin.

...bi, bad; ugly; nasty; obscene; foul.

Bibilia, (ba), Bible. (also Cipingo).

–bifya (bifishe), sin; do wrong.

–bîka (bikile), v.t. put aside; lay; place; save (e.*g.* money). *–bikapo* (bikilepo), add; continue; persevere.

–bîkila (bikile), v. appl. of **–bika** *–bikila mani,* lay eggs.

–bikula (bikwile), announce, used in the expression: *–bikule mfwa,* announce the death of somebody.

–bila (bilile), sew.

–bile mbila, announce; declare; publish banns; make proclamation.

–bilauka (bilawike), 1. v.i. boil; boil over. 2. v.i. turn all round.

–bilaula (bilawile), v. caus. of –bilauka.

...bili, two; double; a pair of.

–bilikisha (bilikishe), shout after somebody.

–bilulula (bilulwile), unstick; unsew.

–binda (bindile), bar; forbid. *–binda ku,* suspend from.

–bîpa (bîpile), be bad; ugly; nasty; foul; obscene.

–bîpila (bipile), 1. v. appl. of –bipa. 2. be harmful.

...bishi, green; unripe; uncooked; fresh; raw (fruit, etc.).

bobo wa kanwa (ba–), indiscreet person; babbler.

–bola (bolele), rot; decay; be rotten; decayed.

boma (ma–), government district headquarters.

–bomba (bombele), 1. work. 2. be wet; damp; moist; soaked.

bombwe (ba–), biceps of the arm.

–bomfya (bomfeshe), v. caus. of –bomba. 1. *– bubi bubi,* make bad use of; 2. make wet.

bonaushi wastage; destruction.

bongobongo (ba–), brain.

–bongoloka (bongolweke), v.i. crumble; fall into pieces or ruin.

–bongolola (bongolwele), v. caus. of –bongoloka. *–bongolole cibili,* break up a kiln.

–bonsa (bonsele), fade; wilt; wither; be tender; soft; feeble; weak.

–bosa (bosele), bark; bark at.

bôwa, mushroom. pl. *môwa,* kinds of mushroom.

buba, plant for making fish-poison.

bubâni, incense.

bube, larva.

bubenshi, white ant.

bubi, 1. n. wickedness; evil; harm; disadvantage. 2. adv. badly. *bubi bubi,* very badly.

buce, n. smallness. *ubuce,* adv. adj. tiny.

bucende, adultery. *mwana wa mu bucende (ba),*

bastard. *–cito bucende,* commit adultery.

bucenême, adv. wide open.

bucenjeshi, deceit; cleverness; fraud.

bûci, honey.

bucibinda, skill; cleverness; craft; art; handicraft.

bucibola impotence of man.

bucibulu, dumbness.

bucibusa, friendship. *–bikana bucibusa,* start a friendship.

bucindami, dignity; respectability.

bucinga, game-pit.

bucipena, madness.

bucishinka, honesty.

bucûshi (ma), suffering; passion; affliction; pain.

bufi, lie; falsehood. *–bepo –bufi (bepele),* v.t. lie. *–bwesho bufi (bweseshe),* retract a lie. *–fwa bufi,* pretend to be dead. *–lapo bufi,* commit perjury. *–soso bufi,* same as *–bepa, ca bufi,* false. *pali bufi,* all the more; particularly; especially. *wa bufi,* liar.

bufuba, jealousy.

bufukême, kneeling position.

bufuma cûmi, truth. *–ba no bufuma cumi,* be truthful.

bufumo, thickness; width; breadth.

bufumu, chieftainship; kingdom; reign.

bufundi, same as bucibinda.

bufyashi, parenthood.

bufyompo, marrow (of the bone).

–bûka (bûkile), wake up; rise or get up from bed; start again (v.g. of school). *–bûke ciwa,* change one-self into an evil spirit after death.

–buka (bukile), evoke spirits; divine.

bukaêle, innocence.

bukafundisha, job of a teacher.

bukalamba, old age; greatness in all senses.

bukâkâshi, chicanery.

bukali, pain; severity; anger; ferocity.

bukambone, bearing of witness.

bukankâla, wealth; prosperity.

bukapitao, job of a foreman.

bukasha, longing for food, (especially meat, fish.)

bukashana, maidenhood; youth of girl.

bukata, priviledge, respectability. *–ikala bukata,* have a honourable position.

bukaya, citizenship.

buko (mako), the "in-laws"; parents-in-law.

bukoloci, very old age.

bukombe, message.

bukonge, sisal; fibre of –.

bukope, debt; loan.

bukota, 1. advocate; intercessor; helper. 2. feminine sex.

bukote, old age.

bukilishityani, Christianity. *bukilishityani bukilishityani,* in a Christian way.

bukula, millet field; garden.

bukulu, width; breadth; largeness. *–lêpa mu bukulu,* be bulky. *–ba pa bukulu,* be in advanced pregnancy.

bukumanino. (ma) place where things meet; junction.

bukumanisho, perfection.

bukupeme, adv. flat on the ground.

bukushi, small apron worn by women as underskirt.

bukwakwa indiscretion; slanderous tongue.

bukwe, (ba–), brother-in-law; sister-in-law.

bukwebo (ma), barter; trade.

bula pl. mala, bowel; intestine.

–bula (bulile), lack; need; fail.

–bûla (bûlile), take; fetch.

bulalo (ma), bridge.

bulamba, energy.

bulambo, platform for smoking meat or fish.

bulamu, laziness. *wa–* lazy person.

bulanda, poverty; misery; sadness; grief; sorrow; calamity. *ca bulanda,* it is sad. *–lilo bulanda,* weep for grief.

bulangeti (ma), blanket.

bulangisho, show.

Bulaya, Europe.

bulebe, paralysis.

bulembo, habit of smoking.

bulendo, journey; tour.

buleshi, art of nursing; education.

–bulila (bulile), be missing; be incomplete.

bulili, greediness; gluttony.

bulilishi, sadness.

bulimbo, birdlime.

bulimi, agriculture.

bulo (malo), sleeping place.

bulobo (ma), hook; fish-hook.

buloshi, witchcraft; sorcery.

–bulubusa (bulubushile), stammer; lisp.

bulubushi, redemption.

–bulukuta (bulukwite), v.i.

thunder.

bulûlu, hardheartedness.

bululu (ba–), relative.

–buluma (bulwîme), growl; roar; purr.

bulumendo, youth of boy.

bulundo, increment.

–bulunga (bulungile), 1. make round. 2. suppose.

bulungani, immodesty.

bulungu (ma), bead.

bulunshi, hunt (with gun, etc.).

bulwani, enmity; hostility.

bulwele (ma), disease; illness; sickness. *bulwêle bwa kushipula,* sleeping sickness. – *bwa cifyalilo,* hereditary disease. – *bwa lwambu,* contagious disease.

bulwi, fight; fighting mood.

bulya, that yonder, cf. T. III.

bumama, sisterhood.

–bumba (bumbile), create; mould; shape.

bumfisolo, mu –, secretly.

bumfutete, backwards.

bumi, life. *–ba no bumi,* be alive. *bumi bwa pe,* eternal life.

bumukubwa, the being in charge.

bumulungu, divine nature; divinity.

bumuntu, human nature; humanity.

bumunyina, brotherhood.

bunangani, laziness; idleness.

–bunda (bundile), v.i. capsize; sink.

–bundama (bundeme), be upset; cloudy; stormy.

–bundwa (bundilwe), be flooded; inundated.

bune with ta pa, how nice.

bunga, flour; powder; meal.

buŋumba, sterility.

bunkalwe, harshness; hard-heartedness; brutality; cruelty; verocity.

bunkole, state of being a prisoner.

buno, this here, cf. T. III.

bunonshi, commerce; trade. – *bwa mu bantu*, slave trade.

–bunsha (bunshishe), v.t. capsize; sink.

bunte, evidence; testimony.

buntu, humanity.

bununko, odour; smell.

bunwenshi, drunkenness.

bunya, infancy; first childhood.

bupatilisho, priesthood.

bupe, gift; present; generosity. *–ba no bupe*, be charitable. *wa bupe*, a generous person.

bupena, craziness; madness.

bupete, docility; obedience; submission. *–ba no bupete*, be docile; willing; submissive.

bupîna, poverty.

bupingushi, judgement.

bupofu, blindness.

bupulumushi, immorality; fornication; perversity. *–cito –*, commit fornication.

bupumbu, stupidity; folly; silliness; lack of intelligence.

bupuba, stupidity.

bupûpu, theft; robbery.

bupusano, difference.

bupusaushi, inattention; carelessness.

bupyani, inheritance; patrimony.

busa, adv. lavishly; profusely.

busafya, uncleanliness; un-tidiness.

busaka, neatness; tidiness; beauty; elegance; charm; order.

busaka busaka, adv. neatly; tidy; carefully.

busâlo (ma), fur.

busâli, filth; dirt; excrement.

busangu, treason; apostasy.

busanku, negligence; carelessness. *–ba no –*, be careless; negligent.

busanshi (ma), bed.

busanso, accident, danger, invasion, death.

busenême, adv. backwards; on the back. *–lala busene-me*, to lie on the back.

busha, slavery.

–bûsha (bûshishe), 1. awaken. 2. ask advise; consult; inquire. *–busho lubuli*, provoke a fight.

bushe, interj. of introducing a question.

bushikofu, bishopric.

bushiku, day; night; date. *bushiku*, adv. at night; during the night. *bulya bushiku*, day before yesterday; day after tomorrow. *bushiku bwantanshi*, previous day. *bushiku bushilile kantu*, unexpectedly; on an unexpected day. *bushiku bwakonkapo*, the following day, *bushiku bubiye*, same as bushiku bwakonkapo. *bushiku nshi*, on which day? *bushiku pakati*, midnight. *cila bushiku*, every day; each day; daily.

bushilika, soldiering. *–ingilo –*, enlist as a soldier.

bushilu, madness; epilepsy; craziness.

bushimbe, widowhood; unmarried state; celibacy.
bushishi, thread.
busôlo (ma), tail of snake; claw of python.
busokololo, Apocalypse.
busuma, bounty; kindness.
busulwishi, commerce.
busungu, venom of snake; poison.
buta (mata), bow. *buta bwa mfuti,* trigger of a gun.
–bûta (bûtile), be white; clear; light in colour; clean. *–bûta tûtu,* be very white, etc.
butakatifu, sanctity; holiness.
butala (ma), grain bin; barn.
butali, height; length.
butali, height; length. *butali bwa câlo,* height of a country, altitude. *butali panshi,* depth.
butanda (ma), reed-mat. *–paso –,* make a mat.
butani, meanness. *wa butani,* miser.
butanshi, sharp pain as of snakebite.
butekeshi, administration; government.
butobatoba, brutality.
butonge, cotton plant thread; twine.
–butuka (butwîke)), run; run away from; flee.
–butukila (butukîle), run to for protection.
–butuluka (butulwike), be whitish; greyish; fair (in colour).
bûtulushi, stoutness; corpulence.
butumpe, stupidity; silliness. *–cito butumpe butumpe,* act foolishly.

butungulushi, leadership.
butûtu, savageness; rusticity; bad manners.
buwelewele, silliness; folly; stupidity; foolishness.
buyantanshi, progress; development.
buyo, destination; end of a journey.
bwa, prep. of. cf. T. I.
bwabi, soaked cassava.
bwaca, it is dawning.
bwafya, difficulty; hardship; trouble. *–ba no bwafya,* be troublesome.
bwaice, childhood; *fya –,* childish.
bwaila, nightfall; dusk; it is getting dark.
bwali, mush.
bwalwa, beer, fig. mâlwa, big quantity of beer.
bwamba (mâmba), fishing weir.
bwamba, nakedness; naked.
bwana (ba–), master.
bwanakashi, womanhood.
bwanga, witchcraft sorcery; magic; charm; spell. *–kweleko muntu bwanga,* bewitch. *–pando bwanga,* practice witchcraft.
bwangu, quickly. *bwangu bwangu,* very quickly; suddenly.
bwâto (mâto), boat; canoe; ship.
bwaume, manhood.
–bwekelapo (bwekelepo), return; go back.
–bwekeshapo (bwekeshepo), repeat; start again.
–bwela (bwelele), return; go back; retreat.
bwêma, scent; smell of animal.
bwembya, rod; lash.
bwendo, hole of rats, etc.

–**bwesha** (bweseshe), return something; give back.

bwikalo, domicile; residence; abode.

bwîle, riddle; cobweb. –*pikululo bwile* (pikulwile), solve a riddle; mystery.

bwîna, species; race; of clan. –*bwina bantu*, mankind; human race. – *ŋandu*, of the ŋandu clan.

bwinga, wedding; marriage ceremony.

bwingi, abundance; plenty; quantity; lot.

bwino, adv. well; nicely. –*ba bwino*, be precise; correct; exact.

bwino, bwino, very well; carefully; thoroughly.

bwipi, shortness; smallness.

bwite, invitation; call; vocation.

–**byala** (byele), plant seeds as beans, etc.

–**byata** (byâtile), flash; lighten.

–**byola** (byolele), belch.

–**byutula** (byutwîle), sprain.

— C —

–**Ca** (ele), dawn.

cabamo (fy), contents.

cabe, adv. freely; gratis; without pay; in vain.

cabu (fy), port; harbour; crossing place, ford.

ca cine (fya), truth.

cacilukako (fy), surplus.

cafwilisho, (fy), help; aid; assistance; support.

ca fye (fya), trifle; worthless object.

cakufwala (fy), clothes; garment; habit.

cakulya (fy), food (prepared); meal; nourishment.

cakunwa (fy), beverage; drink.

cala (fy), corpse.

calenga, cj. this causes; therefore.

calici (ma–), church.

calo (fy), earth; world; country; district; land; climate. – *cakaba*, hot climate. – *ca mpepo*, cold climate.

camfu (fy), palate.

canangwa (fy), useless thing or person; good-for-nothing.

candaluwa (fy), 1. mosquito-net. 2. silk/nylon wedding dress.

canga (ba–), greater galago; bush-baby.

cangalo (fy), play; game.

cango (fy), bundle; heap.

câni (fy), grass; straw.

canso (fy), weapon; fire arms.

–**capa** (capile), wash clothes.

capwa (fy), it is empty; it is finished.

cashala (fy), surplus, remainder.

cau, bad temper. –*ba ne cau*, be quarrelsome.

cawama, it is good; well done.

–**ceba** (cebele), v.i. glance.

–**cebaceba** (cebacebe), look all around.

cebo (fy), law; order; command; precept; rule. –*pêle cebo* (pêle), give a law, etc.

–**cebuka** (cebwike), be on the alert.

–**cebula** (cebwile), call attention by giving a sign.

−**cefya** (cefeshe), shorten; diminish: abbreviate; lessen; reduce; curtail. −*cefya cakulya* (cefeshe), fast. *bushiku bwa kucefya cakulya*, fast day. −*icefya*, be humble.

−**ceka** (cekele), notch; chop.

cela (fy), iron; metal.

cele, dysentery.

−**celeketa** (celekete), gnaw (like a mouse).

−**celela** (celele), 1. greet; salute. 2. rise early.

−**celenganya** (celengenye), talk quickly and indistinctly.

−**celesha** (celeshe), delay; retard.

−**celwa** (celelwe), be late.

−**cema** (cemene), herd.

cembe (ba−), fish eagle.

−**cemeka** (cemeke), filter; strain.

cêna (fy), aroma; scent.

−**cena** (cenene), wrestle; injure −*icena* (icenene), hurt or bruise oneself.

−**cenama** (ceneme), be wide open.

−**ceneka** (ceneke), grin.

−**cenga** (cengele), be stingy; **cengelo** (fy), light.

cêni (fy), lap; bosom.

−**cenjela** (cenjele), 1. be clever; intelligent; bright; cautious; beware. 2. have reached the age of reason.

−**cenjesha** (cenjeshe), cheat; deceive; outwit; fake.

−**censa** mêno (censele), show the teeth; grin; smile.

−**cepa** (cepele), be short; small; little: rare; insufficient; less or **few**.

cesaula (cesawile), cut off with teeth; gnaw off.

cesulo (fy), chisel.

ceswa (fy), broom.

−**ceta** (cetele), same as −cesaula.

−**cetekela** (cetekêle), rely on; count on; trust.

cibala (fi), scar.

cibale (fi), kind of palm tree.

cibamfi, greeting, cf. T. VII,

cibanda (fi), devil; evil spirit; demon.

cibangwampopo (fi), kind of bird, "woodpecker".

cibansa (fi), large courtyard. − *ca ndeke*, aerodrome.

cibelelo (fi), custom.

cibelushi (fi), eve; vigil; *pa Chibelushi* or *mu Chibelushi*, Saturday, also on −.

cibengele (fi), winged white ant.

cibi (fi), evil; wrong.

cibi, very much.

cîbi (fi), door.

cibili (fi), brick kiln.

cibili, pali Chibili or muli Chibili, Tuesday.

cibiliti (fi), matches.

cibimbi (fi), cucumber.

cibinda (ba−), 1. craftsman; expert. 2. responsible person.

cibingu (fi), harpoon.

cibola (ba−), impotent man.

cibolya (fi), deserted village.

cibombelo (fi), tool; implement; instrument.

ciboshi (fi), tatter; rag.

cibote, peace.

cibubi (fi), cataract (of eye).

cibukisho (fi), memory; remembrance. *ca cibukisho* (fya), memorial.

cibukulo (fi), goitre.

cibulu (ba−), dumb person.

cibulukutu (fi), thunder.
cibumba (fi), wall.
cibumbwa (fi), creature.
cibungwe (fi), congregation; society.
cibusa (ba–), friend.
çibushimabwe (fi), klipspringer-antelope.
cibwabwa (ba–), pumpkin leaves used as relish.
cibwanse (fi), square; public place in village (for women).
cibweshi, greeting, cf. T. VII.
cibyalilo (fi), charm for seeds.
cieya (fi), kind of skin disease.
cifine (fi), cold in the head; catarrh.
cifinga (fi), faggot.
cifu (fi), stomach.
cifuba (fi), chest; cough.
cifukushi, discontent; anger.
cifulefule, adv. lukewarm; tepid.
cifulo (fi), home; residence; abode.
cifumbule (fi), area of trees sprouting again after having been lopped.
cifunda (fi), parcel; packet.
cifundo (fi), knot. –fundike cifundo, tie a knot.
cifunga (fi), skirt; underwear.
cifungalashi, cramp with the sensation of "pins and needles".
cifungo (fi), prison; jail.
cifunshi (fi), fist used in the expression: –ume cifunshi, hit with the fist.
cifuti (fi), brush.
cifwaikwa (fi), condition.
cifwambo (fi), empty container; matchbox.

cifwani (fi), old millet field.
cifwile, adv. possibly; may be; perhaps; it is worth while.
cifyalilo (fi), hereditary quality; inborn –.
cikabilila, heat.
cikalishi, adv. adj. stagnant.
cikamba (fi), patch.
cikanda (ba–), edible tuber used as relish.
cikanga, ni –, almost; nearly, cikanga pe, mostly.
cikayo (fi), mill.
ciko (fiko), dirt; filth; –ba ne fiko, be dirty; filth.
cikôla (fi), mucus; mucoid expectoration.
cikolomino (fi), windpipe; larynx; throat.
cikolwe (fi), ancestor; forefather.
cinkolwankolwa (fi), poison.
cikombe (fi), chalice; cup.
cikombola (fi), mould.
cikondo (fi), toe.
cikongwâni (fi), piece work.
cikonka kantengesha, ring finger.
cikonko (fi), 1. peanut butter. 2. resentment; discontent; grudge. 3. knot in tree, bamboo, etc. –enda ne cikonko, hold a grudge.
cikope (fi), copy; photograph.
cikopo (fi), tin can.
cikoti (fi), whip; cane.
cikoto (fi), cord of firewood.
cikuko (fi), epidemic; plague.
cikûku, kindness; tenderness; gentleness; mildness.
cikûku (fi), hurricane, gale.
cikulu, adv. provided that; on condition that.
cikuma (ba–), frequented

path.

cikungulupepo, July.

cikumbi (fi), big cloud. 2. eyebrow.

cikumo (fi), thumb.

cikutika, cloudy weather.

cikwa (fi), trap for moles.

cikwakwa (fi), sickle.

–cila (cilile), 1. v.t. excel; exceed; go beyond; surpass; be superior to. 2. v.i. be more.

cila, adv. adj. each; every;

cîla (fìla), n. dance.

cilafi, forgetfulness. *–ba ne –,* be forgetful. *ku –,* out of forgetfulness; inadvertently; involuntarily.

cilaka, thirst. *–ba ne cilaka,* be thirsty. *–fwe –,* be very thirsty; die of thirst.

cilala, dry spell in rainy season.

cilamba (fi), tear. *–lile filamba,* weep.

cilambanshila (fi), nightadder.

cilambu (fi), reward; tip.

cilandelande, nonsense.

cilandushi, vengeance; revenge.

cilangililo· (fi), example; model; sample; specimen.

–cilanya (cilenye), make different; vary.

cilapilo, penance. *nsakalamenta ya –,* sacrament of penance.

cilapo (fi), oath. *cilapo ca bufi,* perjury.

cilashi (fi), potato.

cilaso (fi), wound caused by a spear, etc.

cilayo (fi), promise.

cilayano (fi), mutual promise.

cilea (fi), dissonant singing. *wa cilêa,* poor singer.

cilêla, kindness; compassion. *–ba ne cilêla,* be mild; kind.

cilema (fi), cripple; lame person.

cilemba, s. class "mu/ba", bean.

cilembo (fi), letter, (alphabet). *cilembo ca musalaba,* sign of the cross.

cilende (ba–), adulterer.

cilesha (fi), impediment; hindrance; obstacle.

–ci–, (adv. infix), still.

ciliba (fi), trap for rats.

cilifye, it does not matter.

–cilika (cilike), plug; stop a hole; bar.

–cililila (cililile), overtake.

cililîshi, sadness; affliction.

cililo (fi), funeral.

cilimba (fi), musical instrument.

cilindo (fi), snare for animals.

cilime (fi), fiield *shicilime* (ba–), owner of a field.

cilimi (fi), blade (of knife, spear, millet) big tongue.

–cilimuka (cilimwike), be startled, jump aside.

cilindi (fi), hole; pit; tomb.

cilinganya (cilingenye), bar; obstruct; lay across; interrupt; take a shortcut; raise obstacles.

cilingile, sufficient.

cilola (fi), 1. mirror; looking glass. 2. habit of looking. *–ba ne cilola,* be attracted by a scene easily.

cilolo (ba–), witness; councillor.

cilonda (fi), sore; wound.

cilonganino (fi), gathering; meeting.

cilongoma (fi), tunnel.

25

cilôto (fi), dream.

cilu (fi), pole.

cilubo (fi), mistake; error; fault. –cite cilubo, make a mistake.

cilubula, redemption.

–ciluka (cilwike), jump over; step over.

–cilula (cilwile), open up a hole; uncork; unplug.

cilumba (fi), pride; arrogance.

cilumbulo, confession; also sacrament of –.

cilume (fi), male of animal.

cilunda (fi), beehive.

cilundu (fi), bark cloth.

cilungi, straightforwardness. muntu wa cilungi, straightforward person.

cilya, 1. that yonder, cf. T. III. 2. cj. because; when. e cilya, that is why.

cilye, council; court. – biko muntu mu cilye, bring somebody to court. –cite cilye, hold a council. wa mu cilye, coucillor.

cilyo (fi), food.

cima, adv. together.

–cimaula (cimawile), bite repeatedly.

–cimba (cimbile), surrender; capitulate; give in; yield.

cimbala (fi), rest of food.

cimbi, something else. cimbi cimbi, something extraordinary; extraordinarily.

cimbo (fi), pick; pick-axe.

cimbusu (fi), latrine; water closet; lavatory. –ya ku –, go to the latrine.

cimbwi (ba–), hyena.

–cimfula (cimfwile), sip.

cimfulunganya, disorder; pell-mell; mix up; confusion.

cimfundawila, same as cimfulunganya.

–cimfya, (cimfishe), conquer; defeat; overcome.

–cimfyanya (cimfyene), 1. v. rec. of –cimfya. 2. v.t. compete.

cimisha, sourness of the stomach.

cimo, num. one. pali Cimo or muli Chimo, Monday; on Chimo. cimo cine, it is the same; just the same; cimo na cimo, same as cimo cine.

cimpangilile (fi), flat roof; ceiling.

cimpapila (ba–), leaves of beans used as relish.

cimpatanya, cause of hatred.

cimpûsa (fi), shoots from stumps of trees.

cimuntu (fibantu), giant.

cimuti (fi), stick; pole; big tree.

–cina (cinine), rub; massage.

cinanashi (fi), pineapple.

cinanda (fi), harmonium; piano. –lishe –, play –.

–cinangwa (fi), same as canangwa.

–cincila (cincile), be active; lively; quick; hurry up; hasten. –cincila ku milimo, be zealous.

–cincisha (cincishe), v.t. hasten; hurry up; urge; incite.

–cinda (cindile), v.i. dance.

–cindama (cindëme), be respectable; honourable; venerable; noble.

cindele (fi), bracelet made of grass.

–cindika (cindike), respect; esteem; honour; celebrate.

cine, muli Cine or pali Cine,

Thursday.

cine cine, certainly; truly; surely; at least. *wa cine cine,* faithful.

–cinga (cingile), screen; shelter; protect; shade; come between.

cingililo (fi), entrance.

cingolongolo (fi), metal ring.

–cinguka (cingwike), v.i. get out of the way; move away.

–cingula (cingwile), v.t. get out of the way; move away.

cingulungula (fi), monster.

–cinja (cinjile), 1. slaughter. 2. change; exchange.

cinkolobondo (fi), hollowed log used as mortar.

cinkolwankolwa (fi), poison; poisonous mushroom.

cinkukuma (fi), earthquake.

cinkûla (fi), child who grows first tooth on the upper jaw.

cinkuli (fi), pipe made from a calabash.

cinkupiti, large crowd or quantity.

cinkwingili (fi), bracelet made of metal.

cino, this here, cf. T. III.

cinse, irritability; fit of anger, *wa cinse,* irritable person.

cinseketa (fi), cheetah.

cinshi, what? why? what is the matter?

Cinshikubili, November.

cinshingwa (fi), shadow.

cinshoko (fi), curve; bend.

cintamba (fi), platform; scaffold.

cintamfu (fi), flat roof; ceiling.

cintefwîla melancholy.

cintelelwe, shade.

cintengulusha (fi), circle; circumference.

cintobentobe, adv. in disorder; pell-mell.

cintomfwa (ba–), stubborn person; indocile.

cintu (fi), thing; object; matter; article *cintu conse,* anything.

cintwëno (fi), thing the name of which one does not remember.

cinungi (fi), porcupine.

cinunkilo, taste of food; flavour; odour.

cinunshi, odour; scent.

cinwa (fi), large mouth.

cinyamuti (fi), resin; gum.

cinyantilo (fi), sole of foot. – *ca ncinga,* pedal.

cipa ca linso (fi), eyelid.

cipaka (fi), kick.

cipampa (fi), poster; signpost.

cipampa (ba–), marabou stork.

cipande (fi), piece; portion; share.

cipandwa, 1. same as *cipande.* 2. chapter (of a book).

cipanga (fi), bone which covers the brain; skull; shell, e.g. of tortoise.

cipangano (fi), agreement; contract.

cipansankola (fi), locust bird (kind of stork).

cipâpa (fi), shell of egg, bean, etc.; husk. – *ca muti,* bark of tree.

cipashi (fi), bee (small kind).

cipasho, likeness; resemblance.

cipata (fi), 1. gate; opening (in a fence). 2. sheath e.g. of a knife.

cipatâla (fi), hospital; dispensary.

cipato, hatred; rancour.

cipe (fipe), 1. load; luggage; charge; burden. 2. small basket. *wa cipe* (ba fipe), carrier.

cipêle (fi), turtle dove; green pigeon.

cipelebesha (fi), butterfly.

cipembele (ba–), rhinoceros.

cipûpe (fi), honeycomb.

cipesha mâno (fi), miracle; wonder; mystery.

cipensepense, –fwa –, faint.

cipimo (fi), scale; measure; size; weight. – *ca pakati*, average.

cipinda bushiku, Milky Way.

cipingano (fi), bet.

cipingila (fi), "quail" bird.

cipingo, covenant; Bible.

cipingulo (fi), advice; judgement; verdict.

cipobe (fi), horsefly; hippofly.

cipolopôlo (fi), bullet; ammunition.

cipôma (fi), waterfall.

cipompa (fi), deserted house.

cipondo (fi), murderer; criminal; manslayer.

ciponshi (fi), gum (socket of teeth).

ciponti (fi), calf (young of a cow).

cipôwe, famine; hunger.

cîpu (fi), bug.

cipuba (fi), fool; idiot; simpleton.

cipuki, stuffy air.

cipululu (fi), owl.

cipumba (fi), swelling.

cipumbu (fi), same as *cipuba*.

cipuna (fi), stool; seat.

cipunda (fi), hole in cloth, wall, etc. – *ca cushi* chimney.

cipungu (fi), bateleur eagle.

cipushi (fi), pumpkin.

cipusho (fi), question.

cipute (fi), boil; abscess; ulcer.

cipya, forest with isolated trees and tall grass.

cipya, adv. anew. *cipya cipya*, anew; over again.

cipyu, anger; wrath; impatience. *–ba ne cipyu*, be angry; impatient. *cipyu cipyu*, angrily.

–cisa (cishile), iron clothe.

cisakulo (fi), comb.

cisakuta (fi), hut with walls made of grass.

cisalatîni (fi), dynamite.

cisâmo (fi), decorations; ornament; fine clothes.

cisangu (fi), bunch.

cisanguka (ba–), manslayer. going about in a lion skin; traitor.

cisankonde (fi), sugarcane.

cisani (fi), coarse mat.

cisaniko (fi), torch.

cisâno, muli Chisano or pali Chisano, Friday.

cisansa (fi), palm of hand; hand.

cisansâla (fi), nest. *–pike cisansala* (pikile), build a nest.

cisasa (fi), enclosure.

cisele (fi), floor tile.

cisenshi, paganism; heathendom.

cisesea (fi), ringworm.

–cisha (cishishe), v.t. surpass; outdo.

cishala (fi), rubbish heap; remnant.

–cishanya (cishenye), 1. v. rec. of *–cisha*. 2. give preference.

cishi (fi), island.

cishiba (fi), pool.

cishibilo (fi), sign; mark; badge; identification mark; – *icishifwaluka*, uneffaceable sign.

cishibisho (fi), notice.

cishiki (fi), stump of a tree.

cishîlano (fi), heredity; inherited quality; testament; tradition; last will.

cishilwa (fi), a drawn line. –*shile cishilwa* (shilile), draw a line.

cishima (fi), fountain; spring; well; water hole.

cishimu (fi), caterpillar. –*kole* fishimu (kolele), gather caterpillars.

cishinde (fi), sod.

cishinino (fi), proof.

cishinka, honesty; loyalty. *wa cishinka* (ba–), faithful / trustworthy / honest / sincere person.

cishinte (fi), origin; cause; rootstock.

cishishi (fi), 1. – *ca mulilo*, firebrand. 2. receptacle for spirits.

cishishi (fi), insect.

cisokopela (fi), weaverbird.

cisongo (ba–), bushbuck.

cisongo, skin disease (kind of –).

cisongo (fi), cartridge; bullet; ammunition.

cisonso (fi), thicket of high grass that remains after bushfire has passed.

cisonta bantu (fi), first finger.

cisôso (fi), rubbish, pl. more used.

cisote (fi), hat. – *ca mfumu*, crown.

cisu (fi), bladder.

cisubilo, hope; expectation.

cisubo (fi), act of anointing. – *ca balwele*, sacrament of the sick.

cisuma, adv. well; all right; it is good. – *sana*, excellent very good; very well.

cisumi (fi), any insect that stings.

cisumino, faith; belief; creed.

cisungu, European race. ... *cisunqu*, adj. European.

cisungu, first menstruation. –*wa cisungu* (wile), have first menstruation.

cisungusho (fi), miracle; wonder; marvel.

cisushi (fi), breaking of wind; flatulence. –*nya cisushi* (nyele), break wind.

ciswango (fi), ferocious animal.

ciswebêbe (fi), dry land; desert.

-cita (citile), do; act; make. –*cita nga*, pretend to; treat as.

cita (fita), patrol; warrior.

cîta (fita), sacrifice; offering.

citabataba (fi), plait. –*luke* – (lukile), make a plait.

citabo (fi), book.

citambala (fi), piece of cloth; towel; napkin. – *ca kufyonenamo*, handkerchief. – *ca kufutilako*, duster.

citatu, muli Chitatu or pali chitatu, Wednesday.

cîte (fîte), lame person; cripple; weakness in the legs.

citêkwa (fi), domestic animal.

citele (fi), dove cot.

citembo (fi), snare for

animals.

citemene (fi), place where branches have been cut for a garden.

citemwiko, love; charity.

citende (fi), heel.

citendekelo, beginning.

citendwe, weariness; disgust; boredom.

citente (fi), section.

citeyo (fi), trap; snare.

citesheni (fi), station.

citetekelo (fi), trust.

citindi (ba–), manure; dung;

citobelo, relish.

citumbi (fi), corpse; carcass.

citundu (fi), basket made of bamboo.

citungu (fi), cape; promontory.

cituntu (fi), bank (of a river).

citupa (fi), identification card (in the col. government of Central Africa).

citusha (fi), blister; hard skin. – *pya* –, have a blister.

citwalo (fi), fruit.

ciwa (fi), evil spirit; devil.

ciwelewele (fi), simpleton; idiot; fool.

ciya (ba–), kind of tree.

ciyeyeye, –ya –, go aimlessly or with no sense of direction.

ciyongoli (fi), centipede.

co, interj. introducing a riddle.

–cofa (cofele), pedal.

côfi (fy), 1. land between a confluence of rivers. 2. lap. *–bika mu –*, encircle.

–coka (kokele), leave; go away (obscene).

côko (ba–), chalk. *–wa seléti*, slate pencil.

–coleka (coleke), riddle.

colwa (ba–), zebra.

...comba, crop left over from last year.

combo (fy), boot.

cona (ba–), domestic cat.

congo, 1. n. noise. 2. interj. "stop noise". *...congo*, noisy.

conse pamo (fy), amount; total.

conto (fy), fire in the open.

coso (fy), wild duck.

cûla (ba–), frog.

–cûla (cûlile), suffer; be afflicted.

cûlu (fy), anthill (bigger type); big boil.

cuma (fy), possession; treasure; wealth.

cumbu (fy), sweet potato.

cumfwano, agreement; pact; treaty.

cumfwila, obedience; docility.

cumi, 1. n. truth. 2. adv. truly. interj.: "it is true."

cungulo, evening; afternoon.

cuni (fy), bird.

cupo (fy), marriage; married state. *–putule* –, v.t. divorce *–lekana mu* –, v.i. divorce.

–cûsha (cùshishe), make suffer; afflict; persecute; molest.

cushi (fy), smoke, steam.

cuswe (fy), waterbuck.

— E —

e, 1. it is; they are. 2. interj. "hey!"

ê or **ee**, interj. "yes".

e e! interj. of disapproval.

–eba (ebele), say; tell;
make a remark; mention;
suggest; bid; inform. *–eba
libéla,* give notice.
–ebaula (ebawile), reprimand; rebuke; reproach;
scold.
êco, hence; therefore.
ehe, interj. of surprise, and
of disapproval.
efyo, like that.
. . .eka, alone; only; apart.
. . .eka . . .eka, pure; absolute; only.
Ekelesia, Church.
eko, there.
–ela (elele), winnow.
–ele sabi, v.t. fish with a
basket.
–elela (elele), float.
–elenganya (elengenye), imagine; guess; invent.
elyo, then; thereupon; afterwards.
emo, therein.
. . .êna, as for; as regards;
but for; however.
–enda (endele), walk; go;
travel. *– cende ende,* loiter
about.
–endauka (endawike), roam
about.
–endela (endele), v. appl. of
*–enda, –endela pa ncinga,
motoka,* etc., go on
bicycle, motor car, etc.
–endela pa tukondo, walk
on tiptoe.
–endesha (endeshe), v. int.
of *–enda.*
endi or **endita,** ves.
–enekela, (enekele), foresee; anticipate.
–enga (engele), extract by
boiling.
engula (engwile), polish;
plane.
. . .êni, of foreign origin.

–ensha (enseshe), v. caus.
of *–enda.*
. . .enu, your(s).
epela, that is all.
epo, here. *epo ndi,* I am here.
–esha (eseshe), try; attempt;
experiment; dare; risk.
. . .esu, our(s).
Evangelyo, Gospel.
eya, interj. "well done!" *eya
mukwai,* interj. "thank
you!"
eye filyako, interj. of satis-
faction; "good enough".
eyo, interj. of assent "just
so"; "yes".

— F —

famu (ma–), farm.
–fenenkesha (fenenkeshe),
jam; squeeze; pinch.
fibashi, leprosy. *wa –,* leper.
fibûla, branches cut in a
citemene for fertilising a
garden.
fifumbule, place where
trees were cut.
–fika (fikile), arrive; reach;
come about; chance;
happen.
fikansa, dispute; quarrel;
argument. *–ba ne –,* be
quarrelsome; have an
argument. *–bikane fikansa,*
v. rec. debate; argue; dispute. *–bikapo –,* object;
contradict. *–cite –,* quarrel
wa –, a contradicting person.
fikisha (fikishe), bring to
end; fulfil; succeed.
fiko; dirt; filth.
fikôti s. cikoti, beating; chastisement. *–pêle fikoti,*
apply a beating.

–filwa (fililwe), be unable
incapable; cannot; fail.
–filwana (filwene), n. rec.
of –filwa; fail to come to
an agreement; be a draw
(in sport).
filya, 1. those cf. -T. III. 2.
cj. as; in such a number.
filya fine, accordingly.
–fimba (fimbile), 1. v.t.
cover (with blanket, etc.).
2. v.i. swell; be swollen.
–fimbila (fimbile), envy.
–fimbula (fimbwile), un-
cover; remove cover.
–fimfya (fimfishe), v. caus.
of –fimba, cause to swell.
–fina (fininĕ), be heavy.
– môlu, be slow is walk-
ing.
–finda (findile), refuse greeting or answer.
fine, num. pl. four.
fino, 1. these, cf. T. III. 2.
adv. like; thus.
–finya (finishe), v. caus.
of –fina, overburden;
overwhelm.
–fipa (fipile), suck or sip
fruit.
–fisa (fishile), v.t. hide; disguise.
fisabo, crop.
fisako, branches cut in a citemene for fertilising a
garden.
fisama (fiseme), v.i. hide;
conceal.
fisâno, num. pl. five.
fisense, bran.
–fisha (finishishe), v. caus.
of –fika, fulfil; accom-
plish. –fishe cipe, carry a
load to destination. –fisha
mashiwi, report.
–fisha (fishishe), blacken;
make black.
fishikisa, potash.

fita, army; patrol. –soke –,
send out patrols.
fita (fitile), be black;
– fititi, be very black. –
nga maluba, be green. –
nga matipa, be blue-black.
– ngo lufungo, be purple.
namufita, it is dark (in-
side a room). napafita, it
is dark (at night).
fitatu, num. pl. three.
fituluka (fitulwike), be
blackish.
–fitwa (fitilwe), be cross;
dissatisfied; displeased.
–fole mpia (folele), receive
pay.
–fôla (fôlele), scratch; claw;
foloko (ba–), fork.
–fôma (fômene), snore.
–fonka (fonkele), be hollow.
–fonkola (fonkwĕle), hol-
low out; excavate.
–fonsha (fonseshe), same
as –fonkola.
fosholo (ba–), shovel.
–fota (fotĕle), fade; wilt.
–fuba (fubile), be inter-
rupted, hindered, delayed
(of work). –fube myuba,
blow the bellows. –fubo
môno, empty a fish-trap.
–fûba (fûbile), snatch; grab;
catch.
–fubata (fubete), put under
something.
fubefube, mist; fog.
–fufuma (fufwime), be
mouldy. ...fufuma, moul-
dy.
–fufya (fufishe), hinder;
prevent; interrupt (e.g.
work).
–fûfya (fûfishe), make blunt.
–fûka (fûkile), 1. rise (of
smoke, etc.). 2. be calm;
gentle; polite. 3. be sullen;
moody.

–**fuka** (fukile), fold; bend (knee, etc). –*fuke mbalala, ntoyo.* etc. dig or gather groundnuts, peas, etc.

–**fukama** (fukeme), kneel down.

–**fukatila** (fukatile), embrace.

–**fukilisha** (fukilishe), incense; smoke out.

–**fukula** (fukwile), turn inside out (of a bag); remove borings; chisel; hollow out.

–**fukumuna** (fukumwine), pour out solid matters; empty.

–**fula** (futile), 1. v.t. forge iron. 2. v.i. be many; sufficient; enough; plenty; ample; abound.

–**fûla** (fûlile), undress strip off clothes. *fûle cani,* fetch grass.

–**fulubana** (fulubene), be uncombed; stand on end (of hair).

–**fuluka** (fulwike), be homesick; long for.

–**fulumuka** (fulumwike), run away; flee.

–**fulumuna** (fulumwine), scare; startle.

–**fulungana** (fulungene), be in disorder.

–**fulunganya** (fulungenye), bring in disorder; disarrange; muddle up; confuse entangle.

–**fulwa** (fulilwe), be angry; displeased; impatient.

fulwe (ba–), tortoise.

–**fuma** (fumine), go out or away; come out or come from; leave; originate.

–**fumba** (fumbile), give generously.

–**fumbate minwe** (fumbete), fold or close hand; grasp with hand.

–**fumbatule minwe** (fumbatwile), open the hand.

fumfwe, in great number.

–**fumpula** (fumpwile), grab; snatch; take by force.

–**fumuka** (fumfike), 1. be exhausted; worn out. 2. quieten down.

–**fumuna** (fumwine), lose strength, energy; become stale; flat.

–**fumya** (fumishe), take away; remove; absolve; expect; subtract.

–**funa** (funine), v.i. break (leg, etc.).

–**funda** (fundile), v.t. teach; educate; instruct; preach; exhort. v.i. be fertile –*fundo lushishi,* make a rope from bark. –*funde nama,* skin an animal.

–**fundauka** (fundawike), be muddy (of water).

–**fundaula** (fundawile), stir up (mud).

–**fundawila** (fundawile), v. appl. of –*fundaula.* – *mulandu,* muddle up a case.

fundi (ba–), craftsman; expert; artisan.

–**fundike cifundo** (fundike), tie a knot. –*fundiko mushili,* manure the soil.

–**fundikana** (fundikene), be entangled like thread.

fundwefundwe, inflammation; pustules.

–**funga** (fungile), lock.

–**fungaula** (fungawile), v.t. break into pieces. v. stat. –*fungauka* (fungawike).

–**fungula** (fungwile), unlock.

–fungulula (fungulwile), unrol; unfold.

–funika (funike), v. stat. be broken, fractured.

–funka (funkile), shake hands.

–funtuka (funtwike), withdraw; go aside; lose foothold; fall down.

–funtula (funtwile), push aside.

–funya (funishe), v.t. fracture, break (leg, etc.).

–fûpa (fûpile), be blunt.

–fûpula (fûpwile), discourage; dishearten.

–fusha (fushishe), multiply; augment.

–futa (futile), pay up (debts, etc.). – mu kulinganya, compensate. – pa mulandu, pay fine.

–fûta (fûtile), wipe; wipe out; rub out; erase; delete; brush. – fifunshi, punch.

–futila (futile), v. appl. of –futa, expiate; atone for.

–futata (futete), turn one's back on.

–futuka (futwike), retract; contradict oneself; break a promise.

–fûtuka (fûtwike), be clean; neat; tidy.

–futula (futwile), 1. knock down. 2. release a spring.

–fwa (fwile), 1. die; decease. 2. be out of order. 3. when used as adj.: dead. – bufi, pretend to be dead. – cipupu, faint pretend to be dead. – mfwa isuma, die peacefully. – mfwa Lesa, die a natural death. – ncentu, die in childbirth (child being delivered). – ncila, die in childbirth (child not be-

ing delivered). – pambili-bili, die without assistance. – cilaka, die of thirst; be very thirsty. – nsala, die of hunger; be very hungry.

–fwa (fwile), be worthy of; deserve; merit; be capable of; ought; should. (past tense is used only).

–fwaikwa (fwaikwe), v. pass. of –fwaya, be wanted; needed; necessary.

–fwaila (fwaile), v. appl. of –fwaya, supply somebody with; provide.

–fwaisha (fwaishe), v. int. of –fwaya, be eager; fond of; desire much; look eagerly forward to.

fwâka, tobacco.

fwâla (fwele), v.i. dress; wear clothe.

–fwalula (fwalwile), rub slightly. – macishi, strike a match.

–fwampuka (fwampwike), spring up (like a trap).

–fwampula (fwampwile), release (a trap or spring).

–fwanta (fwantile), bruise; injure.

–fwaya (fwaile), look for; seek; want; wish; fetch; intend; desire.

fwe, we (abbrev. of ifwe).

–fwena (fwenene), scratch.

–fwika (fwikile), v.t. dress; clothe.

–fwila (fwilile), v. appl. of –fwa. – Lesa or Mulungu, die a martyr.

–fwilwa (fwililwe), lose somebody through death.

–fwîsa (fwîshile), spit.

–fwîta (fwîtile), refuse to accept a gift or – to answer; disdain; ignore.

–**fyala** (fyele), bear; give birth to; **beget**.

–**fyalila** (fyalile), v. appl. of –*fyâla*.

–**fyalwa** (fyelwe), v. pass. of –*fyâla*.

–**fyama** (fyeme), be jammed; squeezed; wedged in.

–**fyamika** (fyamike), jam; squeeze; wedge in.

fyantalala, unsalted food.

fye, adv. only; merely; simply; but ...*fye*, common; ordinary. *wa fye* (ba), commoner. *ca fye* (fya), rubbish; useless thing.

–**fyenga** (fyengele), v.i. harm; wrong; treat unjustly.

–**fyompa** (fyompele), suck e.g. honey.

–**fyôna** (fyônene), blow the nose.

–**fyontoka** (fyontweke), pop off (like a cork).

–**fyuka** (fyukile), escape; flee; run away.

— I —

–**iba** (ibile), steal; rob.

+**ibaka** (ma–), jump; leap. –*ime baka* (imine), v.i. jump; leap. –*cile baka* (cilile), same as –*ime baka*.

+**ibala** (ma), 1. garden; field. 2. spot of colour.

+**ibalabala** (ma), kind of snake: "boomslang".

+**ibalaka**, benediction; blessing.

+**ibanda** (ma), ritual hunt. –*sowe banda* (sowele), make a ritual hunt.

+**ibange** (ma), hemp.

ibata (ma), domestic duck. also see mbata.

+**ibaka** (ma), jump; leap.

–**ibêla** (ibelele), differ; be different; be an exception.

+**ibêle** (ma), breast; udder.

+**ibeli** (ma), firstborn.

+**ibende** (ma), mortar for pounding.

–**ibila** (ibile), dive; plunge.

+**ibimbila** (ma), same as *ibaka*.

+**ibotôlo** (ma), bottle.

ibu (mabu), liver.

–**ibukisha** (ibukishe), remember; remind; commemorate.

+**ibûku** (ma), book.

+**ibûla** (ma), leaf; page of a book; banknote. –*leme bûla* (lemene), make a drinking cup with a leaf.

+**ibumba** (ma), 1. group; herd; swarm. 2. clay.

+**ibundu** (ma), jigger.

+**ibungwe** (ma), gathering; mob.

+**ibutukilo**, refuge.

ibwe (ma), stone, as in pebwe.

–**icefya** (icefeshe), be humble.

+**icela mpundu** (ma), parrot (big kind).

+**iceleta** (ma), cart.

–**icena** (icenene), v. refl. hurt, bruise, injure.

ici, this, cf. T. III.

icikini (ma), kitchen.

icila (ma), hammock.

+**icinka** (ma), sheepfold; cowshed; kraal.

ico, 1. that, cf. T. III. 2. which, what, cf. T. IV. 3. cj. for; because. *e ico*, that is why; therefore; consequently; hence. *ico teco*,

that is not what you mean.
+**icungwa** (ma), orange.
−**icusha** (icushishe), work in vain; make oneself suffer.
ifi, 1. these, cf. T. III. 2. what; that; which; cf. T. IV.
+**ifufu** (ma), fluff.
+**ifulo** (ma), froth; foam.
+**ifuka** (ma), handful.
+**ifumo** (ma), abdomen; belly; womb; pregnancy; foetus, −*ba ne fumo*, be pregnant. *ifumo lyakula*, advanced pregnancy. −*pose fumo*, have a miscarriage, abortion. −*ponye fumo*, cause abortion. *ifumo lyauma*, be constipated.
+**ifunde** (ma), advice; exhortation; lesson; teaching.
+**ifundo** (ma), knot.
+**ifungu** (ma), swarm, e.g. of bees.
+**ifupa** (ma), bone.
+**ifwa** (ma), notch.
+**ifwafwa** (ma), puff-adder.
−**ifwanta** (ifwantile), v. refl. of −*fwanta*, get injured.
+**ifwasa** (ma), anthill (small kind).
...**ifwe** with "ku" or "pa" watering place e.g. *pefwe*, *kwifwe* etc.
ifwe, we, cf. T. II.
ifyo, 1. those, cf. T. III 2. which; that;. cf. T. IV. 3. cj. as; how; so; thus; such. *ifyo tefyo*, one does not act like that, *te ifyo iyo*, it is not so, *ifyo fine*, quite so, *ifyo...efyo*, as ...thus. *pa fyo*, according to.
ii. this; these; cf. T. III.
−**ika** (ikile), come down;

get −; go −; descend.
−**ikala** (ikele), sit; live; reside; dwell; stay quiet; abide. − *busaka na*, live well together with.
+**ikalashi** (ma), tarantula.
+**ikanga** (ma), guinea fowl.
−**ikasha** (ikeshe), fasten.
−**ikata** (ikete), v.t. hold; lay hold of; arrest; retain; keep; catch. v.i. be fixed.
−**ikatana** (ikatene), v. rec. of −*ikata.* −*ikateni minwe*, hold one another by hand.
−**ikatisha** (ikatishe), hold tight. −*ikatishe shiwi*, speak louder.
+**ikêtulo** (ma), kettle.
+**ikôbili** (ma), penny.
+**ikôfi** (ma), fist. −*leme kôfi* (lemene), close the fist.
+**ikolongo** (ma), kind of bird (crane family).
ikonala (ma), corner.
+**ikope** (ma), shoulder blade; scapula. −*tensha makope* (tenseshe), shrug the shoulders.
+**ikôsa** (ma), bracelet (made of ivory).
+**ikoshi** (ma), nape.
+**ikubi** (ma), vulture.
+**ikufi** (ma), knee.
−**ikula** (ikwîle), breakfast.
−**ikulika** (ikulike), kill oneself by hanging.
+**ikumbi** (ma), cloud.
+**ikumi** (ma), num. ten.
+**ikunkutu** (ma), stump of amputated limb, *makunkutu* more used.
−**ikuta** (ikwite), be full; satisfied.
−**ila** (ilile), 1. v. appl. of −*ya.* 2. v i. fall (of night): *bwaila*, nightfall.
+**ilanda**, s. lentil.
+**ilangi** (ma), paint; colour.

+**ilata** (ma), sheet iron.
+**ilaya** (ma), shirt; robe. – *lya mwanakashi*, dress. –*bile laya* (bilile), make a shirt.
ili, this, cf. T. III.
–**ililila** (ililile), leave for good; depart definitely.
+**ilindi** (nindi), grave; tomb.
+**ilinga** (ma), fence; enclosure; hedge.
ilingi, adv. often.
–**ilishanya** (ilishenye), complain; grumble; murmur.
+**iloba** (ma), mud; clay.
+**ilonda** (ma), wasp; hornet.
+**ilonde** (ma), lath.
+**iluba** (ma), flower. –*cita maluba*, blossom.
+**ilungu** (ma), smelting furnace.
ilya, that yonder, of ili, T. III.
+**ilyabantu** (ma), cannibal.
+**ilyashi** (ma), talk; chat; gossip, rumour; conversation. –*pume lyashi* (pumine), v.i. chat; gossip.
ilyo, 1. that, cf. T. III. 2. that; which, cf. T. IV. 3. cj. when.
–**ima** (imine), stand up; get up; start out; leave on a journey.
–**imana** (imene), betroth a girl definitely.
+**imata** (ma), stain; blot of ink.
–**imba** (imbile), 1. sing. 2. dig.
–**imika** (imike), put upright.
–**iminika** (iminike), stop; detain somebody.
–**iminina** (iminine), stand still; halt.
–**imisha** (imishe), fecundate; fructify; render preg-

nant.
–**imita** (imite), conceive.
imwe, you.
–**imya** (imishe), raise; lift. –*imye ` calo*, improve a country.
...**îna**, ...belonging to e.g. umwina Africa.
–**ina** (inine), be fat.
–**inama** (ineme), v.i. bend; bow; incline.
–**inamika** (inamike), v. caus. of –*inama*.
+**indyata** (ma), small bell worn by children round ankles.
ine, I.
...**ine**, self.
...**ine** ...**ine**, real; true; absolute; very.
...**ingi**, much; many; a lot; numerous; a great deal.
...**ingi cikanga** ...onse, most.
–**ingila** (ingile), enter; come or go in; penetrate.
ingini (ma–), engine.
–**ingisha** (ingishe), bring in; put in; enclose; include; introduce.
–**inika** (inike), bend down. –*iniko mutwe*, bend the head. –*inike shina*, give a name; name.
inki, ink.
+**inkolobwe** (ma), orange like wild fruit.
ino, this near. cf. T. III.
+**inongwa** (ma), scale, e.g. of fish.
–**inuka** (inwike), 1. cease a day's work. 2. straighten oneself.
–**inuna** (inwine), v.i. raise; lift. – *menso*, look up.
–**inusha** (inwishe), relieve from a day's work.
+**inwanwa** (ma), whiskers.

–inya (inishe), fatten.

–ipaila (ipaile), v. appl. of –ipaya.

–ipaiwa (ipaiwe), be killed.

+ipaki (ma), sacrifice.

+ipala (ma), baldness. –sebe pala (sebele), become bald. –ba ne pala, be bald.

+ipampa (ma), shoulder-blade.

ipandi (ma), yard of cloth.

–ipakisha (ipakishe), satiate; eat well.

+ipapao (ma), pawpaw.

+Ipasaka, Easter. mwaka we Pasaka, Eastertide.

–ipaya (ipeye), kill. –iipayo mwine, commit suicide.

–ipekanya (ipekenye), foresee; prepare oneself.

+ipêla (ma), guava fruit.

+ipendo (ma), number; digit.

+ipenga (ma), 1. trumpet; bugle. 2. half a day's work. – lya lucêlo, work during the morning. –lya cungulo, work during the afternoon.

+ipepala (ma), paper.

+ipepo (ma), religion; Church.

+ipesa (ma), coin; penny.

...ipi, small; short.

–ipifya (ipifishe), shorten.

–ipika (ipike), cook; boil; stew.

+ipinda (ma), parable; proverb; refrain of a song. –ume pinda, tell a parable. –poke pinda, take up a refrain.

+ipindo (ma), wing. –nyunsa mapindo, stretch out the wings; start to fly.

–ipipa (ipipe), be short; low; narrow; small.

+ipitawa (ma), button.

–ipoka (ipokele), justify one's actions.

ipôma (ma), government. district headquarters; see also boma.

+iposo, rations.

Ipukutu, August.

+ipula (ma), wax.

+ipulanga (ma), plank; board.

+ipulu (ma), mongoose.

–ipununa (ipunwine), knock against, e.g. a toe against a stone.

–ipusha (ipwishe), ask; inquire; question; consult; request.

+ipusukilo, salvation; place of refuge.

–isa (ishile), come.

+isâba (ma), mantle; cloak.

+isabi (li), fish. isabi lingi, many fish. isabi libili, two fishes. fimasabi, many big fish. –ipaye sabi, kill fish. –lobe sabi, fish with a line. –ele sabi, fish with a basket. sakile sabi, fish with a net. –fube sabi, take fish out of a trap. –sungile sabi, kill fish with the "buba" plant. –pangule sabi, open up a fish. isabi lilume, fish without scales. isabi likota, fish with scales.

+isâka (ma), sack.

+isakamika (ma), anxiety; worry.

+isako (ma), feather; hair of animal.

–isala (isele), close; shut.

–isalila (isalile), v. appl. of –isala, shut somebody/ something up.

+isâli (ma), prayer.

–isalwa (isalilwe), v. pass. of –isala

isamba (ma), bottom. *kwisamba* or *pe samba* (lya), at the bottom (of); at the foot of. *mwisamba*, under; below.

+**isambi** (ma), sin. *–cite sambi*, commit a sin.

+**isâno**, chief's compound.

+**isaya** (ma), cheek. *–sosela mu masaya*, talk indistinctly.

+**isembe** (ma), axe. *–kwike sembe*, put handle to axe. *kwikule sembe*, remove handle from axe.

+**isense** (ma), edge or bank of a river.

+**isente** (ma), grimace.

+**isese** (ma), group. *–ende sese*, walk in a group.

–**isha** (ishishe), lower. *–isha panse*, spend the evening outside. *–ishe shiwi*, lower the voice.

ishi, these, cf. T. III.

+**ishâmo** (ma), bad luck; misfortune.

+**ishati** (ma), shirt.

ishiba (ma), 1. pond; pool; 2. milk. *–kame shiba*, v.t. milk.

–**ishiba** (ishibe), know; recognize be aware of something. *–ishiba ca cine* know for certain; be sure or certain. *–ishiba ku mutwe*, know by heart.

–**ishibikwa** (ishibikwe), v. pass. of *–ishiba*.

–**ishibila** (ishibile), be accustomed; adapted; acclimatized.

–**ishibisha** (ishibishe), inform; let know; acknowledge; give notice.

–**ishibwa** (ishibwe), v. pass. of *–ishiba*.

+**ishiko** (ma), hearth; fire-place.

+**ishiku** (ma), scandal. *–cite shiku*, scandalize.

+**ishilu** (ma), lunatic; mad person.

+**ishilya**, side. *kuno ishilya*, on this side, e.g. of a river. *pe shilya*, on the other side, e.g. of a river. *kwishilya*, across

+**ishina** (ma), name, signature. *–inike shina*, give a name; name. *ishina lya mutoto*, name given at birth.

+**ishinda** (ma), trace; track.

+**ishinte** (ma), stump of a tree; family stock.

+**ishipi** (ma), goose.

+**ishitôlo** (ma), store.

+**ishiwi** (ma), word; voice; monition. *–ishe shiwi*, lower the voice. *–imye shiwi*, raise the voice; *–shimpe shiwi*, articulate; accentuate. *–ikatishe shiwi*, speak louder. *ishiwi lyakoma*, be hoarse; mute. *ishiwi lya pa mulu*, soprano. *ishiwi lya panshi*, bass voice.

isho, 1. those, cf. T. III. 2. which, cf. T. IV.

ishôpo ma), shop.

ishûko (ma), chance; good luck; fortune.

+**isonde**, earth; world. *pano isonde*, on earth.

+**isopo** (ma), soap.

–**isosha** (isoseshe), grumble; murmur; complain.

–**isuka** (iswike), be open.

+**isukulu** (ma), school.

–**isula** (iswile), 1. v.t. open. 2. v.i. be full.

–**isula pâ**, to be full to the brim.

+**isumbu** (ma), net. *–pike*

sumbu, make a net. *–tea –masumbu,* set nets. *–andula masumbu,* remove nets.
isunga, dispersion. *–cite sunga,* disperse.
–isusha (iswishe), fill.
–ita (itile), 1. call; cite; summon; invite. 2. flow into (of river).
–itaba (itebe), answer a call.
+itabo (ma), step in staircase.
+itâbwa (ma), board; plank.
+itafwâli (ma), brick. *–tama matafwali* (tamine), make bricks.
–itakisha (itakishe), boast; brag.
+itako (ma), buttock.
+itamba (ma), wave.
+itama (ma), same as itabo.
+itamina (ma), state.
+itanda (ma), small hut for young people.
+itanga (ma), stable; shed; cattle pen; kraal.
itanki (ma), tank.
+itanta (ma), thigh.
+itanuna (ma), brick kiln.
+itêbulo (ma), table. *–tantike tebulo* or *anse tebulo,* set the table. *tantule tebulo* or *fumye mbale pe tebulo,* clear the table.
–itêka (itêkele), be independent.
+itembe (ma), rectangular hut.
+itenga (ma), deep water.
+itepe (ma), tin can (of 4 gallons).
+iteshi (ma), thick forest; thicket; thorny place.
+itete (ma), reed.
itikiti (ma), ticket.
–itika (itike), v. stat. of *–itila.*

–itila (itile), spill; pour out (liquid matter).
+itoloshi (ma), trousers.
+itoni (ma), drop; dot; mark (results).
+itotoli (ma), dung of birds.
itumba (ma), pocket; bag.
+itungi (ma), angle; corner. *–ba na matungi,* be at an angle.
+iule (maule), harlot; prostitute; wench.
+iwindo (ma), window.
+iyembe (ma), mango fruit.
+iyongolo (ma), kind of snake.
–iwaminisha (iwaminishe), justify oneself.
iwe, thou, cf. T. II.
iye or iye tata, interj. of wonder: "is it so!"
iyo, 1. those, cf. T. III. 2. which, cf. T. IV.
iyô, no.

— K —

ka, 1. of, cf. T. I. 2. sign of diminutive.
–kaba (kabile), be hot; warm. *–kaba se,* be very hot.
kabali, pneumonia; pleurisy.
kabalwe (ba–), horse.
kabanga, East; orient.
kabâsa (ba–), carpenter.
kabati (ba–), cupboard.
kabe, interj.: "let him be".
kabeci, cabbage.
kabêla, in advance; beforehand; already. (dim. of *libela.)*
Kabengele kanono, January.
Kabengele kakalamba, February.
kabeshamulilo (tu), glow

worm.

kabila (ba–), tailor.

kabila wa mbila (ba–), herald.

–kabila (kabile), be in need of; want; require.

kabili, 1. cj. moreover; then; also. 2. adv. again; once more; anew. *na kabili,* again.

kabilo (ba–), coucillor of a chief.

kabinge, then; thereupon.

kabiye, pl. kabiyeni, imp. go!

kabokoshi (tu), chickenpox.

kabuka (ba–), evocator (of spirits).

–kabula (kabwile), exchange; barter; bargain.

kabulubulu (tu), honey-fly.

kabungwe (tu), gathering; group.

kabushi (tu), small goat.

–kabushanya (kabushenye), bargain; barter.

kabwa (tu), small dog.

kabwe (tu), small stone.

kacele (ba–), favourite child.

kacêlo, early in the morning. *kacêlo cêlo,* very early.

kacema (ba–), herdsman; shepherd.

kacemeko (tu), small filter.

...kaêle, innocent. *wa kaêle* (ba), innocent person.

kafi (ba–), spitting cobra.

kafîfi, nightblindness.

kafikênipo, greeting, "good bye", cf. T. VII.

kafula (ba–), blacksmith.

–kafula (kafwile), strangle.

kafundisha (ba–), teacher; catechist.

kafwa bufi (ba– or tu), insect which pretends to be dead when touched.

kâfwa (ba–), helper.

–kafya (kafishe), 1. v.t. heat; make warm; boil. 2. v.i. be noisy.

kaimbi (ba–), kind of tree "Erythrophleum".

kaice (twaice), little child. *–ba nga kaice,* be childish.

–kaka (kakile), tie; bind; fasten; arrest; imprison.

–kâkâta (kâkête), 1. be very brave or bold. 2. be insubordinate.

kakandamatipa (tu), kind of bird "snipe".

–kakatika (kakatike), v.t. stick; adhere to.

–kakatila (kakatile), v.i. stick; adhere to.

–kakatuka (kakatwike), be unfixed; detached.

–kakatula (kakatwile), unfix; detach.

kaki, khaki.

kakolenkole (tu), kind of bird "crowned plover".

kakoma wa ŋômbe (ba–), butcher.

kakondo (tu), little toe. *–endela pa tukondo,* walk on tiptoe.

kakonkote (tu), praying mantis.

kakoshi (tu), kind of bird, "chanting go-hawk".

kakoshi-musa, epilepsy.

kakoshi kanika (tu), kind of bird "pale harrier".

–kakuka (kakwike), be loose; untied; unfastened.

–kakula (kakwile), untie, unfasten; loosen.

kakûla wa njelwa (ba–), bricklayer.

kalâle, mines in Zambia and Rhodesia.

kalaliki (ba–), clerk.

...kalamba, great; important; long; elder; adult.

kalanda, interj. used as: *ne kalanda*, I am a poor fellow.

kalata (ma-), letter; card. *kalata lya mu ndeke*, air letter. *kalata lye shina*, label. *-laisha kalata* (laishe), send a letter by hand. *- bwesha kalata* (bweseshe), answer a letter.

kale, adv. formerly; once; once upon a time; long ago; already.

kale fye or kale na kale, very long ago; in old times; in no time. *na kale*, even formerly, *ca kale*, anything in the past.

kale na kêpi, up to the last.

...kale, ancient.

kalebelebe (tu), lobe of the ear.

kalefulefu (tu), chin.

kalenga (ba-), painter.

...kali, fierce; wild; cruel; ferocious; severe; dangerous.

-kalifya (kalifye), cause pain. *- mutima*, make angry; annoy.

-kalika (kalike), stop (of rain only).

kalinda (ba-), guardian; watchman.

-kalipa (kalipe), 1. be angry; wild; severe. 2. be painful; sore; hurt; ache. 3. be strong (as drink).

-kalipila (kalipile), scold; rebuke; blame; reproach; reprove; chide.

kalombo, interj. "I am present".

kalondolola (ba-), one who explains a matter.

kalongwe (tu), kind of tree.

kalubi (tu), idol; fetish; doll.

kalukuluku (ba-), turkey.

kalulu (tu), hare; rabbit.

kalume (ba-), lad; page (of a chief).

kalundwe, s. class "mu/ba", cassava; tapioca.

kalunga (ba), hunter (with a gun, etc.).

...kalwe, harsh; cruel.

kalya, that yonder, cf. T. III.

kalyati (tu), handcuff.

-kama (kamine), . 1. v.t squeeze; milk. 2. v.i. be dry; be dried up.

kamana (tu), brook.

-kambatika (kambatike), v. t. stick; fix; attach; glue.

-kambatila (kambatile), v.i. adhere; be fixed or attached.

-kambatuka (kambatwike), be unstuck; unglued.

-kambatula (kambatwile), v. t. unglue; unfix.

kambili (tu), kind of palm tree.

kambone (ba-), witness. *-ba kambone*, be witness; give evidence; testify.

kamela (ba-), camera.

kamême, stomach trouble.

kamfulumende, government.

kamimbi (tu), swallow (bird).

kamini (tu), scorpion.

kamonkola (ba-), inflammation of the gums.

kampanda (ba-), "so and so"; "what's his name"; (a person).

kampandwe (tu), weasel.

kampasa, smallpox.

kampu (ma-), camp.

kamuntu (tubantu), dwarf.

kana (twana), little child; baby; infant.

-kâna (kêne), refuse (to do or agree); oppose; deny; abstain; resist; renounce. *cakâna*, it does not work out.

-kana (kanine), sprinkle; spray.

kanabesa, interj. of great respect.

kanama (tu), small animal; small piece of meat.

kanapini (tu), safety pin.

kancelelya (tu), sparrow.

kancindu (tu), kind of palm tree.

-kanda (kandile), 1. knead. 2. thrash. *–kando bunga bwa mukate*, knead dough.

-kanga (kangile), dry something over fire; roast on a platform. *–kange nama*, smoke meat.

-kangala (kangele), tie laths on roof.

...kankala, rich; noble.

kankungwe (ba–), whirlwind.

kâno, cj. unless; except; only if; but; save.

kano, this here, cf. T. III.

kanono, (tu), little thing; trifle.

kanônonôno (tu), a very little thing.

-kansana (kansene), argue; dispute.

kanshi, therefore; consequently; then.

kanshilye (ba), sable antelope. `

kanshimonamitenge (tu), very poisonous kind of snake.

kantele mafwasa (tu), pigmy.

kantengesha (tu), little fin-

ger. *cikonka kantengesha*, third finger.

kantu (tu), small thing.

kantimba (tu), blue duiker.

kantwa (ba–), "so and so" (a person). ...*uti kantwa*, on such and such a day.

kanwa (tu), mouth; snout; opening. *ku kanwa*, orally.

kanweno (tu), small clay pot.

kanya (tu), baby; infant.

-kânya (kênye), disagree; disapprove; dissuade; disavow.

kanyelele (tu), small ant.

kanyense (tu), onion.

kapafu (ba), calf (of leg).

-kapakapa (kapakapile), blink (with eyes).

kapalwilo (tu), small pot.

kapanda mâno (ba–), good adviser.

kapanga (ba–), kind of rat.

kapâso (tu), grasshopper.

kapaso (ba–), messenger.

kape (tupe), small basket.

kapekesa (tu), splint.

kapêle (tu), small turtle dove.

kapêpa (ba–), smoker.

kapepa (ba–), worshipper.

Kapepo kanono, May.

Kapepo kakalamba, June.

kapeshi (tu), kind of bird; "Frankolin".

kapilibula (ba–), interpreter.

kapinda ka ku kulyo, South; to the –.

kapinda ka ku kuso, North; to the –.

kapingula (ba–), adviser; judge.

kapisha (kapishe), wink; warn.

kapitao (ba–), headman; foreman.

kapokoshi, kitchenpox; kaffirpox.
kapôli (ba–), wild pig.
kapôpo, adv. –sosa mu –, whisper.
kapumba (tu), pustule; pimple; freckle.
kapumpe (ba–), eagle.
kapunda (tu), small hole. *kapunda ke pitawa,* button hole.
kapundu (tu), shrill shouts of welcome. *–aulo tupundu,* utter shrill shouts of welcome, joy.
kaputula (ba–), pair of shorts.
kaputula wa milandu (ba–), judge.
kapyelele (tu), whistle. *–lisha kapyelele* (lishishe). v.i. blow a whistle.
Kasakantobo. August.
–kasha (kashishe), v.t. chill.
–kashakasha (kashakeshe), delay; hold back.
kasele (tu), 1. dim. of muscle. 2. oribi (small gazelle).
kasembele (tu), tsetsefly.
kasesema (ba–), a possessed person who prophesies.
kashîka wa bwato (ba–), boatsman.
–kashika (kashike), be red. *–kashika ce,* be very red.
–kashikila (kashikile), be redish.
–kashisha (kashishe), make red.
kashîshi (tu), small insect.
kashita (tu), moment; instant.
kashitisha (ba–), merchant.
kashiwa (ba–), orphan.
kaso, avarice; meanness. *wa kaso* (ba), mean or avaricious person.
kasobela (ba–), prophet.

kasokopyo (ba–), 1. black jack (kind of stick-seed). 2. sty on eyelid.
kasoma, pleurisy.
kasote (tu), cap.
kasôwa (ba–), hunter with nets.
kasuba, sun; sunlight, daylight. *kasuba katula,* sun rise. *kasuba kawa,* sun set. *kasuba pakati,* midday. *kasuba konse,* all the day long. *pa kasuba,* in the sun; in the open.
kasuli (ba–), last born.
kasunga (ba–), host; nurse; orderly.
kasûsu (tu), bat.
–kata (katile), be chilled.
katapa, cassava leaves used as relish.
katêka wacalo (ba–), governor; administrator.
katekenya (ba–), driver. → *wa bwâto,* pilot.
katende (tu), heel.
kati with "mu" or "pa", inside.
katile akantu, once upon a time. (used to introduce a fable).
katili (tu), steinbuck.
katîna, reverential fear.
katolika, catholic.
katungulula (ba–), leader; president.
katungwe ((tu), abscess; withlow.
katunka (ba–), seducer; tempter; bad councellor.
katutwa (tu), small dove.
katwishi, interj. of doubt or unconcern: "I do not know".
katyetye (tu), wagtail.
–kaula (kawile), barter; exchange.
–kauka (kawike), be salty;

bitter.

kawêle (tu), shouts of derision; hooting.

–kaya (kaile), mince; mill; chop.

...kaya, indigenous; native.

kebela (ba–), intercessor.

kêla (twêla), small iron; needle.

kensha (ba–), driver.

kêpika (ba–), cook.

kêtwa (ba–), harlot; prostitute.

Kilishitu, Christ.

ko, suffix to verbs; 1. dim. of *uko,* here; there: e.g. *talukako,* go off here. 2. a mere suffix without any meaning; e.g. *abombako* instead of abomba.

...ko, its; their, (with nouns of all classes except class "mu/ba".)

–kobeka (kobeke), hang.

–kobekela (kobekele), betroth; engage (when man).

–kobekelwa (kobekelwe), betroth; engage; (when girl).

–kobola (kobwele), unhook. – *nyanje,* break off a maize cob.

kofi, coffee.

–kofola (kofwele), sink in.

–kofoloka (kofolweke), be dragged out.

–kofolola (kofolwele), pull out somebody (of mud).

–kokesha (kokeshe), urge on; press on. – *lubuli,* stir up a quarrel. – *lyashi,* keep on a lively conversation. – *nseko,* cause a laughter.

–kokola (kokwele), linger; dawdle; tarry; delay; last long.

–kokosha (kokweshe), postpone; delay; put off.

–kokota (kokwete), gnaw.

–kokwesha (kokweshe), misha, put off payment of debts.

–kola (kolele), 1. v.t. scrape. 2. v.i. intoxicate. – *fishimu,* gather caterpillars.

–kôla (kôlele), 1. v.t. scrath like thorns. 2. v.i. cough; have a cold.

–kolokota (kolokwete), gnaw a bone.

–kolola (kolwele), scrape off.

–kololoka (kololweke), become sober.

kolona (ba–), rosary. –*salika pali kolona* (–salike), say the rosary.

–kolongele nkolonga (kologele), v.t. barricade.

–kolopa (kolwepe), scrub (floor etc.).

–kolwa (kolelwe), be drunk.

kolwe (ba), monkey; ape.

kolyokolyo (ba–), blue headed lizard.

–koma (komene), hit; kill; slay. – *lulembo,* make incision for applying remedy. – *matwi,* be deaf. – *shiwi,* be hoarse; be out of tune.

komaki (ba–), cup.

–komboka (kombweke), v. stat. of –*kombola,* fall off e.g. plaster.

kombokombo, adv. in turns.

–kombola (kombwele), v.t. chip; break off; detach, e.g. bark of tree.

–komboshanya (komboshenye), relieve one another at work.

–komoka (komweke), be

cured from hoarseness.

kompaundi (ba–), compound.

–komya (komeshe), v. caus. of –*koma matwi*, deafen.

–kondenkana (kondenkene), be flexible; pliable.

–kondekanya (kondenkenye), make flexible or pliable.

–konga (kongele), hinder; prevent work by talking.

–kongama (kongeme), be curved; crooked.

–kongamika (kongamike), v.t. curve; bend like a crook.

–kongola (kongwele), borrow. (used for money only).

kôni (tûni), little bird.

–konka (konkele), follow; come with; go along. – *mashiwi*, obey; observe.

–konkapo (konkelepo), be following; come after; next.

–konkanya (konkenye), go on; continue; keep on.

–konkela (konkele), go and meet.

–konkelela mu fibi, yeild to temptation.

–konkomeka (konkomeke), barricade.

–konkomesha (konkomeshe), admonish; exhort; stimulate.

–konkomoka (konkomweke). 1. run down (of liquid. 2. be pulled out (*nail*, etc.). 3. resound; ring (of instrument).

–konkomona (konkomwene), caus. of –*konkomoka*.

–konkonsha ku cibi (konkonseshe), knock at door.

konsekonse, adv. every-

where; on all sides.

konto (ba–), grass tick.

–kontoka (kontweke), v. stat. of –*kontola*.

–kontola (kontwele)), v.t. break off; snap off.

–konya (koneshe), tease.

–kopa (kopele), 1. copy; photograph; ape. 2. borrow.

–kopesha (kopeshe), loan; lend. – *na kulipilisha*, lease.

–kosa (kosele), be hard; tough; solid; strong. – *ndi*, be very hard. – *mu kanwa*, be insolent. – *mutengo*, be expensive; dear. – *mutwe*, be obstinate; stubborn; hard-headed. *bushiku bwakosa*, the night is advanced.

–koselesha (koseleshe), encourage.

–kosha (koseshe), harden; strengthen; fortify. – *mulilo*, light fire. – *mutengo*, raise the price. – *shiwi*, raise one's voice. – *mutima*, encourage,

–koshamo lupi, slap. –*muntu bwanga*, bewitch; cast a spell.

kôsha (koseshe), pester with demands; insist upon; give insistent recommendations. – *cimo cine*, repeat something many times.

–kota (kotele), be old; worn out.

..kota, female.

... kote, be old.

kôti (ma–), court.

ku, 1. prep. to; towards; against; at; by; for; from; out of 2. pr. there, cf. T. II, 2b.

–kubatila (kubatile), pave.

kubeya (ma), shoulder.
kubili kubili, on both sides.
kuboko (ma), arm; forearm; railing.
kufyalwa, birth.
–kûka (kûkile), change residence; migrate.
kûki (ba–), cook.
kûkû, greeting used by women only.
–kula (kulile), 1. v.t. drag; pull. 2. v.i. grow; develop; become adult; mature; come of age.
–kûla (kûlile), build; construct.
kuli, prep. cf. ku.
kulici, greeting, cf. T. VII.
–kulika (kulike), kill by hanging.
kulila, cj. provided that; on condition that.
kûlu (mólu), leg; hindleg of animal.
...kulu, big; large; great; thick; important; serious.
–kulunkunta (kulunkuntile), rattle; rumble.
kulya, 1. prep. over there. 2. that yonder; cf. T. III.
kulyo, right. *ku kulyo*, to or on the right side.
–kumana (kumene), v.i. 1. meet. 2. be sufficient; suffice.
–kumanya (kumenye), v.t. meet.
–kumba (kumbile), stir.
–kumbatila (kumbatile), embrace.
kumbi. adv. elsewhere; *kumbi kumbi*, quite elsewhere; far away.
–kumbinkana (kumbinkene), v. stat. of –kumbinkunya.
–kumbinkanya (kumbinkenye), link up; connect; join.

–kumbusuka (kumbuswike), provide or care for somebody. –balanda, give alms.
–kumbwa (kumbilwe), desire; covet; long for something.
kumfwa, cj. provided that; on condition that; in case.
–kuminkanya (kuminkenye), place end to end.
kumo, adv. together; at one time.
kumona, adv. in case.
–kumpa (kumpile), shake roughly. – *cani*, slash grass. – *tushishi*, pull off bark rope.
–kumuna (kumwine), kick aside.
–kumya (kumishe), touch.
–kungama (kungeme), v.i. stick on (like stick-seed).
–kungula (kungwile), v.t. 1. shake down (fruits). 2. clear ground.
kungumfwi (ba–), kind of mushroom, not edible.
–kunkilisha (kunkilishe), push ahead (with hand).
–kunkuluka (kunkulwike), v.i. roll over and over.
–kunkulukila (kunkulukile), v.i. roll down.
–kunkulula (kunkulwile), v.t. roll.
–kunkulusha (kunkulwishe), same as –kunkulula.
kuno, here; hither. *kuno kwine*, just here.
kunonse, here outside.
kuno ishilya, on this side.
kunse, outside; external. *ca kunse* (fy), appearance; surface. *wa kunse* (ba), foreigner. *–ya kunse*, go to the latrine.
kunshi, what for?
–kunta (kuntile), shake off

(dust etc.). – *mutwe*, shake the head in denial. – *cani*, beat dew down in grass.

ku ntanshi, in future; ahead; henceforth; farther on.

–kupa (kupile), cover (book ect.). – *milandu*, expose oneself to trouble. – *mulilo*, beat fire down with branches.

–kupauka (kupawike), be unemployed.

–kupaula (kupawile), whitewash; sprinkle.

–kupika (kupike), cover with a lid. – *citabo*, shut the book. – *kanwa*, keep a secret. – *nshinde*, turn sod over in cultivating.

–kupukula (kupukwile), uncover; take lid off. – *citabo*, open a book.

–kupukumyo mutwe (kupukwimye), shake the head.

–kusa (kushile), clean up.

–kusa (kushile), scrub; rub; file. – *méno*, brush the teeth.

–kusha (kushishe), enlarge; augment, increase; aggravate. – *mwâna*, bring up a child. – *mulandu*, aggravate a case. – *muntu mutwe*, disgrace or shame somebody. –*ikusha*, think highly of oneself.

kushika, depth (of water).

kushipa, courage.

kuso, left side. *ku kuso*, to or on the left side. –*ba no kuso*, be lefthanded.

–kûta (kûtile), screem; call or shout for help; summon; recruit. –*kûta ku kóti*, summon to court.

kutali, adv. far; afar; far away. – *na kuno*, far from here.

kuti, can; must; should; may; could; might; probably; possibly; ...*kuti*, such; such a kind. *kuti wati*, pl. *kuti bati*, one would think that, *takuli wa kuti*, there is none who could. *takula ca kuti*, there is nothing that could. *ni mukuti*, that is to say, *no kuti*, but.

–kutika (kutike), 1. listen attentively. 2. be cloudy.

–kutula (kutwîle), eat mush without relish.

–kutumana (kutumene), be undecided; be at a loss.

Kutumpu. March.

kutwi (ma), ear.

–kuwa (kuwile), bark; be barked at; howl.

kûwe (ba–), 1. go-away bird. 2. cóward.

kwa, 1. prep. at; from (with proper nouns). 2. particle which follows the prep. "of", cf. T. I.

Kwacha (ba), (Zambian currency), note worth 100 ngwee.

kwaita, interj. "I am present".

–kwakwanya (kwakwenye), ɛ̀ be loquacious and saying lies.

kwalepa, it is far or high.

kwani, whose? at whose place?

kwapa (mâpa), armpit.

–kwapila (kwapile), carry under the arm.

Kwaleshima, Lent.

–kwata (kwete), have; own; possess.

kwati, one could think that.

kwempe, adv. hardly; narrow.

kwena, 1. cj. in that case.

2. interj. "it is true".
–kwika (kwikile), set tool to handle.
–kwikuka (kwikwike), become unfixed; loose.
–kwikula (kwikwile), remove handle from tool.
–kwila (kwilile), work for something; gain; merit; earn.
kwindi (ba–), rat.
kwinini, quinine.

— L —

–laba (labile), forget.
–lafya (lafishe), distract, divert attention of (somebody, something).
–laisha (laishe), inform; notify; send for. – kalata send a letter by hand/by courtesy of.
laiti (ma–), light.
–lala (lalile, 1. v.t. break; crack. 2. v.i. (aux.), for ever; entirely.
–lâla (lêle), 1. v.i. be asleep; go to bed; lie down. 2. be at a standstill; be idle. – ubukupeme, lie on the stomach. – ubuseneme, lie on the back. – kabafu, lie on the side. – ne nsala, go to bed without food. – panse, sleep in the open. – panshi, sleep on the floor. – pa nshila, sleep on the road. –tulo twa nenqo, sleep like an antbear.
–lalika (lalike), be broken; cracked.
–lâlila (lâlilile), lie in.
lâlila (lâlile), hatch; sit on eggs.
–lâlila (lâlilile), lie in wait.

–lâlisha (lâlishe), sleep soundly.
lâmba (ba–), spleen.
–lamba ((lambile), 1. v.t. avoid; shun. 2. v.i. be dirty; untidy (body or clothes).
–lambalala (lambalele), v.i. stretch oneself on the ground; lie flat on the ground.
–lambalika (lambalike), v.t. lay out flat on the ground.
–lambula (lambwile), reward.
–lamfya (lamfishe), make dirty; soil; pollute (body or clothes.).
lampi (ma/ba), lamp.
–lamununa (lamunwine), stop a quarrel; separate fighting.
–landa (landile), talk; speak; – na, talk to; address somebody.
...landa, poor.
–landikisha (landikishe), speak frankly.
–landula (landwile), revenge; avenge.
–langa (langile), show; instruct; illustrate.
–languluka (langulwike), be sad; sorry for; mournful; repent; pity; feel compassion.
–lapa (lapile), swear. – bufi, commit perjury.
–lapika (lapike), flog; thrash.
–lapila (lapile), regret; repent.
–lapisha (lapishe), curse.
–lasa (lashile), wound; stab. – nshindano, vaccinate.
–lâsa (lâshile), appoint.
lasenshi (ma–), licence.
–lâshika (lâshike), appoint as representative.

–**latuka** (latwike), v.i. explode; shoot forth rays.

–**latula** (latwile), v.t. explode.

–**laya** (laile), to promise.

–**lebelâ** (lebele), mistake a person for another.

–**lêfya** (lêfeshe), lengthen; widen; broaden.

–**leka** (lekele), leave alone; let be; let go; abolish; give up; cease; stop; omit. – *mulimo*, abdicate. – *bupe*, give a present. – *cita*, offer a sacrifice. – *mafuto*, pay fine.

–**leka**, let (aux v.) followed by subjunctive, e.g. *leka ncite*, let me do.

–**lekana** (lekene), v.rec. of –*leka*, differ; part; be apart; cease fighting.

–**lekanalekana** (lekanalekêne), differ greatly.

–**lekanya** (lekenye), separate; distinguish.

–**lekelesha** (lekeleshe), neglect; forsake; abandon. *pa kulekelesha*, finally; at last; at the end. ...*pa kulekelesha*, the last.

–**lela** (lelele), stay up (of scale). –*mwana*, bring up a child.

lelo! pl. lelwêni, interj. "hey"; "take care"; "look out".

lelo, cj. but; now.

lêlo, to-day. *lelo line*, this very day; just today, *lelo te lyo*, not to-day. *lelo lyena*, as for to-day. *na lelo*, to-day also or again.

–**leme ŋoma** (lemene), fix a skin on drum. – *ŋana*, make a wreath with grass or leaves. – *bucinga*, set a gamepit. – *bula*, make a drinking cup with a leaf. – *lukondwa*, make a hole in mush for sauce. – *makunda* squat down. – *mwana*, spoil a child. – *kofi*, close the fist. – *mu buta*, draw the bow; pull the trigger of a gun.

–**lemana** ((lemene), be maimed; crippled; lame; paralysed; infirm.

–**lemba** (lembele), write; design.

lembalemba (ba–), kind of spider; film spun by it.

–**lembelelo lulembo** (lembelele), make incision on body to apply remedy.

–**lemyo mulandu** (lemeshe), exaggerate.

–**lenga** (lengele), 1. cause; produce. 2. design; paint; *icalenga*, this causes; therefore.

–**lengama** (lengeme), be clear like water or sky.

–**lengamika** (lengamike), make clear (water, etc.).

–**lengela** (lengele), v.t. peep; spy.

–**lengula** (lengwile), check; examine; inspect; explore.

–**lepa** (lepele), be tall; large; far. – *mu butali*, be high; tall. – *panshi*, be deep. – *mu bukulu*, be large; bulky; wide; broad. *kwalepa*, it is far or high.

–**lepuka** (lepwike), be split; cracked; torn; burst.

–**lepula** (lepwile), split; halve in width; saw.

Lesa, God.

–**lesha** (leseshe), forbid; prevent; cancel; prohibit.

–**leshalesha** (leshaleseshe), talk evasively.

–**leshiwa** (leshiwe), v. pass.

of *-lesha.*

-lêta, (lètele), bring; deliver here.

-letelela (letelele), bring into trouble.

libe (ma), sweat, perspiration.

libela (adv.), in advance.

libila (libile), whirl; go or turn round.

libili libili, often; frequently.

libu (ma), liver.

libwe (ma), stone, rock.

lifi (ma), leave temporarily from job.

lifumo (ma), spear; lance.

-lîka (lìkile), be edible.

-lila (lilile), v.i. make sound; weep; cry (of people); sing (of birds); bleat, call (of animals); ring (of bells); roar etc. *-lile misowa,* bewail; mourn.

lilali, when?

-lîlamo (lìlilemo), make a profit out of something.

-lîla (lilîle), eat good food.

-lilila (lilile), v. appl. of *-lila,* lament.

-lilisha (lilishe), weep bitterly.

-lilîshika (lilîshike), be very sad; afflicted.

lilya, 1. adv. when. 2. that yonder, cf. T. III.

lilya line, at that moment.

-lima (limine), v.t. cultivate; grow; produce. *- ne ŋombe,* plough.

-limba (limbile), transplant.

limbi, another time; later on. *na limbi,* again; a second time.

-limbuka (limbwike), v.i. 1. uproot. 2. (of plants) begin to grow after transplanting.

-limbula (limbwile), uproot; pull out (plants).

-limbuluka (limbulwike), be elastic; sticky; gummy.

-limbulula (limbulwile), stretch (rubber, etc.).

limbwelimbwe (ba–), green, filmy scum growing in or on water; green colour. *–ba ŋga limbwelimbwe,* be green.

limo, once; one time.

limo limo, sometimes; once in a while. *– fye,* seldom.

-limuka (limwike), be clever.

-linda (lindile), await; wait for; stay; remain; watch; guard.

-lindika (lindike), keep waiting; delay.

liŋa (maŋa), crack in the skin of heels.

-linga (lingile), 1. v.t. measure correctly; estimate; compare; adapt. 2. v.i. be capable; able; sufficient; satisfactory; accurate; convenient.

linga, how often?

-lingâna (lingêne), be equal; level; even; compare; make or treat alike; measure against an equal; be just; impartial; pay back; retaliate.

lîni (mani), egg. *– lya kukumba,* scrambled egg. *– lya kusalula,* fried egg. *– lyasuka,* the egg is bad. *–bikila mani,* lay eggs. *–lâlila mani,* sit on eggs. *łota mani,* hatch.

lîno (mêno), tooth. *– lya nsofu,* ivory.

lino, how long? (expressing impatience). *na lino*

still.

–linsha (linshishe), same as *lindika*.

lînso (mênso), eye; grains in ear of corn, any spot in an object that looks like human eye. *–isula menso*, open the eyes. *–ipaye linso*, aim with one eye. *–shibatike menso*, blindfold. *–shine linso*, close one eye. *–tumbula menso*, stare. *ku menso*, by sight; in sight. *pa menso ya bantu*, openly; to everyone's knowledge.

lintu, cj. when.

linwanwa (ma), whiskers of cat; dog; etc.

–lipa (lipile), pay; reward;

–lipila (lipîle), same as *–lipa*.

–lipilisha (lipilishe) charge (ask payment), fine.

lipôti (ba–), report.

–lisha (lishishe), v.t. ring; play an instrument. *–cinanda*, play harmonium or piano. *– mfuti*, shoot a gun. *– ɣoma*, beat a drum. *– penga*, blow a trumpet.

–lisha (lishishe), 1. v.t. feed; nourish. 2. v.i. eat much.

lishîti (ba–), receipt.

–liwa (liliwe), 1. v. pass. of *–lya*. 2. v.i. be edible: eatable.

–loba (lobele), 1. v.t. fish with a line. 2. v.i. disappear.

–loboka (lobweke), reappear (of things that appear in seasons.)

–lofya (lofeshe), ruin; annihilate; enslave.

–loka (lokele), rain.

loko (ba–), lock.

lokwishoni (ba–), location.

–lola (lolele), v.i. 1. be

awake; see. 2. go or lead to. 3. face. 4. mean. *–lola ku*, be inclined to.

–lolana (lolene), face one another.

–lolekesha (lolekeshe), look carefully; fix; gaze.

–lolela (lolele), wait for; expect.

–lolesha (loleshe), look; face.

–lomba (lombele), ask for; beg; demand.

–lombela (lombele), v. appl. of *–lomba*; pray for someone.

lôna (ba–), lady; madam.

–londa (londele), inspect; correct; watch; superintend; look for. *–londe nama*, track game.

–londoka (londweke), v. stat. of *–londa*, be found; recovered; returned.

–londoloka (londolweke), be clear; become comprehensible.

–londolola (londolwêle), explain; describe; illustrate; clear up (a case).

–longa (longele), pack. *– bwalwa*, brew beer. *– fipe*, pack loads.

–longâna (longêne), v.i. gather; assemble; hold a meeting.

–longanya (longenye), v.t. gather; assemble; accumulate; make addition.

–longola (longwele), interpret (a dream).

–longolola (longolwele), unpack.

longololo lwa numa; spine; dorsal.

–lonsha (lonsheshe), follow a spoor.

–looloka (loolweke), remove a spell.

–loolola (loolweke) same as –looloka.

–losha (loseshe), v. caus. of –lola, cause to go or turn. – menso ku, turn eyes towards. mashiwi, mean.

–lôsha (lôsheshe), mourn; bewail.

lôta (lôtele), dream.

–lowa (lowele), 1. v.i. bewitch; cast a spell. 2. v.i. be sweet; tasty.

–lowekwa (lowekwe), pass. of –lowa.

–luba (lubile), 1. be lost; err! disappear; wander. 2. make a mistake; blunder; be wrong.

lubafu (m), rib; one side of ribs.

lubalala (m), nut; groundnut; peanut.

lubali, adv. on the side; half; partly; lubali lwa, on the side of. lubali kwi, in what direction? on what side?

lubali...lubali, partly... partly; on the one side ...on the other side.

–lubana (lubene), v. rec. of –luba; be stranger to one another, be unacquainted.

–lubâna (lubêne), be confused; incomprehensible, unrecognisable. umutima walubana, be upset; ill at ease.

lubango (mango) flexible rod; lath; withe.

lubansa (mânsa), courtyard.

lubao (m), fence, enclosure.

lubatisho, baptism. mwana ma –, godchild. wishi wa

–, godfather. nyina wa –, godmother.

lubêlo (m), razor.

lubembo (m), gong.

lubembu (m), adultery.

–lubika (lubike), pass unnoticed; be hidden.

lubilo, 1. n. speed (in running. 2. adv. fast (running).

lubingu (mingu or mabingu), flame; blaze.

lubola (m), sting of an insect.

lubondo (mondo), hoof.

lububa, thicket; thick undergrowth.

–lubuka (lubwike), v. stat, of –lubula.

lubuko (m), divination; evocation of spirits.

–lubula (lubwile), redeem; set free; deliver.

lubuli, quarrel; fight; provocation; assault; battle; clash. –cito –, have a fight, etc. –bûsho –, cause a fight; provoke. –songo –, incite to a fight. –ba no –, be quarrelsome. wa –, quarrelsome person.

lubuli lubuli, provokingly.

–lubulula (lubulwile), explain or defend a case.

lubungu, decay of teeth.

–lubwila (lubwile), 1. v. appl. of –lubula, 2. v.t. return something borrowed. – misha, pay debts.

luce, smell of fish.

lucebu, forboding.

lucêlo 1. n. morning. 2. adv. early in the morning. lucêlo cêlo, very early.

lucene (n), tiger fish.

lucengo (n), cave; cavern.

luceshi (n), pillar; column.

lucu, suffering; ill-treat-

ment. *–cito –*, ill-treat.
lufine (m), pimple; pustule.
lufuba (m), hut for spirits.
lufungo (m), wild plumlike fruit.
lufungulo (m), key.
lufukutu (m), black soil.
lufwi (m), white hair.
lufwinyemba (ba–), chameleon.
–lufya (lufishe), lose; mislay.
–lufyanya (lufyenye), 1. v. rec. of *–lufya.* 2. v.i. do wrong. *–lufyanyo mulandu,* muddle up a case.
lufyengo, injustice; harm; wrong. *–ba no –,* be unjust.
lufyo (m), kidney.
–luka (lukile), 1. v.t. weave. 2. v.i. vomit. *– bushishi,* twist thread. *– mpóto,* plait hair. *muti wa kuluka,* vomitive; emetic.
Lukalisitiya, Eucharist.
–lukana (lukêne), be entangled (of thread).
–lukanya (lukenye), v.t. entangle.
lukasa (ma), foot; paw. *ku makasa* or *ku nkasa,* on foot; foot-print.
lukasu (n), hoe. *– lwa ŋombe,* plough.
luko (nduko), tribe; clan.
lukombo (n), gourd-cup.
lukoma (n), kind of bird: "hornbill".
lukomo (n), notch made in trees to show the way. *–komo tukomo,* mark the way by cutting notches in trees.
lukondwa (n), hole made in mush for relish. *–lemo lukondwa,* make a hole in mush for relish.

lukopyo (n), eyelash.
lukose (n), snare for birds.
lukoshi (n), Shikra hawk.
lukufu (n), tick.
lukuni (n), firewood.
lukungu (n), dust.
lukûngu (n), verandah.
lukûso, used in the expression; *–beo lukuso,* shave all the head.
–lula (lulile), be bitter.
–lûla (lûlile), disown; disregard; shun.
lulamba, shore; beach; coast.
lulembo (nêmbo), incision on body for applying medicine. *–kome* or *–lembe nembo,* make incisions for applying medicine.
lulimi (ndimi), tongue; language. *–ba ne ndimi shibili,* be deceitful.
lulumbi, fame; renown.
lulya, that yonder, cf. T. III.
lûma (ŋuma), bruise; blow.
–lumano (mano), pliers; pincers; tongs.
–lumba (lumbile), praise; extol; glorify.
–lumbanya (lumbenye), extol; sing the glory of.
lumbâsa (ba–), nightjar.
–lumbuka (lumbwike), 1. v. v. stat. of *–lumbula.* 2. v.i. be famous; illustrious; well known; renowned; distinguished.
–lumbula (lumbwile), pronounce; enumerate; mention; confess. *–filembo,* spell a word.
lumbwe (ba–), fiancé, consort of a queen.
–lumbwisha (lumbishe), 1. v.t. make famous; renowned. 2. v.i. articulate,

pronounce distinctly.

...**lume**, male (of animal).

lumembe, kind of sweet beverage from "mpundu" fruit.

lumene (mene), kind of fish.

luminuminu (minuminu), blindsnake.

lumono (mono), castor bean.

–lumpa (lumpile), go afar; travel abroad.

–lunda (lundile), add; join; repair.

–lundikanya (lundikenye), join; solder.

–lunduluka (lundulwike), v. stat. of –*lundulula*.

–lundulula (lundulwile), 1. widen; lengthen. 2. spread (news). 3. aggravate; make worse.

–lundumana (lundumene), be steep; precipitous; elevated (as elevation from surface); protrude.

–lundumanika (lundumanike), raise; elevate; make higher.

–lunga (lungile), 1. hunt (with a gun, etc.). 2. season food.

–lungama (lungeme), 1. be right; correct. 2. be level, straight; even. 3. go straight to; start off to a place; go or come to.

–lungamika (lungamike), straighten; set right.

–lungatana (lungatene), be parallel.

–lungatanika (lungatanike), make parallel.

–lungika (lungike), 1. v.t. put in line; aim at (shooting). 2. v.i. be exact; precise; right; straightforward; correct. – *pa kusosa*, say the truth.

–lungisha (lungishe), 1. v. int. of –*lunga*. 2. v.t. repair; mend.

–lungula (lungwile), v.i. be burnt (of food).

–lungusha (lungwishe), burn food in cooking.

lûni (ŋuni), honey-bird.

lunkoto, dog-grass.

lunkumbwa, concupiscence; lust.

lunse, sickness in a child caused by the mother because she becomes pregnant before the child is weaned.

lunshi (ba–), house fly.

lunshingwa, dizziness; giddiness; vertigo. – *lwaba pa menso*, feel giddy or dizzy.

lunweno (nweno), small earthenwear.

lunyungo (nyungo), sieve.

lupako (m), hallow in a tree.

lupanda (m), forked pole.

lupande (m), kind of necklace, pl. more used.

lupanga (m), sword; sabre.

lupango (m), bride price; –*leko* –, pay the bride price. pl. mpango, more used.

lupapo, hedge; fence.

lupashi (m), red ant; "army" or "soldier" ant.

lupantila (m), flea.

lupapo, amazement.

lupato, hatred; antipathy; dissension.

lupe (ndupe), winnowing basket.

lupele (m), scabies; itch.

lupemba (m), white clay; chalk.

lupemfu (m), cockroach.

lupese (m), weevil; boring

beetle.

lupeta (m), seed of "mupeta" tree, used in native games.

lupi (ndupi or mapi), palm of hand. *–tóta– mapi*, applause. *–ombe ndupi*, clap hands. *lupi pa*, a handful. *–umo lupi*, slap; smack.

lupili (m), mountain; hill.

lupimpi (m), amulet.

lupingu (m), knuckle; joint; knot in reed or bamboo, etc.

lupiya (m), money; shilling; rupee. *–fole mpiya*, receive wages.

lupofu (m̀), mouthful.

lupoloto (m), tattoo on abdomen. *–shile mpoloto*, v.t. tattoo.

lupôpo (m), peg, tent peg; beacon.

lupóto (m), curl of hair; lock.

lupu (ndupu), bag made of bark.

lupuma (m), honeycomb when full of honey.

lupuma (ba–), fit of pielepsy; stroke; fainting fit.

lupumo (m), blow; stroke.

lupungu (m), hut built on a platform; two or more storeyed house. *– lwa njelwa*, tower; spire.

lupupo (m), ceremony in honour of a deceased. *–pupo lupupo* (pupile), perform the ceremony.

luputa (m), round mound. *– lwa muntu*, grave; tomb.

luputu (m), kind of fern.

lupwa (ndupwa), family.

lusa, permission. *–kwato –*, have permission; be authorised. *–nelo –*, give permission; allow. *–lombo –*, ask permission. *–poko –*, obtain permission.

lusale (n), wire.

lusambo (n), bracelet made of copper wire.

lusâmu (n), rag; tatter.

lusani (n), shelf placed above fire place.

lusaniko (n), torch made of grass or reeds.

lusanshilo (n), strainer.

lusanso (n), same as *lusanshilo*.

lusapato (n), shoe.

lusasa (n), fence made of grass, reeds, etc.

lusase (n), spark.

lusâshi (n), bullet.

lusato (n), python.

luse, mercy; pardon; dispensation. *–ba no luse*, be merciful. *–belelo* (or *–kwato) luse*, have mercy; pardon. *–cito luse*, same as *–belelo – wa luse*, (ba), merciful person.

lusebo, tale – bearing. *wa lusebo* (ba), tale bearer.

luseke (n), grain; seed.

luseko (n), laughter; joke. pl. more used.

lusele (n), insult; reviling. *–tuke nsele* (tukile), insult; use abusive language.

luse luse, meekly; with kindness.

lusenga (n), grain of sand.

lusengo (n), horn.

lusengu (n), bamboo.

lushembe (n), kind of small fish.

lushimi (n), fable; legend.

lushimu (n), bee.

lushindano (n), needle, pl. more used.

lushindo (n), sound of footsteps.

lushinga (n), rope made of

hide.

lushipa (n), nerve; sinew.

lushishi (n), rope made with the bark of trees. *–fundo –*, make a rope with the bark of trees.

lusomo (n), fee of a witch-doctor.

lusongwa (n), cape goose-berry.

lusoni (n), shame, shyness; modesty. pl. more used.

lusonta (n), roof pole; rafter.

lusuba, dry or hot season. *– lunono*, September. *– lukalamba*, October.

lusuka (n), tail of fowl or bird.

lusuko (n), cloud of dust.

lusuko, dropsy.

lusundu (n), wart.

lusunga (n), nail; screw.

luswa (n), winged white ant. *–kole nswa*, gather winged white ants.

lutambo (n), string; wick.

lutampulo (n), step; pace; yard (measure).

lutanda (n), star.

lutesu (n), sneeze.

luto lwa buci, pure liquid honey.

lutobatoba, brutality.

lutobaula (ba–), brutal person.

lutombo (n), bud; blossom.

lutoshi (n), lump.

lutoyo (n), groundpea. *–fuke ntoyo*, dig out –.

lutungu (n), hip.

lutwe (ndutwe), end; extremity (local). *ku lutwe*, at the end (locally).

lwa, prep. of, cf. T. I.

–lwa (lwile), fight; resist; clash.

lwala (ngala), finger nail; claw.

–lwala (lwele), be ill; suffer from.

lwalala, open court. *–biko muntu ʼmu lwalâla*, try somebody in public.

–lwalika (lwalike), cause to be ill.

–lwalilila (lwalilile), be sickly; feeble; infirm.

lwambo, slander.

lwambu, 1. contagion; infection. 2. charm set to guard a field. *bulwêle bwa –*, contagious disease.

...lwani, ferocious; hostile; wicked.

lwelele, emptiness; sky; atmosphere.

lwendo (nyendo), journey; trip; tour.

lweo, kind of fine grass.

lwili (njili), oyster.

lwimbo (nyimbo), song; hymn. *–bûlo –*, intone a song. *–lusho –*, sing a song badly. *–poko –*, take up a refrain. *–shiko –*, invent a song.

lwingwe (ma), door post.

lwino (nyino), shelf placed above fire place.

lwinso, sight. *–ba no –*, be sharpsighted.

–lwisha (lwishishe), fight; attack; charge; assault.

–lya (lile), 1. eat; consume; 2. gain.

lya, prep. of, cf. T. I.

lyashi, conversation; gossip.

lyena, cj. in that case.

lyeshi, flood; inundation.

lyonse, adv. each time; always.

— M —

m, I; me, cf. T. II, 2, a & b.
macaca, daybreak; dawn.
macishi, matches.
mafi, excrement; feaces.
– *ya ɲombe*, cattle manure.
mafina, pus.
mafisa kanwa, bribe. –*cita mafisa kanwa*, v.t. bribe.
mafundisho, sermon; instruction.
mafuta, oil; grease; fat; lard. *mafuta ye shiba*, butter.
mafuto, fine; penance; compensation. –*leka mafuto*, pay fine.
mailo, yesterday; tomorrow, *na mailo*, to-morrow also. *mailo telyo*, not to-morrow. *mailo lyena*, as for to-morrow.
mainsa, rainy season.
maka, strength; power; force; effort; authority; right. –*ba na maka*, be strong; can. –*pela maka*, authorize. *wa maka* (ba), a strong person. *maka maka*, energetically with force; hard. *na maka* or *pa maka*, interj.: "put on all your strength".
makalashi, spectacles. –*fwala* –, wear spectacles.
makanta, locust used with singular and class "mu/ba".
makasa, pl. of lukasa; footprints; traces; spoor. –*lengula makasa*, v.t. trace; follow spoor.
makashi, scissors.
mako, parents-in-law.
makumanino, appointed place of meeting.

makunda, –*lema* –, squat down.
makunga, exaggeration.
makungwe, kind of edible mushroom.
makunkutu, stump of amputated limb. *wa* –, mutilated person. –*teta* –, mutilate.
makwebo, objects of trade. *wa* – (ba), tradesman.
makwelelo, suspenders.
malaika (ba–), angel. – *mulinshi*, guardian angel.
malaila, song of triumph.
malale, trickery.
malasha, coal.
male, finger millet, pl. of bule.
malekano, place where roads part.
malêle, pretence; pretext; fraud; trickery.
malelya, malaria.
malîla, feast; banquet.
malilo, wailing.
malimino, garden.
malipilo, wages; pay; salary.
malisawa, shot for shotgun.
malitili (ba–), martyr.
malo, camping or sleeping place. *pa malo ya*, in the place of; on behalf of; instead of. –*ikala pa mâlo ya*, take the place of; represent.
malumbo, praise; glory; litany.
maluti, gunpowder.
malwa, sufferings; sorrows.
mâlwa, big quantity of beer.
malyo, good omen.
mama (ba–), grandmother; wife; Sister.
mamafyala (ba–), my mother-in-law / daughter-in-law.

mamba, forest cobra.
mambalushi, water cobra.
mambepa, pretext.
mangimêla (ba–), surveyor.
–manika (manike), grip as with pincers.
manda, kind of fish.
mâno, intelligence; wisdom; cleverness; common sense; intellectual ability. *–ba na mâno,* be intelligent; wise. *–pelwa mâno,* be dull; not intelligent; have no common sense. *–pesho muntu amâno,* be beyond one's understanding. *–twalako mâno,* pay attention to. *mâno yafulungana,* be cofused.
mâno mâno, wisely.
mansansa, small grass hut built by children to play housekeeping.
mapili, mountain chain.
–masa (mashile), plaster; mud.
masaka, white sorghum.
masako, fur; coat of animal.
masamba, West.
masambi, pl. of isambi. *wa –* (ba), sinner.
masange, joke; teasing.
masansa, bifurcation in road.
mashi, dregs of beer.
mashindano, examination.
mashinjala (ba–), messenger.
mashini (ba–), machine.
mashiwi, 1. pl. of ishiwi. 2. speech. *–ba na –* have something to say or report. *–fisha –,* report. *–bwekeshapo –,* repeat; insist on one's words. *–konka –,* obey.
mashutu, cakes of groundnuts after oil has been extracted.

–masuka (maswike), v. stat. of *–masula.*
–masula (maswile), take plaster away.
mataki, boasting; brag.
mate, saliva; spittle.*–fwisa, –,* spit. *–pâla –,* bless.
matomato (ba–), tomato.
matipa, mud; swamp.
matololo, desert.
matunda, strawberries.
mawilo, confluence.
mayo (ba–), my mother.
mayosenge (ba–), my paternal aunt.
mayo-mwaice, my maternal aunt.
mba, adv. at least.
mbafi, nicely forged axe.
mbalaminwe (m), finger ring.
mbale (m), 1. plate. 2. serval cat. *– yafonka,* bowl; dish. also *– yafongomana.* *– yasenama,* plate. also, *– yapapatala.*
mbali, ku *– ya,* nearby; around. *mu mbali,* secretly.
mbao (m), board; plank. *– ya kwikalapo,* bench.
mbata (m), spurwing goose.
...mbi, other; another; else; following.
...mbi, ...mbi, the one, the other; some, others.
...mbi ...mbi, different; strange.
mbila, announcement; proclamation; banns; *–bile mbila,* make a proclamation.
mboboyo, sore ears; earache.
mbone (m), witness.
mboni ya linso, pupil of eye.
mboo (m), buffalo.

mbulu (m), monitor (iguana lizard).

mbulushi (m), blindsnake.

mbushi (m), goat.

mbuto (m), seed; grain.

mbwa (m), domestic dog. *–kuwishe mbwa pa,* set dog on.

mbwili (m), leopard.

mêlu, mail. *wa mêlu* (ba), mailman. *mêlu ya mu ndeke,* air mail. *mêlu ya panshi,* surface mail.

–mena (menene), germinate; sprout.

–menda (mendele), mend.

mêno. 1. pl. of lino. 2. wound caused by a bite.

menshi, water; sap; juice; *– makasa,* ice. also *–yakambantana. – ya cikalishi,* stagnant water. *–tapa menshi* (tapite), draw water.

menso, pl. of linso; sight. *–ba pa –,* be in sight. *ca ku menso* (fya), appearance, *–ishiba ku –,* know by sight. *ku menso,* face. *–linda ku –,* keep in sight. *pa menso,* at first sight. *pa menso ya,* in the presence of. *pa menso ya bantu bonse,* openly; to the knowledge of all.

mfifi, obscurity; darkness.

mfubu (m), hippopotamus.

mfuko (m), mole.

mfula, rain; *mabwe ya –,* hail, n.

mfumu (ma or bashamfumu), chief; king. *– yanakashi,* queen.

mfundato, discretion.

mfungo (m), civet cat.

mfuti (m), gun; rifle. *– ya ciwaya,* machine-gun. *buta bwa mfuti,* trigger of a gun. *–lishe* (or *–pose*),

mfuti, shoot.

mfwa, death.

mfwalashi, horse.

mfwi (m), reedbuck.

mfwila, *–ume –,* beat to death.

mfwilwa (m), person in mourning. *muka –* (ba–), widow; widower.

mibombele, way of doing.

micitile, behaviour; way of acting.

mikalile, way of sitting.

miku, times. *miku inga,* how often. *miku imo imo,* sometimes; once and again. *miku imo imo fye,* seldom; rarely; a few times only. *miku ne miku,* often. *miku ingi,* many times. *miku te ya kupenda,* innumerous times.

–mikula (mikwile), multiply (math.); times (math.).

milandile, ways of talking.

milandu, history, (pl. of *mulandu). – ya kale,* ancient history. *– ya nomba,* modern history.

milangwe, funny stories; jokes.

milioni (ba–), million.

milomo, edge; brim of container.

milumbe, 1. kind of bird: "bee-eater". 2. pl. of *mulumbe.*

milumbelumbe, kind of bird: "speckled coly".

–mima (mimine), drizzle.

mimonekele, appearance.

–mina (minine), v.t. swallow.

minsa, Mass. *–umfwe –* attend Mass.

–minya (minishe), dislocate; sprain. *–minyo mucila,* wag the tail.

minwe, pl. of munwe. *minwe mikutwa,* empty handed.

miponto reviling; abuse; insolence. *–ba ne miponto,* be ungrateful.

misakalala, skeleton.

misango, character.

misasatwe, in great number.

miseke. 1. pl. of museke 2. change in silver.

misekele, way of laughing.

misha, debts. *–ba ne misha,* have debts; owe. *–fûte misha,* pay debts.

misokolo, village in construction.

misu, urine.

misûla, disregard; contempt; insolence; abuse; offence; reviling. *–ba ne misûla,* be disrespectful; insolent.

mîtamîta, adv. in rapid succession.

mitanda, huts in the gardens.

mito, ashes. *nshikunkulu ya mito.* Ash Wednesday.

mo, 1. dim. of umo: talimo, he is not in here. 2. with which; on which: *nshila bayamo,* the road on which they went. 3. mere suffix without additional meaning.

...mo, 1. num. one. 2. adj. same.

...mo ...mo, some; the one, the other; one by one; one after another; each one; few; several.

...mo ...ine, just the same.

mobe, ku –, at thy home.

mófu, kind of tree.

–mokoalue (mokawile), break into several pieces. (as bread).

–mokoka (mokweke), n. stat. of *–mokola,* be broken.

–mokola (mokwele), v.t.

môlwa (ba–), long mounds.

môna nose; nostrils. *–sosela mu myona,* speak through the nose.

–mona (mwene), see; notice; look; find; have. *– ku menso,* be eyewitness.

–monana (monene), v. rec. of *–mona,* meet; face one another; visit one another.

–moneka (moneke), be visible; appear; become manifest; be clear; found. *–nga,* seem; look like.

mono, pl. of lumono, castor bean. *mafuta ya mono,* castor oil.

môno (myono), fish trap. *–têko –,* set a fish trap. *–fûbo –,* remove a fish trap.

monse monse, everywhere; in all things; on all sides.

motoka, motorcar.

mpaka (m), wild cat.

mpaka na, adv. till; until.

mpakilo (m), tunnel.

mpala (m), mpala antelope.

mpali, polygamy. *wa –.* polygamist *–upe –,* marry in polygamy.

mpâlume (m), defender; saviour.

mpanda, 1. pl. of lupanda. 2. straightforward or honest person.

mpanda mâno (m), good advisor.

mpande matete (mi), kind of fish.

mpande, pl. of lupande.

mpande ye kufi, knee-cap.

mpânga (m), bush; forest; country: *mwina –,* country man. *mpanga yonse,* everywhere; anywhere.

mpanga (m), 1. sheep. 2. pl.

of *lupanga. na mpanga,*
ewe.

mpango, 1. pl. of lupango. 2.
bride-price. *–leke mpango,*
pay the bride-price.

mpao, food for journey;
rations.

mpapa (m), hide; leather;
skin (of animal).

mpasa, kind of tree.

mpatila, hatred.

mpasase (m), revolt; uproar; strike; trouble.

mpela (m), end; limit. *pa –
ya,* at the end of.

mpele, pl. of tupele.

mpelembe (m), roan antelope.

mpelwa mâno (ba–), fool;
idiot.

mpemba, pl. of lupemba.

mpembwe (m), trench or
ditch round village or
garden for protection.

mpende (m), kind of fish.

mpendwa (m), number;
qauntity.

mpendwa, adv. in small
number. *–ba –,* be just a
few.

mpepo, n. cold; cold weather or – season; frost; fever.
–lwale mpepo, have a
fever. *bulwele bwa –,* malaria.

mpini (m), kind of poisonous viper.

mpilipili, pepper.

mpofu (m), blind person.

mpombo (m), duiker.

...mpomfu, of good quality.

mpongolo (m), gate.

mpuka (m), small group;
regiment.

mpuku (m), mouse.

mpulumushi (ba–), rascal.

mpumfya (m), kind of
edible mushroom.

mpumi (m), forehead; front;
face. *wa mpumi yakosa,*
thickheaded person.

mpumpumpu (ba–), onoma-
topaeic name for motor-
cycle.

mpundu (ba–), twins. *–pasa
–,* bear twins.

mpundu (m), fruit of "mupundu" tree.

mpungu (m), bateleur.

mpusho (m), any unit over
ten.

mputi (m), anus.

mpyani (m), heir; successor.

mu, 1. you; him; her, cf. T.
II. 2. a & b. 2. prep. in;
within; into; across; during; on the point of.

muba (my), bellows.

mûba (my), coffin.

mubale (mi), branch of
"cibale" palm tree.

mubamba (mi), elephantiasis.

mubanga (mi), kind of tree.

mubango wa kanwa (mi),
jaw.

mubanse (mi), kind of fish.

mubêle (mi), habit; custom.
– usuma, virtue. *– ubi,*
vice.

mubifi (ba), scoundrel;
rogue; sinner.

mubîle (ba), favourite;
friend.

mubili (mi), body.

mubiye (ba), his/her companion.

mubiyo (ba), thy com-
panion.

mubomfi (ba), worker;
servant.

mubongola, bilharzia.

mubumbishi, creator.

muca, toothache.

mucanga, sand.

mucapi (ba–), quack doctor.

mucele, salt. –*engo* –, make salt. –*lungo* –, v.t. salt.
mucence (ba–), parrot.
mucende (ba), adulterer.
mucendwa (mi), jaw.
mucenja (mi), kind of tree.
mucila (mi), tail.
mucindami (ba), honourable or respectable person.
mucinshi, honour; politeness; respect; esteem; good manners. –*ba no* –, be respectful; polite.
mucinshi mucinshi, adv. respectfully.
mucisha cinani, partiality.
mufimbila, jealousy; envy. –*ba no* –, be jealous; envious.
mufito (mi), charcoal.
mufôlo (mi), furrow; ditch; canal.
mufuki, perseverance.
mufukila kubili (ba–), flatterer.
mufuko (mi), bag; sack.
mufula (mi), trench for foundation.
mufulo, malice; deliberate wickedness. *kù mufulo*, deliberately; intentionally; wilfully.
mufumbi (mi), rainy day.
mufundo, manure; compost.
mufungo (mi), kind of tree.
mufutu (mi), kind of tree.
mufwi (mi), arrow.
mufyala (ba), cousin (child of father's sister or mother's brother).
mufyashi (ba) parent (father or mother).
muka (ba–), spouse; wife or husband of.
muka mfwilwa (ba)–), widow; widower.
mukaka, milk.
mukakashi (ba), insolent or

quarrelsome person.
mukakwa (ba), prisoner.
mukalamba (ba), elder brother or sister.
mukanda (mi), pit.
mukanga (mi), pelican.
mukâni (ba), one who refuses all he is asked.
mukankala (ba), rich or honourable person.
mukashana (ba), maid.
mukashi (ba), wife.
mukate (mi), bread; loaf of bread.
mukati, adv. inside; into.
mukaya (ba), native; citizen.
mukobe (mi), otter (small kind).
mukolamfula (mi), rainbow.
mukole (mi), kind of tree.
mukôli (mi), the seed in a one-seed fruit.
mukolo (mi), tin basin.
mukolo (ba–), first wife of a polygamist.
mukoloci (ba), old person.
mukolobwe (mi), snare for animals made with rope.
mukolwa (mi), small furrow.
mukolwe (ba–), cock.
mukome (mi), kind of tree.
mukondo (mi), path made by game; hollow log used as trough.
mukonko (mi), gorge; dry riverbed.
mukosela (mi), importunity.
mukoshi (mi), neck; collar; throat.
mukote (ba), old person.
mukôti (mi), mine (excavation in earth).
mukoto (mi), dried fruit.
mukôwa (mi), totem; clan.
mukilishityani (ba), Christian.

muku (mi), time (in enumeration).

mukuba (mi), copper.

mukubwa (ba–), the one in charge; superior.

mukubi, perseverance.

mukufi; kind of bird: "roller".

mukuku (mi), rapid; strong current.

mukunyu (mi), wild fig tree.

mukupo mi), hide.

mukusao (mi), broom made of twigs.

mukuta (mi), cougal bird.

mukuwe (mi), kind of tree.

mukwa (mi), piece of bark used as a tray.

mukwai. 1. sir; madam. 2. answer to a call: "present". 3. interj. of surprise: "is that so!"

mukwakwa (ba), indiscreet person; tale bearer.

mulaba (mi), scratch; cut.

mulale (mi), crack in wall, etc.

mulalu (mi), hissing sandsnake.

mulamba (ba–), torrent.

mulamba (mi), track; trail.

mulambo (mi), tribute. –*leko* –, pay tribute.

mulanda (ba), poor unfortunate person. *ne* –, interj.: "what a poor person I am".

mulando (mi), log.

mulandu (mi), case; affair; fault cause; reason; purpose; aim; lawsuit. concern; business; offence; crime. cf. –*ampa mu mulandu; ampo mulandu –ampulo mulandu. –ba no mulandu*, be guilty. –*cefya* –, excuse. –*cito* –, commit an offence. –*citilo muntu* –, accuse. –*fisho* –, report

a. case. –*fundawilo* –, muddleup a case. –*futa pa* –, pay a fine. *ku mulandu wa*, on account of; for the sake of. *lelo* –, what does it matter! –*lemyo* –, exaggerate. –*lundululo* –, announce something. *mu* –, *uyu*, in this point; herein, *mulandu nshi?* why? – *wakosa*, the case is insoluble. *pa – wa*, on account of; for the sake of; as regrads. –*pindo* –. ask for compensation. –*putulo* –, judge or settle a case. –*sendeko* –, alter a case. –*shininkisho* –, study a case. –*sosa mu* –, give evidence. –*sula pa* –, excuse or disregard a case. *te* –, interj.: "don't mind"; "it does not matter". –*lumbulo* –, let out a secret. *wa mulandu* (ba), accused person.

mulanga, morning-star.

mulanga (mi), club.

mulao (mi), last will; testament.

mulapo (mi), oath. –*lapo* –, take an oath. –*onaulo* –, break an oath.

mulâsa (mi), compulsory work for a chief.

mulashi (ba), vassal; governor; administrator.

mulebe (mi), kind of tree.

mulêle, laziness; negligence.

mulemba, 1. suppuration of the ear. 2. flight (of birds).

mulembe (mi), trunk of elephant.

mulembwe, dried leaves used as relish; relish so made.

mulemfwe (m), new grass after burning.

mulendo (ba), traveller.

mulenga (ba–), 1. divin

of the Babemba. 2. hunter (with a dog).

mulengesha (ba–), dragon fly.

mulenshi (ba), handsome boy or girl.

mulesha citendwe, pastime.

muleshi (ba), nurse; orderly; fosterfather or foster-mother; custodian.

muleya (ba–), long-tailed widow bird.

muli, prep. in; into.

mulilo (mi), fire; matches. *–wa pe*, hell. *–kosho –*, light fire. *–kupo –*. beat fire down with branches. *–paso –*, scatter fire to put it out. *–shiko –*, make fire by friction. *–shimyo –*, extinguish fire.

mulima (mi), fruit bat.

mulimba (mi), trough; riverbed.

mulimi (ba), farmer.

mulimo (mi), work; job; duty; task; obligation; use. *–ba no –*. be busy. *–lwa no –*, be very busy. *–bombo –*, work. *fwayo –*, look for work. *–inuka ku –*, cease a day's work. *–inusha ku –*, relieve from a day's work. *–leko –*, leave work; abdicate. *–pélo –*, give work! engage; employ.

mulinda fipe (ba–), watchman for goods.

mulinganya, impartially. *–ba no –*, be impartial.

mulinshi (ba), guardian.

mulinso (ba), lizard.

mulolâni (mi), mirror; looking glass.

mulolo (mi), kind of tree.

mulombwa (mi), kind of tree.

mulombwe (ba–), masked weaver bird.

mulomo (mi), lip. *– wa cûni*, beak of bird. *–ba no –*, be insolent; provocative. *–shintiko – ku*, kiss.

mulondo (ba), fisherman; tracks; traces.

mulonga (mi), running water.

mulonge (mi), kind of fish.

mulongo (mi), row; line; file. *–tantamo –*, line up. *–enda –*, walk in a single row.

mulongóti (m), flag-staff; tent pole.

mulongwe (ba–), kind of bird: "fly catcher".

mulopa (m), blood. *–súko –*, excret blood. *–súmo –*, bleed. *–sundo –*, pass blood.

mulopwe, interj.: "master"; "Lord".

muloshi (ba), sorcerer; witch.

mulowa (mi), kind of bird: "kingfisher".

mûlu, heaven; sky; top. *pa –*, on top; above; in addition.

muluba (m), pollen.

mulubushi, saviour; redeemer.

mululu (mi), kind of tree.

mulumbe (mi), fable; tale; story; legend. *–umo –*, tell a fable, etc.

mulume (ba), husband.

mulumendo (ba), youth.

mulundu (mi), elevated distance up a hill or mountain.

mulundubwi (mi), soft stone, slate pencil.

Mulungu, God.

mulungu (mi), week. *milungu ibili*, fortnight.

mulungulwa (mi), ghost;

spook.

mulunguti (mi), kind of tree.

mulunshi (ba), hunter (with gun, etc.).

mulwani (ba), enemy; foe; adversary.

mulwele (ba), sick person.

mulyabantu (ba), cannibal.

mumana (mi), river; stream. – *upita pe*, perennial stream. – *uwauma mu lusuba*, seasonal stream. *ku mulu wa* –, upstream. *kwisamba lya* –, downstream.

mumbo, deliberatness.

mûmbu (my), yam.

mumbulu (mi), wild dog.

mumbwe (ba—), jackal.

mume (mime), dew.

mumena (mi), germinated millet.

mumena (ba), abscess; boil; tumour.

mûmi (bômi), healthy person. –*ba mûmi*, be healthy; alive.

mumo, adv. alike; of the same kind/manner/character.

mumo mumo, here and there.

mumono (mi), castor oil plant.

mumpanda (ba), otter (big kind).

munabi (ba), prophet.

munabo (ba), their companion.

munandi (ba), my companion.

munaŋani (ba), lazy person.

munani, relish.

munankwe (ba), his/her companion.

mundowendowe, agreeable aftertaste.

mune (bane), friend; companion; fellow; mate.

munensu (ba), our companion.

munenu (ba), your companion.

mûnga (my), thorn. – *we sabi*, fishbone.

muŋomba (mi), kind of bird; hornbill.

mungu (my), marrow (gourd).

munjili (ba–), warthog.

munkalwe (ba), brute; heartless person.

muno, in here.

munobe (banobe), thy companion.

munofu (mi), flesh; lean meat.

munonko (ba–), thy brother.

munshanya (ba–), ungrateful person.

munshebwa (ba–), person who does not stand a remark.

munshele (mi), kick. –*panta* (or *nyanta*) –, v.t. kick.

munshumfwa (ba–), person who does not want to listen.

munsôli (mi), sound of whistling. –*lisho* –, v.t. whistle.

muntekunteku, hiccup.

muntontonkanya, imagination; idea; thoughts. – *wa mpofu*, mere imagination.

muntu (ba), human being; person belonging to the 'Bantu' race. *muntu onse*, anybody; everyone. *muntu* with poss. pr. relative; akin; e.g. *muntu wandi*, my relative. *muntu wa mibêle isuma*, gentleman.

muntu, adv. wherein; the place in which.

muntunse (ba), commoner.

munungwe (ba), person of an opposite clan.

munwe (mi), finger. – *ukalamba*, second finger.

munwena (mi), 1. reed for drinking beer. 2. poison put into drink.

munwenshi (ba), drunkard.

munyama (ba), vampire; ritual murderer.

munyamata (ba), gentleman.

munyangâla (mi), furrow.

munyina (ba–), 1. his/her brother or sister. 2. his/her cousin (child of father's brother/mother's sister).

munyinane (ba–), my brother/sister/cousin.

munyinabo (ba–), their brother/sister/cousin.

munyinefwe (ba–), our brother/sister/cousin.

munyinenwe (ba–), your brother/sister/cousin.

munyololo (mi), chain.

muomba (ba), singer.

muombo (mi), kind of tree.

mupabi (ba), commoner.

mupaka (mi), boundary; border; demarcation line; frontier.

mupakwa (mi), same as *mupaka*.

mupamba (mi), bad omen.

mupando (mi), chair.

mupâpa (mi), kind of tree.

mupashi (mi), soul or spirit of a departed. –*pepe mipashi*, worship spirits.

mupata (mi), gorge; ravine.

mupatili (ba), priest.

mupêla (mi), guava tree.

mupemo (mi), respiration; breathing; breath.

mupêpi, adv. near; nearby; close; beside. – *na*, near

to; about; approximately.

mupeto (mi), wheel; tyre.

mupika (mi), iron pot.

mupila (mi), rubber; rubber tyre; ball. –*to mupila*, play football; –*umo mupila*, kick a ball.

mupina (ba), poor or unhappy person.

mupindo, colic.

mupini (mi), handle of a tool.

mupokapoka (mi), gorge; gap.

mupu, breath; air in tyre.

mupukila, insolence.

mupundu (mi), kind of tree.

Mupûndu-milimo, December.

mupûpu (ba), thief; burglar; robber.

mupusaushi (ba), flighty or careless person.

mupushi (ba), beggar.

muputu (mi), kind of tree.

muputule (mi), room; partition in a house.

mupya (mi), bush after fire has passed.

musa (mi), draught; liquid; drink.

musâfwa (mi), kind of tree.

musalaba (mi), cross; crucifix. *cilembo ca* –, sign of the cross.

musâlu, vegetable; spinach.

musâlula, insolence; contempt; abuse; reviling –*ba no* –, be insolent; impertinent.

musambashi (ba), wealthy or important person.

musambilila (ba), pupil; apprentice; student; disciple

musambo (mi), branch shoot; twig.

musamwe (mi), amusement

musana (mi), back; loin waist. –*lwalo* –, suffer

from lumbago.

musange (mi), teasing.

musango (mi), kind; manner; method; species; custom; character; example; form; shape; sort; quality. *musango wa kuti*, in such a manner. *musango nshi*, in what manner? how? *te musango iyo*, it is no manner.

musangu (ba), deserter; apostate; traitor.

musanku (ba), untidy or carreless person.

musanse (mi), coarse grass.

musao (mi), pillow; cushion, *–sailo mutwe pa musao*, lay head on cushion.

musase (mi), kind of tree.

musashi (mi), small gourd.

musêbo (mi), road; path; street. *– wa motoka*, motorcar road.

museke (mi), basket made of reeds.

musele (mi), small basket.

musêlu (mi), sick-feeling.

muselwe (ba), friend.

musemo (mi), bunch of bananas.

musenga (mi), sand.

musengele (mi), bed.

musensenga (mi), sand.

musenshi (ba), pagan; heathen; gentile.

museshi (mi), kind of tree.

musha (ba), slave.

mushi (mi), village. *–sokolo mushi*, build a new village. *mwine mushi* (ba), headman of a village.

mushika (ba–), manager. *– wa mfumu*, adviser of a chief.

mushikale (ba), soldier.

mushike (mi), kind of tree.

mushila (mi), root; vine of

a creeper.

mushili (mi), soil. *mushili we lambo*, loam.– *wa mpuma*, virgin soil.

mushilinshi (mi), plateau; flat country.

mushilika (ba), soldier.

mushimbe (ba), unmarried person; spinster; bachelor; celibate; widow; widower.

mushinga (mi), marriage impediment.

mushingo (mi), girdle.

mushipa (mi), 1. kind of small fish. 2. nerve; muscle. *– wa mulopa*, bloodvessel; artery; vein.

mushipi (mi), belt; sash.

mushishi (mi), hair. *–beo –*, cut hair. *mishishi yafulubana*, uncombed hair, *mishishi yanyongâna* or *ya mpolombo*, curled hair.

mushitu (mi), grove.

mushobo (mi), race; tribe; nation.

musoka (mi), murder. *wa misoka* (ba), murderer.

musokela, importunity.

musole (ba), apostle.

musolilo (mi), embers; red hot cinders.

musolo wa nkoko, (mi), young hen starting to lay eggs.

musomali (mi), nail.

musombo (mi), small burrow.

musonga (mi), germ of a plant.

musongole (mi), kind of tree.

musonko (mi), tax.

musôwa (mi), wails, mourning. *–lile misowa*, bewail; mourn.

musuku (mi), kind of tree.

musukupala (mi), bottle; flask.

musula (mi), anus.

musulolo (mi), fire-poker.

musulushi (ba), trader; hawker.

musulwishi (ba), same as *musulushi*.

musumba (mi), city; town; village where a chief lives. *mwina musumba* (bêna), townsman.

musumbo (mi), drill; awl; borer.

musunga, gruel; paste; porridge. *–kumbo musunga*, cook gruel or porridge.

musungu (ba), European.

musungu (mi), chaff.

muswaki (mi), toothbrush.

muswema (mi), kind of snake.

musweshi (ba), light coloured African.

muta (mi), 1. catfish. 2. burrow.

mutaba (mi), kind of tree.

mutakatifu (ba), saint; patron saint.

mutalantanshi (ba), wanderer; vagabond; loafer.

mutanda, 1. num. six. 2. s. of mitanda.

mutande (ba), row; line.

mutani (ba), stingy person; miser.

mutanshi (ba), predecessor.

mutantamfula, swollen gland in groin caused by a septic wound.

mutante (mi), meat without bone.

mutanto (mi), ladder; staircase.

mute, perseverance; courage.

mute mute, perseveringly.

muteke (mi), kind of tree.

mutembo, meekness. *–bo no –*, be meek; amiable.

mutemwikwa (ba), dear or beloved person.

mutemwishi (ba), same as *mutemwikwa*.

mutende, health. *–ba –* or *–endo –*, be healthy; in good health.

mutenge (mi), roof. *–fimbo –*, thatch a roof. *–paliko –*, put a roof on hut/house.

mutengo (mi), 1. forest; 2. price; value; cost; charge. *ca –*, expensive; valuable. *– ni shani?* what is the price? what does it cost? *– wakosa*, it is expensive or dear; it costs much. *– te pa kukosa*, how expensive (interj. of surprise). *– naunake*, it is cheap or of moderate price. *–nasho –*, lower the price. *–pango –*, fix a price. *–umyo –*, raise the price.

mutengu (mi), kind of bird: "Drongo".

mutete (mi), reed for drinking.

muti (mi), 1. tree. 2. medicine; remedy.

mutima (mi), heart; soul; conscience; will; instinct. *biko – ku*, put one's heart into. *–bwesho –*, v.i. calm down; become appeased. *–kosho –*, v.t. encourage. *–lwâla mu –*, be epileptic. *–lwâla pa –*, suffer from diarrhoea. *mutima nteku*, adv. calmly; without haste. *pa – palekalipa*, suffer colic. *–teko mutima*, be careful; pay attention; behave. *mutima nawikala*, be appeased.

mutîti (mi), maggot.

muto, sauce; gravy.
mutobatoba (bi), brute.
mutobo (mi), kind of tree.
mutopoto (mi), green bean.
mutofwe (mi), zink; lead.
mutôlilo, (ba), flute.
mutondo (mi), 1. clay pot. 2. kind of tree.
mutonshi, humidity; moisture; dampness.
mutoto (mi), navel.
mutulo (mi), tribute; tithe.
mutumishi (ba), envoy; servant; emissary; apostle.
mutundu (mi), 1. tribe. 2. lair. 3. small hut for children to play house-keeping.
mutunganya, accusation; suspicion. –*ba no* –, be suspicious.
mutungi (mi), barrel.
mutungu (ba–), ox.
mutunta (mi), beat of the heart; pulse.
mutûtu (ba), savage or rustic person.
mutwâla, purgatory.
mutwe (mi), head. –*ishiba ku* –, know by heart. –*koso* –, be stubborn; hardheaded; obstinate. –*kunto* –, shake the head in denial. –*pukunyo* –, shake the head with astonishment. –*lwalo mutwe*, suffer from headache.
muyembe (mi), mango tree. also *mwêmbe*.
muyenge (mi), deep valley; abyss.
mwa! interj. of surprise "is it so!" "really!"
Mwalabu (ba), Arab.
mwabo, ku–, their home.
mwafi (my), poison used in trial.
mwaice (ba), 1. child (of another). 2. younger sister

or brother. 3. younger person.
mwaka (my), year; season.
...**mwaka**, annual, *cila* –, annually; yearly.
mwakatala (my), ostrich.
mwalimêni, greeting, cf. T. VII.
mwalimu (ba–), catechist; evangelist; teacher.
mwalo (my), beam.
Mwalule, burial place of the Bemba chiefs: Chitimukulu, Mwamba and Nkula.
mwalyêni bwino, greeting. cf. T. VII.
mwambo (my), worm.
mwamfuli (my), umbrella.
mwana (bâna), 1. child (one's own). *mwana mwaume*, son. *mwana mwanakashi*, daughter. *mwana wa lubatisho*, godchild. *mwana wa mu bucende*, bastard. 2. –, the young of an animal, bird etc. e.g. *mwana wa nkoko*, chicken.
mwanakashi (ba), woman.
mwanda, (my), hundred.
mwandi, pl. mwandini, interj. of astonishment "is it so?" "indeed!"
mwandi, ku –, at my home.
mwando (my), rope; string; cord. –*pyato* –, make a rope.
mwâne (ba–), his/her child.
mwangashi (my), vine.
mwankole (ba–), crow; raven.
mwano (ba–), thy/your/ child.
mwansa (my), mane.
mwanshi (my), bundle.
mwapolêni, greeting, cf. T. VII.
mwau (my), n. yawn.
mwaume (ba). man.

mwe, abbr. of imwe.

mwefu (my), beard; moustache; whiskers. –*meno* –, grow a beard. –*beo* –, shave.

mwêla, wind; atmosphere; air; draught. –*lekelo mwêla ukwingila*, v.t. air.

mwele (my), knife.

mwele wa mfula, lightning.

–mwenamo (mwenenemo), obtain; earn; profit; gain; acquire.

mwendalwali (my), filesnake.

mwendo (my), leg of a kill; limb.

mwengele (my), kind of tree.

mwengo (my), chisel.

mweni (bêni), stranger; foreigner; visitor; guest.

–mwensekesha (mwensekeshe), see distinctly.

mwenso, fear; timidity; shyness. –*ba no mwenso*, be afraid; anxious; timid; shy; fear. *wa mwenso*, coward.

mwenu, kù –, your home.

mweo (my), life; soul; spirit. –*leko* –, die. –*mino* –, hold the breath. –*putulo* –, kill. –*pwilisho* –, choke; strangle.

Mweo Mutakatifu, Holy Ghost.

mweshi (my), moon; month; *mweshi waba uwashinguluka*, full moon. *mweshi wamoneka*, new moon. –*ba ku* –, have menstruation.

mwesu, ku –, at our home.

mwi? where? wherein.

mwiko (miko), 1. pallet; trowel. 2. taboo.

mwimba (mimba), burrow (big kind).

mwiminishi (bêminishi), godfather; protector.

mwina (bêna), person or people of a clan or a country, etc. – *fyalo*, stranger. – *Africa*, African. – *Kilishitu*, Christian. – *kufwa*, mortal (of man). *cina kufwa* (fina), mortal (of things). – *mupalamano*, neighbour.

mwina (bêna), husband, cf. T. V.

mwine (bene), person; owner; self, cf. T. II.

mwine mushi, headman; (ba mwine mushi).

mwinga (ba-), second wife; concubine; additional wife.

mwinshi (mi), 1. doorway; entrance. 2. pestle for pounding.

mwipwa (bêpwa), mwaume, nephew; – *mwanakashi*, niece.

mwishikulu (be), grandchild.

myabo, same as mwabo.

myaka, pl. of mwaka; age.

–myanga (myangile), lick.

myendele, customs; behaviour; manners; character.

myenu, same as mwenu.

myesu, same as mwesu.

— N —

n–m, 1; me, cf. T. II, 2.

na, 1. cj. and 2. prep. with. 3. adv. even.

...nabo, their fellow –, e.g. *kafundisha munâbo*, their fellow teacher.

naboya (ba–), molar tooth.

nabwinga (ba), bride.

nacibe, interj. "let it be"; "it does not matter."

nacimbusa (ba-), midwife.

nacine, adv. really; it is a fact; it is evident.

nacisungu (ba-), name given to a girl who passes through the 'cisungu' ceremonies; fiancée; virgin.

naendi, (interj. "indeed"; "certainly"; "exactly"; "quite so".

nafyala (ba-), his/her mother-in-law or daughter-in-law.

nafyalebo (ba-) their mother-in-law or daughter-in-law.

nafyalenwe (ba-), your mother-in-law or daughter-in-law.

–naka (nakile), 1. be tired; dying. 2. be tender; soft.

nakabili, adv. again; once more.

nakabumba (ba-), potter (woman); moulder.

nakabundu (ba-), kind of bird: "quail".

nakabushe, in fact; indeed.

nakalimo, adv. perhaps; possibly; likely; probably; may be.

nakalya, adv. 1. not at all. 2. (with ...onse), completely; entirely.

nakamo, nothing.

nakanga, all the more; with greater reason; particularly.

nakansha, same as nakanga.

nakapelele (ba-), winged white ant.

–nakilila (nakilile), be submissive; docile; meek; obliging.

nakonde (ba-), tattoo on temples. –shila –, v.t.

tattoo.

nakulu (ba-), his/her grandmother.

nalimo, same as nakalimo.

nalume (ba-), his/her maternal uncle.

nalumebo (ba-), their maternal uncle.

nalumefwe (ba), our maternal uncle.

nalumenwe (ba-, your maternal uncle.

nama (n), animal; beast; meat. –sha kulunga, game.

namabula (ba-), kind of green snake.

namba (n), gum; sealing wax –bikapo or –kambatikako namba, v.t. seal.

nampónga, same as nakalimo.

nampundu (ba-), mother of twins.

namufita, it is dark (inside a room).

namutekenya (ba-), driver; pilot.

nana, cj. in that case.

–nanana (nanene), 1. be lazy; idle. 2. be soft.

...**nâŋani**, lazy.

nangu, cj. although; though; in spite of; notwithstanding. – cimo, nothing. – kumo, nowhere. – limo, never. – panóno, not a little. – umo, nobody.

nangu ... nangu, neither ... nor.

nangula, same as nangu.

...**nankwe**, his/her companion/fellow, etc.: kafundisha munankwe, his/her fellow-teacher.

na ... o, also.

naosa (ba-), rudder; oarsman.

napafita, it is dark (at

night.

nasenge (ba–), his/her paternal aunt.

nasengebo (ba–), their paternal aunt.

nasengefwe (ba), our paternal aunt.

nasengenwe (ba–), your paternal aunt.

–nasha (nashishe), v.t. 1. tame; subdue; defeat. 2. tire. 3. persuade. 4. soften. 5. give moderately.

nasuna, inflamation of gums.

–nayo bwali (naile), make mush.

ncemeko (n), filter; strainer.

ncende (n), place; space; site; spot; room. *mu – ya,* instead of.

ncendwa (n), jaw.

ncentu (n), unfaithfulness of wife.

ncila (n), unfaithfulness of husband.

nciliko (n), cork; stopper.

ncilwilo (n), corkscrew.

ncinde (ba–), axe when used as spade.

ncinga (n), bicycle. *–endela pa –,* ride a bicycle. *cofe –,* peddal. *–lungishe –,* repair a bicycle. *–pompe –,* pump a bicycle. *– tamfye –,* accompany a cyclist.

ncito (n), same as mulimo. *–fwaye –,* look for work. *–ingile –,* find/get a job. *–lemba ku –,* enlist for work. *–leke –,* leave a job. *wa –,* worker.

nda (nda), 1. louse. 2. nda, belly. *mu nda,* belly. *–lwalu mu nda,* suffer from belly ache.

ndaka (n), mortar for building. *–kande ndáka*

(kandile), tread mortar.

ndakai, immediately; presently; instantly; at once; at this moment; just now.

ndalama (n), money; cash.

ndale (n), kind of tree.

ndawa (n), medicine; remedy; drug.

ndeke (n), aeroplane.

ndele, (n), house-snake.

ndelema (n), kind of edible mushroom.

ndeleshi (n), woman's dress; frock.

ndi, adv. very hard, used only with *...uma,* dry; strong. *...kosa,* hard.

ndifai, wine.

ndimi, pl. of lulimi. *ba ne ndimi shibili,* be deceitful. *wa ndimi shibili,* hypocrit.

ndo (n), stage on journey; camping place.

ndobâni (n), fish hook.

ndoshi (n), sorcerer.

nduba (n), kind of bird: "Livingstone lourie".

ndubulwîla (ba–), advocate; intercessor; redeemer; mediator.

ndume (n), brother.

ndusha (n), bile; gall.

ndyabuluba (n), griraffe.

ndyato (n), sandal.

ne, abbr. of ine.

...ne, four.

néfwe, abbr. of na ifwe.

nelyo, same as nangu.

nelyo...nelyo, neither ... nor. *nelyo panono,* not a little *nelyo cimo,* nothing.

nêma (n), grace. *– ya kubûta,* sanctifying grace. *– ya kutûla,* actual grace.

nêmwe, abbr. of na imwe.

nengo (n), antbear.

nengu (n), spy.

–nenuka (nenwike), lose

heart.

-nenuna (nenwine), discourage.

nga; 1. cj. when; whether; if; in case; since; as; as if. 2. adv. till; until. 3. as (comparison). *nga filya*, like; as. *nga nomba*, interj. of agreement "as I told you", etc. *nga nshi*, very much. *nga pali*, approximately.

nga ... atemwa, whether ... or.

...nga, how much? how many?

ngalande (n), embarkment; dike.

ngalâwa, rust.

ngamiya (n), camel.

ngashi (n), coconut.

nge fyo, however; nevertheless.

ngôli (n), crested crane.

ngolofwani (n), wheelbarrow.

ngoshe (ba-), common cobra.

ngulu (n), secondary divinity. *wa ngulu* (ba), person supposed to be possessed by "ngulu".

ngulube (n), wild pig.

ngwee (ki–), (Zambian currency), a bronze coin worth 1/100 of one Kwacha.

ni, he/she/it is; they are.

nibu (ba–), nib.

nifi fine, interj. "quite so".

nifyo fine, interj. "it is so".

ni mukuti, cj. that is to say.

nika (n), dambo; treeless place along rivers; plain; meadow.

-nina (ninine), climb; mount; ascend.

...nini, little; small.

-ninika (ninike), v. caus. of *-nina*.

...nini nini, very little.

ninshi, then; thereupon; hereupon.

nja (nja), lechwe antelope.

njelwa (n), brick.

njili (n), warthog.

njuka (n), playing cards.

nkafi (n), paddle; oar.

nkakashi (nĵ, wicked tongue.

nkalamo (n), lion. *–yalubuko*, man-eater lion.

...nkalwe, hardhearted, inhospitable; fierce.

nkâma (n), secret. *–ba ne nkâma*, keep a secret. *–sosa fya –*, reveal a secret; babble. *ca mu –*, confidential.

nkanda (n), human skin.

nkanshi (n), wrinkles on forehead. *–tumbe –*, frown.

nkansu (n), gown; robe.

nkashi (n or ba–), sister.

nkasa, ku –, on foot.

nkatu (n), footmarks.

nkôba (n), tick-bird or heron.

nkoko (n), fowl; hen.

nkokolembe (n), turkey.

nkola (n), snail.

nkole (ba–), prisoner; captive.

nkoloko (n), clock.

nkolokoso (n), ankle.

nkolonga (n), bar; fence made with logs put upon one another.

nkoma-matwi (ba–), deaf person.

nkombe (n), 1. envoy; messenger. 2. sternum; breastbone.

nkomfola-musunga (n), first finger.

nkonde (n), banana; banana

tree.

nkondo (n), war; battle. – ya bukaya, civil war.

nkondokondo (n), green pigeon.

nkongole (n), debts from borrowing. –bwesha fya –, return something borrowed; pay debts.

nkonko, adv. pure; real; hundred per cent.

nkonkoni (n), elbow.

nkonshi (n), hartebeest.

nkonto (n), walking stick.

nkosho, sacrament of Confirmation.

nkuba (n), lightning; thunder.

nkuku (n), dandruff.

nkula (n), red powder.

nkumba (n), domestic pig. nama ya –, bacon.

nkunda (n), pigeon.

nkupiko (n), cover; lid.

nkupo (n), cover (of a book); envelope.

nkuta (n), shout or call for help.

nkwale (n), partridge.

nkwashi (n), fish-eagle.

nkwêla (n), shield.

nobe, with you; you also.

...nobe, thy fellow: kafundisha munobe, thy fellow-teacher.

noko (ba–), thy mother.

nokofyala (ba–), thy mother-in-law/daughter-in-law.

nokokulu (ba–), thy grandmother.

nokolume (ba–), thy maternal uncle.

noko mwaice (ba–), thy maternal aunt.

noko senge (ba–), thy paternal aunt.

nomba, 1. adv. now. 2. cj. but: however. nomba te lyo or te nomba lya, not now; not at this moment. na nomba, 1. adv. still; not yet. 3. interj. 'exactly'. ukufuma nomba, as from now on. ukufika nomba, up to now.

...nomba, recent; modern;

nombaline, same as ndakai.

–nona (nonene), be fatty

...nona, fatty; oily.

–nôna (nônene), sharpen (iron).

nondo (n), 1. hammer. 2. gizzard. 3. kind of water bird and water snake.

nongo (n), clay pot.

–nonka (nonkele), acquire; trade in far countries. –nonkela mu bantu, make slave trade.

...nôno, little; small. nôno-nôno, very little.

nsa (n), hour; watch.

nsaka (n), open rest hut; shelter; sitting room.

nsakalabwe (n), gravel.

nsakalamenta (n), sacrament. –poke –, receive a sacrament. –pêle –, administer a sacrament.

nsakwe (n), hut with walls made of branches; camp shelter. –sake –, build a rough shelter.

nsala, hunger; famine; appetite. –ba ne nsala, be hungry. –fwa ku –, die of hunger; fig. be very hungry.

nsalabubenshi (n), kind of bird, "coqui Frankolin".

nsalamu (n), 1. picture; medal; statue, image. 2. fee a suitor gives to the in-laws of the girl to confirm bethrothal.

nsalu (n), cloth.

nsamba (n), water iguana.
nsambu (n), approval; approbation; right.
nsange (ba–), blue monkey or Colobus monkey.
nsani (n), dish.
nsansa (n), pleasure; joy; happiness; gaity; cheerfulness. –*ba ne nsansa*, be joyful; gay; happy.
nsansala (n), kudu antelope.
nsansalila, adv. forsaken; without shelter.
nsashiko, yeast; ferment.
nseba (n), kind of bird "wax bill".
nsebula (n), puku antelope.
nsefu (n), eland.
nseko (n), laughter; joke; fun. –*ba ne nseko*, be fond of joke. –*kokeshe nseko*, cause a laughter. –*uma ku nseko*, roar with laughter. –*wa ku nseko*, burst out into laughter.
nsele (n), pl. of lusele. –*tuke –*, use abusive language.
nsemwa (n), piece of dried sweet potato.
nsenga pl. of lusenga; sand.
nsenshi (n), cane rat.
nshi, 1. what? what kind? 2. with *pa*, on the ground; down. *ku nshi*? what for?
nshiku, pl. of bushiku. – *ya Mulungu*, Sunday. – *nkulu*, feastday. –*cilile –*, let days pass by. –*shonse*, every day; daily. *mu – mu –*, from time to time. *muno –*, nowadays.
nshila (n), path; footpath; way. –*lube nshila*, go astray. –*sake nshila*, mark out a path for people who follow. *nshila ya tondo*, a small path.

nshilila (n), kind of bird "kingfisher".
nshimbi (n), flat iron; rubber stamp; seal. –*bikapo –*, stamp; seal.
nshindano, pl. of lushindano. –*lase nshindano*, vaccinate.
nshinga (n), kind of fish.
nshinshi (n), graveyard; cemetery; burial place.
nshita (n), time; period; opportunity; chance; occasion. – *nshi*? what time? – *ya kale*, old times; past tense. – *ya nomba*, actually; present tense. – *ikêsa*, or – *ya ku ntanshi*, future tense. – *ya kwaleshima*, Lent. – *yalepa apo...*, it is a long time since. *nshita yonse*, all the time; since. *nshita yonse iyo...*, as long as...; ever since. *mu –*, whilst; meanwhile. *mu – lya*, on that occasion. *mu – ya*, during. *mu – ya nomba*, nowadays; actually; at present. *mu – mu –*, from time to time; sometimes; occasionally. *mu – nshi*? at what time? *pa – inono*, soon. *papita – inôno*, not long ago.
nsobe (n), situtunga antelope.
nsofu (n), elephant.
nsoka (n), snake.
nsokanda (n), tape worm; intestinal worm.
nsolo (n), honey guide.
nsoni, pl. of lusoni. *nsoni nsoni*, shyly. –*ba nensoni*, be shameless.
nsonshi (n), roof-tip; top of a roof.
nsoselo (n), proverb; saying.

nsupa (n), gourd; calabash.

ntambo , pl. of lutambo wick; string. pl. more used.

ntanda-bwanga, lingering disease; consumption; tuberculosis.

...ntanshi, the one in front; first; previous; preliminary. *ku ntanshi* or *pa ntanshi*, 1. adv. at first; before; in future; later on. 2. prep. in front; ahead; farther on; forward.

ntekwe (n), snuff container.

ntenda (n), sickly or infirm person.

nteneshi (n), collar.

ntengele (n), hump of cattle.

ntiku, hiccup.

ntinti, adv. very much and in vain.

ntîpu (n), curse.

ntongwe, pl. of lutongwe (not used), pea.

ntontoka (n), wheelbarrow.

ntontongolo (n), cramp.

ntoyo, pl. of. lutoyo.

...ntu, he or she who; they who; that which. cf. T. IV. 3.

ntulo (n), source.

ntumba (n), cloud of dust or smoke.

ntunga (n), direction.

ntungu (n), castrated animal.

ntungulushi (n), leader; guide; captain.

ntunka-mafi (n), dungrolling beetle.

ntunko (n), incitement to do wrong; temptation.

ntuse (n), dwarf.

ntwanikane (ba–), Mr. so and so; Mr. what's his name.

ntwenokane (ba–), same as

ntwanikane.

ntwilo (n), sauce made with pounded peanuts.

–nukula (nukwile), pluck out; root out; extract; pull out.

numa (n), back. *kunuma* or *panuma*, 1. adv. after; afterwards; later on. 2. prep. behind.

nungo, potash for snuff.

–nunka (nunkile), v.i. smell. – *cisuma*, smell good. – *bubi*, stink.

–nunkila (nunkile), 1. v. appl. of –*nunka*. 2. be tasty.

–nunsha (nunshishe), v.t. smell; sniff; scent.

–nwa (nwene), drink.

–nwena (nwenene), get drowned.

–nwensha (nwenseshe), 1. v. caus. of –*nwa*. 2. v. int. of –*nwa*. 3. v.t. drown.

–nya (nyele), pass stool. –*nya icisushi* no –*nya umwêla*, break wind.

nyali (n), candle; wax.

nyanje (n), maize. –*kopole nyanje*, break off a maize cob.

nyanji (n), railway line.

–nyanta (nyantile), tread; trample; walk on.

nyau (ba–), domestic cat.

nyelele (n), ant.

nyenjele (n), bell. –*lishe –*, ring a bell.

nyense (n), cricket.

nyina (ba–), his/her mother. – *wa lubatisho*, his/her godmother.

–nyonga (nyongele), twist; screw.

–nyongâna (nyongêne), be curled; twisted; coil.

–nyunga (nyungile), sift.

nyunshi (ma–), news.

nyunshipepala (ma–), newspaper.
–nyunsa (nyunshile), extend; stretch out.
–nyunsuluka (nyunsulwike), be stretched out. ...*nyunsuluka*, extensible; elastic.
–nyunsulula (nyunsulwile), stretch (rubber, etc.).

— Ṇ —

ṇana (ṇ), ring or crown (of flowers, etc.).
ṇanda (ṇ or mayanda), house; hut; private room. – *ya Mulungu* church; chapel. – *ntumuna*, rectangular hut. cf. also *itembe*. – *ya filu*, hut made with poles. – *ya kulilamo*, dining room. – *ya kwipikilamo*, kitchen. – *ya ntunti* or – *ya tupungu*, storeyed house. – *ya njelwa*, house built with bricks. – *ya kusendama*, bedroom; dormitory. – *ya ndililwa*, house in which somebody died. – *ya mushiki*, round hut.
ṇandu (ṇ), crocodile (used as term of a totem).
ṇanga (ṇ), witch-doctor; medicine-man; evocator.
ṇanse (ṇ), crab.
ṇanu (ṇ), wheat.
ṇoma (ṇ), drum.
ṇoma ya kalulu (ṇ), kind of inedible mushroom.
ṇombe (ṇ), cattle; cow.*ṇombe ilume*, bull.
ṇonta (ṇontele), groan (like a dying).
ṇumba (ṇ), sterile woman. – *ba ṇumba*, be sterile.
ṇwena (ṇ), crocodile.

ṇwiṇwinsa (ṇwiṇwinshile), hum; mumble.
–ṇwiṇwinta (ṇwiṇwintile), murmur; grumble.

— O —

–oba (obele), paddle.
...obe, thy; thine.
–obelwa (obelelwe), be possessed.
–obola (obwele), lay hold of.
–oca (ocele), bake; burn.
–óca.
–ocewa (ocewe), v. pass. of **ofishi** (ma–), office.
–ofya (ofeshe), surround; encircle.
–olola (olwele), straighten; stretch. *–olole nsalu*, iron cloth.
–ololoka (ololweke), be straight; upright.
–ombe ndupi (ombele), clap hands; applause.
–ombolo muti (ombwele), strip bark from tree.
–onaika (onaike), 1. v. stat. of *–onaula*. 2. v.i. collapse; crash; perish.
–onaula (onawile), spoil; damage; demolish; destroy.
–onda (ondele), be thin; lean; meagre.
–onga (ongele), arrange a body for burial.
–ongesha (ongeshe), add on; give above measure.
–ongoloka (ongolweke), disappear quietly; sneak away.
–onka (onkele), suck.
...onse, all; each; every; any; complete; general; whoever/whatever.

...onse ...bili, both; either.
...onse, ...mo ...mo, all;
one by one.
...onse nakalya, completely.
–onsha (onseshe), give suck;
suckle.
–onta (ontele), warm one-
self. –onto mulilo; –ontela
kasuba.
oti (odi), may I come in.
–owa (owele), bathe; swim;
wash oneself.
owe! interj. of surprise or
distress "ah"; "alas".

— P —

pa, 1. prep. on; upon; at;
among; in. 2. adv. very
(said with –isula). 3. e –,
then.
–pa (pele), give.
...pabi, vulgar; common; ordinary.
pabili, adv. on two places;
double.
pabula, num. nine.
pa fyo, according to.
paipi (ma–), pipe.
–paka (pakile), pack; fill up.
pakalamba, adv. very much;
greatly.
–pakata (pakête), pay re-
spect.
pakati, 1. inside. 2. half; in
the middle. pakati ka, in
the middle of; amidst;
among; between. cipimo ca
pakati, average.
–pakisha (pakishe), v. int. of
–paka. –ipakisha, satiate.
–pakula (pakwile), unpack.
pakuti, in order that; so
that.
–pala (palile), 1. resemble;
be alike. 2. scrape; peel;

plane.
–pâla mipashi (pâlile), invoke spirits. –pâla mate,
bless.
–palama (palême), come
near; approach.
–palamanya (palamenye),
put near one another.
–palamika (palamike), put
near; bring near.
–palana (palene), v. rec.
of –pala.
–palanya (palênye), make
resemble; alike; similar;
compare.
pali, 1. prep. same as ''pa
(used with proper nouns,
pers. pr. and quasi-numerals). 2. there is; there was.
3. perhaps (dubitative),
e.g. pali nkalamo, perhaps
a lion is there.
–palika (palike), become
polygamist.
–pâlika (pâlike), supply
with a roof.
palya, over there. palya pêne, just there.
–pama (pamine), 1. v.t. hit;
strike. 2. v.i. be bold; fearless; brave.
–pambana (pambele), be
active.
pambi, 1. differently; otherwise. 2. elsewhere.
pambilibili, in disorder.
–pamfiwa (pamfiwe), be
urgent; in a hurry; need;
must.
–pamfya (pamfishe), urge
on; annoy; molest; pester;
insist.
pamo, together; at the same
time or place. conse pamo,
total. pamo na, together
with; besides; along with.
na ... pamo, as well as.
pâmo pâmo, here and

there; on same places.

pampa (ba–), kind of edible mushroom.

–pampamina (pampamine), hammer. *–pampaminako musomali*, v.t. nail.

–pampanta (pampantile), feel (like a blind man with hands, etc.).

–pana (pene), aux. v. be on the point to; nearly; almost.

–panda mano (pandile, strive; enlighten. *– bûci*, remove honey from comb. *– bwanga*, throw a spell. *– muti*, concoct a remedy.

–pandaula (pandawile), splinter.

–pandula (pandwile), chop; split.

–panga (pangile), make; manufacture; form fabricate; produce; invent; build. *– mu mutima*, intend; scheme; plan.

–pangana (pangene), come to an agreement; agree.

–pangila (pangile), 1. v. appl. of *–panga*. 2. v.t. threaten; menace.

–panguka (pangwike), v. stat. of *–pangula*.

–pangula (pangwile), v.t. break up; dismantle.

–pangulula (pangulwile), same as *–pangula*.

pani (ma–), pan.

pâni, abbr. of pa ani, at whose place?

–panika (panike), punish; vex.

panîni, a little; slightly. *panínini*, very little.

pano, here. *pano pêne*, just here.

panôno, a little; a bit. *panônono*, very slowly. *pa-*

panôno panôno, little by little; slowly.

panonse, here outside. *– ya calo*, here on earth.

panse, outside.

panshi, 1. n. floor; ground. 2. adv. on the floor; down.

–panta (pantile), kick. *mfula ilepanta*, it is thundering.

pantanshi, in front; farther on.

pantu, 1. cj. because; for. 2. adv. where.

–panya (panishe), v.t. miss; fail to catch.

Pâpa, (ba–), Pope.

–pâpa (pâpile), 1. give birth to. 2. carry on the back. *e pâpa* or *te pâpa*, interj. of agreement "that is it!"; "exactly so!"

–papa (papile), wonder; be astonished; amazed. *ca kupapa (fya)*, it is extraordinary; astonishing.

–pâpâta (pâpête), implore; beseech; beg.

–papâtala (papâtele), be even; flat; level.

–papâtika (papâtike), make even; flatten; level.

–pâpâtila (pâpâtile), v. appl. of *–pâpâta*; intercede; cling to for protection.

pâpi (ba–), surplus.

papita, prep. ago; past.

papo with 'e' or 'te', same as *e papa*.

–pâpula (pâpwile), remove what was carried on the back.

–pasa (pashile), scatter; disperse; level, e.g. mounds.

–pashanya (pashenye), imitate; ape.

pasu (ma–), passport.

–pâsuka (pâswike), go off or leave the road.

–pata (patile), hate; detest; be against somebody; do not fit or suit.

patali, far away. *apatali* from afar.

–patika (patike), force; compel; oblige; coerce.

–patikisha (patikishe), v. int. of –*patika*.

patile　akantu, interj. of introducing a story "once upon a time, there was a little thing".

–pâtuka (pâtwike)), 1. be separated. 2. come from (as river from source).

–patula (patwile), separate; put apart.

paundi (ba–), pound (in money or weight).

pe, always; for ever. *pe na pe,* for ever and ever; everlasting. –*ba pe,* be immortal; perpetual. ...*pe,* adj. immortal; everlasting; perpetual.

–peka (pekele), squeeze oneself through a narrow opening.

–pekanisha (pekanishe), v. appl. of –*pekanya.*

–pekanya (pekeɲye), prepare; arrange; keep ready.

–pêla (pêle), give; grant; allot; contribute; offer; administer.

–pela (pelele), 1. grind; mince. 2. reach end.

–pêma (pêmene), breathe; rest; relax.

–pemba (pembele), wait; await.

–pembesha (pembeshe), keep waiting; put off.

–pemekêsa (pemekêse), be out of breath; gasp; pant.

–pempula (pampwile), visit.

–pena (penene), be mad;

crazy; insane.

–penda (pendele), count; reckon; calculate. *te fya kupenda,* countless; innumerable.

pêne, 1. pr. as for this. 2. adv. very, with *apa, apo, palya:* e.g. *apo pêne,* at this very place or moment.

peni (ba–), penny.

pensulo (ba–), pencil.

–penununa (penunwine), cure from madness.

–pêpa (pêpele), smoke. – *ku myôna,* snuff.

–pepa (pepele), worship; adore; pray. –*ba wa kupepa,* be adorable.

pêpi, same as mupêpi.

–pesa (pesele), bore like a weevil.

–pesha (peseshe), make reach end. – *muntu amâno,* astonish; upset somebody.

–peta (petele), fold; bend.

–petama (peteme), 1. be bent or crooked; bow. 2. be docile; obedient; submissive; obliging.

–peteka (peteke), be flexible.

–petuka (petwike), v.i. deviate.

–petula (petwile), v.t. deviate.

–petulo, petrol.

–petulula (petulwile), unfold; stretch.

pi? where? in what part?

–piba mabe (pibile), sweat.

–pika (pikile), 1. v.t. weave (with grass, reeds, etc.). 2. v.i. be hard; strong; resistant.

pikicala (ma–), movies; picture.

–pikula (pikwile), weave (with wool); knit.

–pilibuka (pilibwike), v.i. turn.

–pilibula (pilibwile), v.t. turn; turn over. – *mashiwi*, interpret.

–pima (pimine), weigh; measure; test.

–pimpa (pimpile), be troublesome.

–pimpila (pimpile), tempt; solicit; annoy; pester; entice.

–pindo muntu (pindile), sue somebody for debts. – *mulandu*, ask compensation.

–pindama (pindeme), lie crosswise.

–pindika (pindikwe, put crosswise.

–pindilo lubao (pindile), make a fence.

–pinduluka (pindulwike), v. i. change direction.

–pindulula (pindulwile), v. t. change direction.

–pinga (pingile), carry a load between two persons' shoulders/hands.

–pinga (pingile), bet.

–pingana (pingene), v. rec. of –*pinga*.

–pingula (pingwile), 1. decide. 2. run across. –*pingulako* (pingwileko), advise.

pini (ba–), pin; safety-pin.

–pinta (pintile), rush about; run to and fro.

pintu (ba–), whistle.

–pipa (pipile), remove dirt. –*pipo mwana*, wipe child after stool.

pipi, adv. badly (used with –*nunka*).

–pisha (pishishe), v. caus. of –*pita*.

–pita (pitile), pass; pass by; flow (of water).

–pofula pofwile), be blind.

–poka (pokele), take; receive; accept; obtain; get; secure.

–pokako (pokeleko), get from; rescue; defend.

–pokana (pokene, v. rec. of –*poka;* take turns (at work).

–pokela (pokele), help out.

–pokelela (pokelele), 1. v.t. take something with both hands. 2. v.i. assent; consent to.

–pola (polele), be in good health.

–polela)(polelele), recover from illness.

polishi (ba–), 1. police; constable. 2. polish.

–pôloloka (pôlolweke), trickle down.

–polomya (polwemye), suffer from diarrhoea.

–pomba (pombele), wind round; envelop; wrap in.

–pomboloka (pombolwêke), v. stat. of –*pombolola*.

–pombolola (pombolwêle), unwind; unrol.

–pompa (pompele), pump.

pompi (ba–), pump; tap.

–pompoloka (pompolweke), v. stat. of –*pompolola*.

–pompolola (pompolwele), let air out (of tyre).

–pona (ponene), fall.

–ponda (pondele) crush; pound.

–pongoka (pongweke), v. stat. of –*pongola*.

–pongola (pongwele), perforate; pierce; bore a hole.

–pongoloka (pongolweke), v.i. pour out; flow out;

burst.
-**pongolola** (pongolwele), v. t. pour out.
-**ponta** (pontele), be rude; say that one owes one nothing; ungrateful to; disrespectful.
-**pontela** (pontele), 1. v. ap- of -*ponta*. 2. v.i. be un- grateful; rude; complain against.
-**ponya** (poneshe), let fall; drop (solid object).
-**pôpa** (pôpele), hammer in; drive in.
-**pôpoloka** (pôpolweke), v. stat. of -*pôpolola*.
-**pôpolola** (pôpolwele), pull out (nail).
-**pôsa** (pôsele), 1. throw; throw away. 2. neglect. 3. overflow (river), – *menso ku*, cast eyes upon. – *mfuti*, shoot a gun. – *ndalama*, spend money.
-**pôsaika** (pôsaike), waste.
-**pôselekesha** (pôselekeshe), abandon.
-**posha** (poseshe), 1. cure; heal. 2. greet; salute; hail.
-**poshita** (poshite), v.t. send by post.
-**pûka** (pûkile), v.i. 1. burst. 2. sprout.
-**pukunya** (pukwinye), v.t. shake.
-**pukusa** (pukwise), rub dirt off; scrub; polish.
-**pukuta** (pukwite), wipe; polish; clean.
-**pula** (pulile), work for food; beg. -*pula mashiwi*, overhear. -*pûlapo*, pass without stopping. -*pula- mo*, disobey; transgress; offend against.
-**pûlama** (pûleme), be hon- ourable; respectable.

-**pulikila** (pulikile), same as -*pumikisha*.
-**pulula** (pululwile), strip off; pull off; e.g. leaves.
-**pululuka** (pululwike), v. stat. of *pululula*.
-**pulumuka** (pulumwike), tumble down; come out of a sudden; miscarry.
-**pulumuna** (pulumwine), v. caus. of -*pulumuka*.
-**puma** (pumine), hit; beat; – *lyashi*, chat; hold a con- versation. – *cilemba*, shell beans.
-**pumbuka** (pumbwike), ago- nize.
pumbwa (ba-), kind of edible mushroom.
-**pumikisha** (pumikishe), take by surprise; come unexpectedly.
-**puminkana** (puminkene), be mixed; put together.
-**puminkanya** (puminke- nye), v.t. mix; put to- gether.
pumpumpu (ba-), motor- cycle.
punda (ba-), donkey, ass.
-**punda** (pundile), shout; yell; call out (for help), names, etc.); exclaim.
-**pungwa** (ba-), kind of hawk "black kite".
-**punuka** (punwike), v. stat. of -*punuma*.
-**punuma** (punwine), grind badly.
-**pûpa** (pûpile), v.i. blow (of wind).
-**pupo lupupo** (pupile), wor- ship spirit of departed.
-**pûpila** (pûpile), sprinkle.
-**pupuka** (pupwike), fly.
-**pûpûta** (pûpûtile), rub; polish.
-**pusa** (pushile), miss; fail

to meet.

-pusana (pusene), 1. v. rec. of *-pusa*. 2. v.i. be different.

-pusanya (pusenye), distinguish.

-pusauka (pusawike), be distracted; absent-minded, lighthearted; careless; misbehave.

-pusaula (pusawile), distract.

pushi (ba–), domestic cat.

-pusuka (puswike), be safe; redeemed.

-pusumuka (pusumwike), slip; escape.

-pususha (puswishe), save; redeem; deliver; rescue.

-pûta (pûtile), v.t. blow.

-putaula (putawile), cut into small pices; chop.

-putuka (putwike), v. stat. of *-putula*.

-putula (putwile), v.t. break; cut; abbreviate. – *pakati*, halve in length.

-pwa (pwile), 1. v.t. finish; achieve; end. 2. v.i. be empty. *pa kupwa kwa*, at the end of (time-limit).

pwapwa (ba–), lungs.

pwilisho mweo (pwilishe), strangle; choke.

-pwishisha (pwishishe), v. int. of *-pwa*, accomplish; fulfil.

-pya (pile), v.i. burn; be burnt; cooked; ripe; fresh. ...**pya**, new; recent; modern.

-pyana (pyene), inherit; succeed.

-pyanika (pyanike), appoint as heir or successor.

-pyata (pyatile), throw to the ground.

— S —

–saba (sabile), pluck; pick (fruits).

–sabaila (sabaile), 1. v.t. talk nonsense. 2. v.i. be delirious.

–sabaula (sabawile), v.t. splash.

–safya (safishe), make dirty; filthy; untidy (not of body or clothes).

–sailo mutwe (saile), lay head; rest head.

–saina (sainile), v.t. sign.

–saka (sakile), 1. v.i. (used in expressions as): *ŋanda yalisaka*, the hut is tabooed (by death). *mushi nausaka*, the village is polluted (by birth of twins). *mpaŋga, naisaka*, the bush is full of dangerous animals. *ibêle nalisaka*, the breast is full. 2. v.t. (used in expressions as): *-sake nshila*, mark out a path for people who follow. *-sake nsakwe*, make a rough shelter; put up a camp. *-saka mate*, spit at.

sakala, measles.

–sakalala (sakalele), be extended fanlike.

–sakalika (sakalike), 1. stick out (feathers); (hair). 2. make angry. *-sakaliko mushishi*, ruffle hair.

–sakamana (sakamene), 1. v.t. care about; be interested in. 2. v.i. be worried about; 2 anxious; mind; bother.

–sakamika (sakamike), 1. v.

caus. of –*sakamana*. 2. v.i. be upset (mentally).

–**sakâna** (sakêne), v.i. mix; mingle.

–**sakanya** (sakenye), v.t. mix; mingle.

sakatila, mumps.

–**sakâtuka** (sakâtwike), v.i. become angry; furious; lose temper.

–**sakula** (sakwile), v.t. comb.

–**sala** (salile), choose; select; sort out; assort.

–**salakata** (salakete), be restless.

–**salangana** (salangene), be dispersed; scattered.

salanganya (salangenye), scatter; disperse; spread. – *mashiwi*, publish news.

–**salapuka** (salapwike), reach the age of reason.

–**sâlika** (sâlike), pray.

–**sâlikila** (sâlikile), v. appl. of –*sâlika*.

–**sâlikishanya** (sâlikishenye), v. rec. of –*sâlika*.

–**salipa** (salipe), rid the country of dangerous animals. *mwasalipêni*, greeting, cf. T. VII.

–**salula** (salwile), roast; fry.

–**sâlula** (sâlwile), abuse; revile; contempt; despise.

–**samba** (sambile), wash; bathe. – *ŋombe*, dip cattle.

–**sambilila** (sambilile), learn

–**sambilisha** (sambilishe), teach; show how to do.

samfwe (ba–), kind of edible mushroom.

–**sâmika** (sâmike), place high up; adorn; decorate.

–**sâmuna** (sâmwine), put down from high up; take decoration off.

–**sâmwina** (sâmwine), to be in working dress (a loin cloth).

sana, adv. much; very; quite; a great deal; absolutely; good. *sana sana*, very much, *sana fye*, same as *sana sana*.

–**sanda** (sandile), be prolific; breed.

–**sanduluka** (sandulwike), v.i. increase; grow numerous; yield; extend; become larger; e.g. a village.

–**sandulukana** (sandulukene), v.i. disperse; scatter.

–**sandulukanya** (sandulukenye), v. caus. of –*sandulukana*.

–**sandulula** (sandulwile), v.t. increase; expand; enlarge; separate.

–**sanga** (sangile), find; discover; come across; invent.

–**sanguka** (sangwike), v.i. change into; turn badly; become or be unfaithful; apostate.

–**sangukila** (sangukile), betray.

–**sangula** (sangwile), v.t. change into; convert. – *ndalama*, give one's share in a collection of money; raise money.

–**sangwa** (sangilwe), v. pass. of –*sanga*.

–**sangwako** (sangilweko), v.i. be present; attend; assist.

–**sanika** (sanike), make light; light; kindle.

saninga (ba–), kind of tree.

...**sano,** num. five.

–**sansa** (sanshile), sprinkle; filter; strain.

–**sansamuka** (sansamwike), be happy; cheerful; rejoice; be delighted.

–sansamusha sansamwi-she), v.t. make happy; delighted; please; cheer up.

–sansaula (sansawile), break; smash to pieces

–sansha (sanshishe), v.t. mix; mingle same kind; blend.

–sanshika (sanshike), 1. raise; lift. 2. put above (on shelf).

–sansuka (sanswike), be elevated; high up; be steep; have a high altitude.

–sansula (sanswile), v.t. raise; lift; elevate. – *menso*, look up. – *mutwe*, lift the head. – *shiwi*, raise the voice.

–santika (santike), thank; be grateful.

santi! interj. "thank you!" –*pika santi*, v.t. thank.

–sapa (sapile), covered with grass; unswept; untidy; neglected (not of body or clothes).

–sapula (sapwile), be in rags.

–sasa (sashile), be sour; acid.

–sâsâtuka (sâsâtwike), v.i. 1. fall off (like whitewash). 2. be very ripe. 3. burst; be fired (gun).

–sashika (sashike), make ferment.

–sashila (sashile), make sauce with pounded peanuts.

–sasuka (saswike), be flat; stale (of beer).

–satula (satwile), v.i. bloom; blossom.

sâwe (ba–), he-goat.

se, 1. interj. with awi, not at all. 2. int. particle with –*kaba se*, be very hot.

–seba (sebele), v.i. 1. talk against. 2. clear (of road). –*sebe pala*, become bald.

–sêba (sebele), to pick fruits one by one; to glean.

–sebânya (sebênye), disgrace; defame; put to shame.

sefa (ba–), sieve.

–sêka (sékele), be numerous.

–seka (sekele), 1. v.t. laugh at: mock; 2. v.i. laugh; smile; be merry. – *cisekeseke*, laugh at nothing; like a fool.

–sekaseka (sekasekele), v. red. of –*seka*, laugh without reason.

–sekela (sekele), be happy; contented. – *cintu*, enjoy something. – *muntu*, be glad to see somebody.

–sekelela (sekelele), welcome.

sekeseke (ba–), mouse with bushy tail.

–sekesha (sekeshe), v. caus. and v. int. of –*seka*.

sekondi (ba–), second.

–sekwîla (sekwile), weed.

–sêla (sélele), get out of way; change domicile; move.

–sêluka (sèlwike), v.i. 1. be open to view; 2. forsake; deny.

–seluka (selwike), v.i. 1. feel sick. 2. boil. 3. be upset (of stomach).

–sembeleka (sembeleke), win over; get in favour.

sementi, cement.

–senama (seneme), 1. be wide; broad. 2. lie flat on the back. 3. be inverted; turned upside down.

–senamika (senamike), v.

caus. of –senama.

–senamina (senamine), bless; favour.

–senda (sendele), carry; bear; take away.

–sendama (sendeme), v.i. lie down; sleep.

–sendamika (sendamike), v. caus. of –sendama, put to sleep.

–sendeka (sendeke), v.t. tilt.

–senga (sengele), flatter; court.

–senganya (sengenye), rub against. – mêno, gnash teeth.

–sengela (sengele), welcome; greet with embracing.

–sengelela (sengelele), v.i. move over (nearer or further).

–sengelesha (sengeleshe), v. t. move over.

–sengeleshanya (sengele-shenye), hand round; pass round.

–sengulwilo muntu (sengu-lwile), have pity and help somebody.

–sensa (sensele), sift.

–sensebula (sensebwile), v. t. winnow.

senti, scent.

–sêpa (sèpele), harvest; reap (millet).

–sesa (sesele), pluck or pull out (feathers).

sêse (ba–), talebearer; tattler.

–sesema (seseme), prophesy (as evokers of spirits).

–sesha (seseshe), v.t. move; transfer.

sha, prep. of, cf. T. I.

–sha (shile), leave; forsake; desert.

–shala (shele), remain;

stay; be left over; missing; wanting.

shalenipo, greeting, cf. T. VII.

–shalikapo (shalikepo), take leave; bid farewell.

–shama (sheme), be unlucky; unfortunate.

shamende, cement.

–shamika (shamike), v. caus. of –shama.

shani? pr. how? however? what? why?

–shêta (shêtele), masticate; chew; munch.

shetani (ba–), devil; satan. kwa shetani, hell.

sheti, separation of hair. –uma sheti, separate hair.

shi, 1. prefix of proper nouns, the father of. shi Bwalya, the father of Bwalya. 2. prefix of nouns expressing a man's occupation: shimalimino, gardener. 3. prefix of imperative (insisting): shitalala, do keep quiet. 4. neg. prefix in rel. sentences and for 1st person in all sentences.

–shiba (shibile), fill up (cracks in wall). dot (wall).

–shibantukila (shibantuki-le), twinkle; blink (of stars).

–shibashiba (shibashibe), twinkle; blink; wink (with eyes).

–shibata (shibete), close or shut eyes.

–shibatika (shibatike), v.t. blindfold.

–shibatuka (shibatwike), v.i. open eyes; awaken.

–shibila (shibile), 1. v. appl. of –shiba, 2. mix (e.g.

sand with clay).

shibo (ba–), their father.

–shibûka (shibwike), v.i. awake; open the eyes; be on the alert; get up (from bed).

–shibûsha (shibwishe), v.i. awaken.

shibwinga (ba–), bridegroom.

shicilye (ba–), chairman.

shicisungu (ba–), fiancé of a girl who goes through the initiation ceremonies.

shifulu (ba–), zero, nought.

shifwe (ba–), our father.

shifyala (ba–), his/her father-in-law/son-in-law.

shifyalebo (ba–), their father-in-law; their son-in-law.

shifyalefwe (ba–), our father-in-law; our son-in-law.

shifyalenwe (ba–), your father-in-law; your son-in-law.

–shika (shikile), bury; fill up a hole. – *mbuto*, cover seeds with earth. – *bwato*, paddle.

–shika (shikile), 1. v.t. bore a hole (in shell, needle, etc.). – *mulilo*, make fire by friction. – *lwimbo*, compose a new song. 2. v.i. be deep (of water).

shiki, vinegar; diarrhoea.

shikofu (ba–), bishop.

–shîkula (shìkwile), disinter; unearth; dig up.

shikulu (ba–), my/his/her grandfather.

–shila cishilwa (shilile), draw a line.

shiliki, silk.

shilili, adv. quiet; silently.

–shima (shimine), 1. v.t.

dig; hoe. 2. v.i. die down (of fire).

shimalimino (ba–), gardener.

shimalonda (ba–), guardian.

shimapepo (ba–), priest; clergyman.

–shimikila (shimikile), v. appl. of –*shimika*.

–shimiko mulandu (shimike), tell a story; relate; report a case.

–shimpa (shimpile), drive in; fix. – *shiwi*, articulate; stress a word. – *munwe*, point out with finger.

–shimpula (shimpwile), pull out e.g. a pole.

shimpundu (ba–), father of twins.

–shimya (shimishe), extinguish; put light out.

–shina (shinine), pinch; reduce to powder; crush.

–shinaula (shinawile), scratch all over.

–shindaila (shindaile), ram in; press in.

–shindana (shindene), sit for an examination; compete with.

–shindanya (shindenye), give an examination.

Shinde, April.

shindika (shindike), accompany; escort.

–shinga (shingile), smear; rub in. – *pakati*, surround; besiege; encircle.

–shingashinga (shingashingile), be slow; waver.

shinanga (ba–), witchdoctor; medicineman; evocator.

–shingauka (shingawike), v.i. rotate; spin round; go round.

–shingausha (shingawishe),

v. caus. of – shingauka;
encircle; fence in; cause a
detour.

–shingilila (shingilile), v.i.
loiter; be slow.

–shingilisha (shingilishe),
keep waiting; put off in-
definitely.

–shingula (shingwile),
whitewash; smear.

–shinguluka (shingulwike),
same as –*shingauka*.

–shingulusha (shingulwishe), v.t. rotate; turn
round.

–shinina (shinine), convict; prove guilty.

–shininkisha (shininkishe),
make certain; verify;
prove. – *mulandu*, study
a case.

–shinko munani (shinkile),
eat relish without mush.

shinsa, epilepsy; epileptic
fits.

–shinsuka (shinswike), die
suddenly.

–shinta (shintile), reach
at; extend to.

–shintika (shintike), v. caus.
of –*shinta*. – *mulomo ku*,
kiss.

–shintilila (shintilile), v.i.
lean.

–shintilisha (shintilishe), v.
t. lean.

shinwe (ba–), your father.

–shipa (shipile), be brave;
courageous; fearless; make
effort; be patient; be energetic.

shipanala (ba–), spanner.

–shipikisha (shipikishe),
same as –*shipa*; (more
used).

–shipula (shipwile), slumber; doze; drowse; be
sleepy; nap.

shisala (ba–), scissors.

–shishîta (shishîte), buzz.

–shita (shitile), buy; purchase.

shitampa (ba–), postal
stamps.

shitima (ba–), steamer. –
– *wa panshi*, train;
railway.

–shitisha (shitishe), sell.

shitofu (ba–), stove.

shitolo (ba–), store).

–shoka (shokele), v.i. make
a detour; take a round-
about; be winding (of
roads and rivers).

–sholoka (sholweke), slip;
skid.

–shôna (shônene), crush to
powder.

–shônaika (shônaike), . v.
stat. of –*shôna*.

–shosha (shoseshe), v. caus.
of –*shoka*.

–shuka, sugar.

–shûka (shûkile), be lucky;
fortunate.

–shûkila (shûkile), v. appl.
of –*shuka*, rejoice in; enjoy; benefit.

–shukuka (shukwile), rise
from death; be disinterred.

–shukula (shukwile), unearth; disinter; exhume.

–shula (shulile), dig up;
unearth; uproot.

–shuluka (shulwike), sulk;
show contempt; eye en-
viously or with hatred.

–shutulwîla (shutulwile),
grind very fine.

sikakonko (ba–), kind of
bird: "sacred Ibis".

sinema (ba–), movies; cinema.

so (ba–), saw.

–soba (sobele), peck like
fowl.

-sobela 89 -sûbila

-sobela (sobele), announce somebody; prophesy.

-sôbolola (sôbolwele), sort out; select; choose; show preference.

sofyala (ba–), thy father-in-law; thy son-in-law.

-soka (sokele) warn; alarm; inform of danger. – *bwanga,* lay a charm. – *fita,* send out patrols.

-sokela (sokele), 1. v. appl. of *–soka.* 2. v.t. load a gun; fill and press in.

-sokoka (sokweke), fall out (tool of handle).

-sokola (sokwele), v.t. 1. remove (tool from handle). 2. decorticate; husk. 3. discover. 4. extract; pull out (tooth). v.i. swarm (of bees). *–sokolo mushi,* build a new village.

-sokoloka (sokolweke), be made known; divulged; come out of hiding.

-sokolola (sokolwele), make known; publish; reveal; bring out of hiding.

-sokomona (sokomwene), pull out, e.g. axe in wood.

-sokona (sokwene), be loose; shake with fever; shiver.

-sokonya (sokoneshe), v.t. loosen.

sokulu (ba–, thy grandfather.

solwesolwe (ba–), pioneer.

-soma (somene), 1. read. 2. cause sharp pain. 3. plant; stick in.

-sombola (sombwele), advertise.

-someka (someke), insert; stick in.

-somona (somwene), same as *–sokomona.*

-sompa (sompele), peck; tear with beak.

-sompola (sompwele), v.t. seize; snatch; catch.

-sonda (sondele), taste.

-songa (songele), sharpen; point.

-songoka (songweke), v. stat. of *songola.*

-songola (songwele), point wood; sharpen.

-songoloka (songolweke), 1. be diluted; watery. 2. be thin; slender; slim.

-songolola (songolwele), dilute; thin out.

-sonka (sonkele), pay tax.

-sonkelesho mulilo (sonkeleshe), poke fire.

-sonkesha (sonkeshe), levy taxes.

sonkwe (ba–), kind of sorghum.

-sonta (sontele), point to/at; nominate; appoint.

-sônteka (sonteke), light fire; set fire to.

-sopesha (sopeshe), hoot; warn; admonish.

-sosa (sosele), say; speak; talk – *na maka,* affirm.

-sosela (sosele), v. appl. of *–sosa.* – *mu myona,* speak through the nose. – *mu masaya,* speak indistinctly.

-sosesha (soseshe), v. int. of *–sosa,* speak distinctly or clearly; speak with conviction.

-sosha (soseshe), v. caus. of *–sosa.*

-sowa (sowele), hunt with nets. – *banda,* make a ritual hunt.

-suba (subile), rub with oil; anoint; grease.

-sûbila (sûbile), hope; trust; rely on; be con-dent.

–**subuka** (subwike), cool off
(water).

–**sûka** (sùkile), pass stool.
–*mulopa*, excrete blood.

–**suka** (sukile), 1. v.t. shake.
2. v.i. be bad (of egg).
3. aux. verb. finally; at
last; at the end.

–**sukunsha** (sukwinshe), v.t.
shake.

–**sukunta** (sukuntile), same
as –*sukunsha*.

–**sukusa** (sukwise), rinse;
gargle.

sukusuku (ba–), ram.

–**sula** (sulile), have flatull-
ence; break wind.

–**sûla** (sùlule), despise;
abuse; contempt; ignore.

–**suluka** (sulwike), be tilted;
slopy.

–**sulula** (sulwile), tilt; incline; turn upside down;
cant; tip.

...**suma**, good; kind; fine;
beautiful; pleasant; pretty;
nice. – *sâna*, excellent;
perfect.

–**sûma** (sûmine), leak; ooze.
– *mulopa*, bleed.

–**suma** (sumine), bite;
sting.

–**sumba** (sumbile), wind up
(of clock); bore.

–**sûmika** (sûmike), v. caus.
of –*sûma*. – *mulopa*, make
bleed; cup.

–**sumina** (sumine), believe;
agree; admit; plead guilty;
consent; accept.

–**suminisha** (suminishe), v.
int. of –*sumina*, allow;
certify; approve.

–**suminishanya** (suminishenye), agree together; give
mutual consent.

sumu, strychnine.

–**sumuna** (sumwine)), wean.

–**sunda** (sundile), urinate;
pass water. –*mulopa*, pass
blood.

–**sundula** (sundwile), dilute.

–**sunga** (sungile), care for;
look after; protect; put
aside for future use; re-
serve; spare.

–**sunguka** (sungwike), be
astonished; amazed; sur-
prised; wonder. ...*ku su-
ngyka*, astonishing; mar-
vellous; amazing; extraordinary; strange.

–**sungulula** (sungulwike),
v. stat. of –*sungulula*.

–**sungulula** (sungulwile),
melt; dissolve; digest.

–**sungusha** (sungwishe), astonish; surprise; amaze;
puzzle.

–**sunka** (sunkile), push
away.

–**sunsa** (sunshile), carry on
shoulder.

–**sunsha** (sunshishe), v.t.
swing; sway; tundle.

–**sunsunta** (sunsuntile), trot
along.

–**sunsuntila** (sunsuntile), to
rock; lull to sleep.

–**sunta** (suntile), v.i. limp.

supuni (ba–), spoon.

–**sûsa** (sûshile), surpass;
outdo.

susu (ba–), sixpence.

–**sûsuka** (sûswike), be
frightened.

suti (ba–), suit (man's
clothes).

–**swa** (swile), 1. v.t. pluck;
pick (fruits). 2. aux. verb.
be about to; be on the
point of; almost.

swelele (ba–), barn owl.

— T —

ta, neg. particle used in all tenses, except 1st person s. and in rel. sentences which take 'shi/sha'.

–ta (tele), ply with. *–to mupila,* play football.

–tâba (tâbile), run away from; wander.

tailoshi (ma–), tile.

...takatifu, holy; sacred; divine.

–takisha (takishe), praise.

takuli, there is not.

–tala (talile), aux. v. 1. begin; start; do first. 2. ever; never.

talaifa (ba–), driver.

–talala (talele), 1. be silent; quiet; peaceful. 2. be cold; cool; fresh.

–talalika mutima (talalike), pacify; appease; calm down.

–talama (taleme), be stiff; rigid.

–talantanta (talantantile), loaf; roam about; totter; wander.

...tali long; tall; high; steep; deep.

–talika (talike), begin; start.

–taluka (talwike), go aside; move aside; keep distance; avoid.

–talusha (talwishe), put into distance; take away; move off.

–talushanya (talushenye), space out.

–tamo mupila (tamine), bounce a ball. *– matafwâli,* make bricks.

–tamba (tambile), admire; look at; regard.

–tambalala (tambalele), be straight.

–tambalika maboko (tambalike), stretch out arms.

–tambika (tambike), hand out to.

–tamfiwa (tamfiwe), 1. pass. of *–tamfya.* 2. mate (when female).

–tamfya (tamfishe), chase; pursue; expel; dismiss; banish; drive away; run after. *–tamfya ...kota,* mate (when male).

–tampa (tampile), begin; start.

–tana (tanine), refuse to give; withhold.

–tanda (tandile), sow.

tandabube (ba–), spider; spider's web; cobweb.

–tandala (tandele), go for a walk. *– ku bantu,* pay a visit.

–tandanya (tandenye), publish; scatter; spread; make known.

–tandasha (tandeshe), v. caus. of *–tandala.*

–tanga (tangile), surpass; outrun; beat (in race).

–tangâna (tangêne), disappear.

–tangana (tangene), compete (in speed); shake.

–tangâta (tangête), welcome.

–tangila (tangile), 1. v. appl. of *–tanga.* 2. v.i. go ahead; precede; lead the way.

–tangisha (tangishe), send ahead; advance.

–tanika (tanike), stretch out and fix. *– pa musalaba,* crucify.

tanki (ma–), tank.

...tanshi, cf. ...ntanshi.

–tanta (tantile), ache; pain; hurt. *– nama,* cut up meat.

-tantalila (tantalile), be far away.

-tantalisha (tantalishe), v. caus. of –tantalila, postpone; adjourn; defer.

-tantama (tanteme), v.i. line up; stand in line.

-tantamika (tantamike), v. caus. of –tantama, put in line; arrange.

-tantawila (tantawile), enumerate; mention.

-tantika (tantike), same as –tantamika.

-tantuka (tantwike), v. stat. of –tantula.

-tantula (tantwile), v.t. set out of line.

-tapa (tapile), take by force; plunder. –menshi, draw water.

-tapata (tapete), v.i. irritate; hurt (as sore).

-tapilila (tapilile), irrigate.

-tapula (tapwile), take out (of a container).

-tasha (tashishe), praise; honour; thank; congratulate; pay compliments.

-tâsha (tâshishe), conquer; take by force.

tata (ba–), my father.

tata mwaice (ba–), my paternal uncle.

tatafyala (ba–), my father-in-law; my son-in-law.

-tâta (tâtile), hum; flutter (as bees).

.tatu, num. three.

tausandi (ba–), thousand.

te, neg. particle, not; it is not. te fyo, interj. asking agreement "is it not so?" te ifyo iyo, it is not so.

tea (têle), set a trap; prepare in advance. –tea njuka, play cards.

-tebe nkuni (têbele), fetch firewood.

-tebeta (tebete), prepare food.

tefwetefwe, quagmire; marsh.

-tefya (tefeshe), whimper; snivel; weep for no reason; be sensitive.

-têka (tekele), put; place; put aside; set aside. – bantu, govern; reign. – câlo, administer a country. – muntu, retain a person. – mutima, behave well; take care; be calm; patient. têkapo bwali (têkelepo), boil water for making mush. mfula naitêka, rain is coming.

-tekanya (tekenye), take care; behave; be attentive; calm; quiet; beware.

-tekelesha (tekeleshe), pet; fondle; coddle.

-tekenya (tekenye), drive; steer; pilot.

...teku, soft (of shoots).

-tekunya (tekwinye), tickle.

tekuti, negative of 'kuti': cannot; should not; must not; be unable.

-telela (telele), be slippery; greasy; smooth or soft in touch.

-telemuka (telemwike), slide down; slip.

-tema (temene), cut or lop trees.

-temba (tembele), be meek; kind.

-tembatemba (tembatembele), treat kindly.

-tembuka (tembwike), be exhausted; faint.

-tembula (tembwile), exhaust.

-temwa (temenwe), 1. v.t. love; like; be fond of

2. v.i. be happy; satisfied; content; pleased; consent. –*ukucila,* prefer.

–temwisha (temwishe), v. int. of –*temwa,* prefer.

–tena (tenene), make a mistake; blunder.

–tendeka (tendeke), start; begin; provoke; attack; charge. –*itendeka,* start on one's own initiative.

–tendusha (tendwishe), v. caus. of –*tendwa,* disgust; cause annoyance.

–tendwa (tendelwe), be disgusted; fed up; tired of.

–tengela (tengele), spare; leave aside.

–tensha (tenseshe), shake; jostle. – *mabêa* or *makôpe,* shrug the shoulders. – *muntu,* jostle; push a person. – *mutwe,* shake the head.

–tênsha (tênseshe), nurse.

–tenta (tentele), tremble; shake.

tente (ba–), kind of edible mushroom.

–tentemba (tentembe), pet; treat kindly; coddle foster. –*itentemba,* look well after oneself.

tenti (ma–), tent.

–tesekesha (tesekeshe), to understand very well.

–tesemuna (tesemwine), sneeze.

–tesha (teseshe), understand; pay attention; listen; hear; feel.

–teta (tetele), moan; groan; sigh.

–têta (têtele), cut; mutilate; amputate.

–tetekela (tetekele), trust; rely on; count on; put hope into.

–tetêla (tetêle), cackle (as hen).

teti contraction of tekuti.

–teula (tewile), take away; remove. – *fipe pe tebulo,* clear the table.

–teulula (teulile), release (snare, gun, etc.).

tî, tea.

–ti (tile), say; think; imagine. *ni mukuti,* that is to say.

–tibila (tibile), genuflect.

–tibinte filamba (tibintile), weep; shed tears. – *mabe,* perspire; sweat.

–tika (tikile), be boggy; muddy; sink in.

–tikama (tikeme), clot; congeal; freeze; be stiff; hard.

–tikula ntiku (tikwile), v.i. hiccup.

–tikuluka (tikulwike), v. stat. of –*tikulula.*

–tikulula (tikulwile), v.t. pull out of mud.

–tîla (tile), say; suppose; signify. *e kutila,* that means.

–timba (timbile), thrash.

–tîna (tinine), fear; be afraid; anxious. *cakutina,* frightful.

–tina (tinine), squeeze; press out.

–tininkisha (tininkishe), press against.

–tinta (tintile), pull; drag; attract.

–tintana (tintene), 1. v. rec. of –*tinta.* 2. v.i. quarrel; dispute; argue.

–tînya (tînishe), frighten; alarm; scare; intimidate; threaten.

–tîpa (tîpile), curse.

–tîpwila (tîpwile), same as –*tipa.*

titi (ba–), **kind of bird**

"small warbler".

–**toba** (tobele), break (plate, etc.);) pull down (hut, etc.); crash; smash. – *lupi*, hit; slap; strike with fist.

–**tobeka** (tobeke), v. stat. of –*toba*.

–**tobela** (tobele), eat relish with mush.

–**tobenkana** (tobenkene), v. i. be mixed.

–**tobenkanya** (tobenkenye), v.t. mix.

–**toboka** (tobweke), hop; leap; jump.

–**tôla** (tôlele), pick up.

–**tôlana mu cupo** (tôlene), live in concubinage.

tôki (ba–), torch.

–**toloka** (tolweke), same as –*toboka*.

tololo, ad.v straight.

tomatoshi (ba–), tomato.

–**tomboka** (tombweke), same as –*toloka*.

–**tombola** (tombele), v.i. bud.

tombolilo (ba–), tadpole.

–**tona** (tonene), v.i. drop; drip.

tondolo, adv. silently; quietly; calmly.

tondwe (ba–), kind of bird "woodpecker".

tonge (ba–), cotton; cotton plant.

–**tongola** (tongwele), v.t. shell (beans, etc.).

–**tonkola menso** (tonkwele), gouge out eyes.

–**tontoloka** (tontolweke), smoothen; soften (with oil); yeild.

–**tontomesha menso** (tontomeshe); stare at; look fixedly; eye.

–**tontonkanya** (tontonke-

nye), think; imagine; consider; reflect; plan.

–**tonya** (toneshe), v.t. drop; drip.

–**tôta** (tôtele), greet; salute. – *mapi*, applaud. – *panshi*, give the royal salute. –*mani*, hatch eggs.

–**tôtela** (tôtele), 1. v. appl. of –*tôta*. 2. v.i. thank; pay homage.

–**tôtôsha** (tôtôseshe), whisper.

tu, 1. pr. cf. T. II, 2. 2. pref. of class "ka/tu".

–**tubula** (tubwile), wade through water.

–**tuka** (tukile), revile; abuse; insult; use obscene language.

–**tuka** (tukile), make small heaps of earth (as moles); dig (as pigs for food).

–**tûka** (tûkile), satiate; vomit (as poison).

–**tukana** (tukene), insult; revile; use abusive language.

–**tukuta** (tukwite), strive hard; endeavour; struggle.

–**tula** (tulile), 1. v.t. pierce; bore a hole. 2. v.i. come from; originate; rise (of sun).

–**tûla** (tûlile), offer; pay tribute; help.

–**tulaula** (tulawile), perforate.

–**tulika** (tulike), be pierced; punctured.

–**tûlika** (tûlike), pile up; put on a heap.

tulo, sleep, n.

–**tuluka** (tulwike), be stout.

tulya, those yonder, cf. T. III.

–**tuma** (tumine), dispatch; send; forward.

-tumba (tumbile), v.i. swell. - nkanshi, frown.

-tumbuka (tumbwike), be revealed; cleared up.

-tumbula (tumbwile), cut open; operate. - menso, stare. - mulandu, reveal a secret. - nkóko, clean out a fowl.

-tumfya (tumfishe), v. caus. of -tumpa.

-tumpa (tumpile), 1. v.t. immerse; dip; plunge into. 2. v.i. be foolish; stupid; silly.

-tumpika (tumpike), 1. v.t. immerse; dip; plunge into. 2. v. caus. make a fool of somebody.

-tumyo bwalwa (tumishe), work for beer.

-tunga (tungile), string; thread.

-tunganya (tungenye), suspect; guess.

-tungula (tungwile), castrate.

-tungulula (tungulwile), show the way; lead; guide.

-tunka (tunkile), tempt.

-tunkana (tunkene), 1. v. rec. of -tunka. 2. v.i. shrink; be drawn up.

-tunkilisha (tunk she), push ahead.

-tunta (tuntile), beat (of heart), palpitate.

...tuntulu, whole; entire; intact; complete; perfect; unhurt; in good health.

-tuntuka (tuntwike), come from; emerge.

tûpa (ba-), file.

-tusa (tushile), be undersized; stunted.

tusanda, furred tongue caused by bile or fever.

-tûsha (tûshishe), 1. v.t. satiate; satisfy hunger or thirst. 22 v.i. rest; relax; repose.

—tusha (tushishe), start from; come from.

tuswende, syphilis; venereal disease.

tuti (ba-), conical hut.

-tutila (tutile), store grain etc.

tûtu, very, used with -bûta.

-tûtula (tûtwile), mend clothe; patch.

-tutuma (tutwime), tremble. shake with fear or cold; shiver.

-tutumuka (tutumwike), be raised like bread.

twa, prep. of, cf. T. I.

-twa (twile), 1. v.t. thresh; pound. 2. v.i. be sharp; cut well.

-twala (twele), 1. v.t. deliver; bring/carry (to); lead (to). 2. v.i. bear (fruit).

—twalila (twalile), v. appl. of -twâla.

-twika (twikile), load; burden; charge.

-twishika (twishike), be unceartain; doubt; hesitate.

— U —

U, thou; cf. T. II, 2.

-uba (ubile), take shelter.

ubo, 1. that. cf. T. III. 2. which, cf. T. IV.

uko, 1. adv. there; where;

-ufya (ufishe), give in marriage.

uko, 1. adv. there; where; when; wherever. 2. cj. the reason why; because. 3. that, cf. T. III. 4. which, cf.

T. IV. *uko kwine,* just
there. *uko no ku,* here and
there. *e uko,* that is why.
uku, this, cf. T. III.
ukuba, adv. very likely;
probably.
ukucila, adv. more; rather;
especially; further.
ukufika na nomba, adv. up
till now.
ukufuma, since. – *nomba,*
from now on; henceforth.
**ukufuma ku...ukufika na
ku,** from ... to.
ukuti, in order that.
ukwa, adv. where; the place
where.
uleke, imp. allow; let; so
that.
ulo 1. that, cf. T. III. 2.
which, cf. T. IV.
ulu, this, cf. T. III.
–uluka menso (ulwike), be
squinted.
–ulungana (ulungene), do
evil with others.
ulya, that yonder, cf. T. III.
–uma (umine), 1. v.t. hit;
strike; beat. 2. v.i. be dry.
–umana (umene), quarrel.
–umanya (umenye), rebuke;
reprimand.
–umfwa, (umfwile), hear;
listen; hark; understand;
feel.
–umfwana (umfwene), 1. v.
rec. of –u mfwa. 2. agree;
come to an understanding.
–umfwikwa (umfwikwe), be
understood; heard; di-
vulged.
...umi, alive; living;
healthy.
umo, adv. in; into; inside;
umo mwine, accordingly.
umwa, in which; wherein.
–umwa (uminwe), v. pass.

of *–uma.* – *nka,* be
thrashed.
–umya (umishe), stress;
strain. – *bufumu,* abuse
one's authority. – *mutengo,*
raise the price.
–undapa (undepe), heal;
cure.
uo, whom, cf. T. IV.
–upa (upile), marry; wed
(when man).
–upwa (upilwe), marry;
wed (when girl).
–upana (upene), married
(speaking of both husband
and wife).
uto, 1. those, cf. T. III.
utu, these, cf. T. III.
uyo, that, cf. T. III.
uyu, this, cf. T. III.

— W —

wa, prep. of, cf. T. I.
–wa (wile), fall; set (of
sun). – *bukupeme,* fall on
all fours. – *buseneme,* fall
on the back. – *cisungu,*
have first menstruation.
– *kabafu,* fall on one side.
– *panshi,* fall to the
ground; crash; collapse.
–wama (weme), be good;
nice; pretty; beautiful;
agreeable; pleasant. –
sána, be excellent; very
good, etc.
waileshi (ma–), wireless.
–wamina (wamine), do
good; be profitable; use-
ful; of advantage.
–waminisha (waminishe),
make pretty; embellish.
–wamya (wemye), repair;
improve; mend; put in
order; clean up.

–**washa** (washile), wash.
–**wina** (winine), win (school term).
we, abbr. of iwe.
–**wêla** (wêlele), jeer; mock; scoff at; hoot.
weweta mulopwe, interj. "yes sir".
–**wikishanya** (wikishenye), v. rec. be reconciled.
wiba (ba–), her husband.
–**wila** (wilile), 1. v. appl. of –*wa*. 2. flow into. – *kumo*, be of the same opinion.
–**wilwa** (wililwe), be possessed.
wine, self.
–**wisha** (wishishe), throw down; knock down.
wishi (ba–), his/her father. – *wa lubatisho*, his/her godfather.
wiso (ba–), thy father.

— Y —

ya, prep. of.
–**ya** (ile), go; leave; depart.
– *ciyeyeye*, go aimlessly.
– *kunse*, go to the latrine.
yaba, interj. of surprise or wonder.
yalya, those yonder, cf. T. III.
yabwe, interj. of disapproval.
yama (ba–), maternal uncle.
–**yana** (yene), v.i. fit; be of proper size.
yangu, interj. of surprise "oh".
yangwe, same as yangu.
yawe, interj. of surprise.
ye, interj. of surprise or admiration.
yengula (yengwile), skim.
yemba (yembele), to be pretty; good looking.
yensa (ba–), big kind of locust.
Yesu, Jesus.

Part II

ENGLISH — BEMBA

— A —

abandon, –lekelesha (leke-leshe); –pôselekesha (po-selekeshe).

abbreviate, –cefya (cefeshe).

abdicate, –leko mulimo (le-kele).

abdomen, ifumo (ma).

abide, 1. (dwell). –ikala (ikele). 2. (remain),–shala (shele).

ability, 1. (physical, maka). 2. (intellectual), mâno.

able, 1. (physically), –ba na maka. 2. (intellectually), –ba na maka; ali na mâno. ali na maka; ali na mâno.

abode, cifulo (fi); bwikalo

abolish, –onaula (onawile); –leka (lekele).

abortion, 1. (have –), –pôse fumo (pôsele). 2. (cause –), –ponye fumo (pone-she).

abortive child, kapôpo (tu).

abound, ...ingi. be abound-ing, –fula (fulile).

about, (there is no proper term. Examples show how to translate it): 1. prep.: pa; pa mulandu wa; pa lwa: talk –, –landa pa; –la-nda pa mulandu wa; – la-nda pa lwa. mupêpi na; – 10.00 hours, nga: what about (me), nga (ine). 2. adv.: nalimo: – 10 men, antu nalimo ikumi. cf. also come about; approxi-mately; be on the point of.

above, adv. & prep., pa mulu.

abscess, cipute (fi); mumena (ba–).

absent, (there is no proper

term. It can be translated by the neg. of –ba): he is –, talipo; lit. he is not here.

absolute, 1. (pure), ...eka ...eka: – falsehood, bufi bweka bweka. 2. (real), ...ine ...ine: he is an – fool, cipuba cine cine.

absolutely, sana; he is – wrong, aluba sana. cf. also completely.

absolve, –fwîsa, –luka –leka (umuntu); –fumya masa-mbi (catholic).

abstain, –kâna (kânine), –le-ke (lekele) followed by inf. It can also be transcribed as in following example. he abstains from beer, ta-nwa bwalwa, he does not drink beer.

abundance, bwingi.

abuse, 1. n. (reviling), mu-sâlula (mi); misûla. 2. v.t. (revile), -sâlula (sâlwile); –sûla (sûlile); –tuke (nse-le) (tukile); (make bad use of), –bomfya bubibubi (bomfeshe). 3. of one's authority – lumyo bufumu.

abyss, muyenge (mi).

accelerate, –angufyanya (angufyenye). – lumya (lu-mishe).

accentuate, –shimpe shiwi (shimpile).

accent, 1. (receive), –poka (pokele). 2. (agree), –su-mina (sumine).

accident, ishâmo (ma); bu-sanso (ma); it happened by –, cafika fye, cacitika fye.

acclimatize, –belela; –bele-sha (beleshe) (belele); ishibila (ishibile): he is –, abelela ne câlo; icâlo calimwishibila.

accompany, –shindika (shindike); *I will – you,* ndemushindika.

accomplish, –pwishishisha (pwishishe).

according to, pa fyo; umo *to your words,* pa fyo musosele; umo asosele.

accordingly, umo mwine; filya fine: *do –,* cita umo mwine; – filya fine.

account, (verb.). 1. (see consider). 2. –lubulula (lubulwile); – lubulwisha (lubulwishe) caus. of above.

account (n) 1. on – of, pa mulandu wa. 2. amapendo.

accumulate, –longanya (longenye); tûlika (tûlike).

accurate, –kumana (kumêne); –ba ...onse; *it is –,* cakumana or cili conse.

accuse, –cito mulandu (cititile): *they accuse him of,* bamucito mulandu wa. *accused person,* wa mulandu (ba).

accuse falsely, –bepesha (bepeshe).

accustom, –belesha (beleshe). *be accustomed,* –belela (belele).

ache, –kalipa (kalipe); –tanta (tantile): *the legs ache,* môlu yakalipa or ciletanta mu môlu.

achieve, –pwa (pwile).

acid, –sasa (sashile).

acknowledge, –ishibisha (ishibishe): *I – your letter,* namwishibisha ukuti kala ta wenu nalipoka.

acquire, –mwenamo (mwenenemo).

across, 1. prep. mu: *he went – the garden,* apita mu malimino. 2. adv. kwishilya:

go – the river, kabiye kwishilya lya mumana. 3. cf. also *come across; put across.*

act, 1. n. micitile; mibombele. 2. v.t. –cita (citile); *one does not act like that,* ifyo tefyo. *act on one's own,* –icita (icitile).

active, –cincila (cincile); –anguka (angwike); –pambana (pambene).

actually, 1. mu nshita ya nomba; nombaline. 2. ukuba kwena.

adapt, cf. accustom.

add, –lundapo (lundilepo); –bikapo (bikilepo).

addition, make –, –longanya (longenye).

address, 1. n. adeleshi (ma-), 2. v.t. –lemba adeleshi. *– somebody,* –landa **na.**

adhere, –kambatila (kambatile); –kakatila (kakatile).

adjourn, –tantalisha (tantalishe).

administer, 1. (give), –pêla (pêle). 2. (– a country), –têke calo (têkele).

administration, butêkeshi, butêko.

administrator, katêka (ba–); mulashi (ba).

admire, –tamba (tambile), –papa (papile).

admit, 1. (agree), –sumina (sumine). 2. (allow entrance), –sumino kwingila.

admonish, –konkomesha (konkomeshe); –sopesha (sopeshe).

adore, –pepa (pepele).

adorn, –sâmika (âmike).

adult, –ba ...kalamba; –kula (kulile): *he is –,* mukalamba or mukulu.

adulterer, mucende (ba);

cilende (ba-).

adultery, bucende; lubembu. *commit* –, –cito bucende or lubembu; –bembuka (bembwike).

advance, v.t. –tangisha (tangishe); v.i. –tangisha (tangile). *in advance,* libela; kabêla: *I give* –, ndepêla libêla or kabêla.

advantage, be of –, wamina (wamine); *schools are of advantage to us,* masukulu yalituwamina.

adversary, mulwani (ba).

advertise, –sombola (sombwele).

advice, ifunde (ma). *ask advice,* –bûsha (bûshishe).

advise, –eba (ebele); –pingulako (pingwileko); –panda mano (pandile); *he advised me,* anjebele or ampingwileko.

adviser good –, kapanda mâno (ba-); mpanda mâno (m), *bad* –, katunka (ba-).

advocate, bukota; ndubulwila (ba-).

aerodrome, cibansa ca ndendeke (fi).

aeroplane, ndeke (n).

afar, kutali: *he is afar,* ali kutali. *from afar,* apatali: *he comes from afar,* afuma apatali.

affair (concern), mulandu (mi), ncito (n): *it is your affair,* mulandu wenu or ncito yenu.

affirm, –sosa na maka (sosele).

afflict, –cûsha (cûshishe). *be afflicted,* –cûla (cûlile); –lilishika (lilishike).

affliction, bucûshi; cililishi.

afraid, –tina (tinine); –ba

no mwenso: *he is afraid,* atina, or ali no, mwenso.

afresh, kabili; nakabili; na limbi; cipya cipya.

African, mwina Africa (bêna). *light coloured African,* musweshi (ba).

after, 1. adv. ku ntanshi. 2. prep. ku numa; 3. cj. ilyo.

afternoon, cungulo.

afterwards, pa numa; ku ntanshi; elyo.

again, cf. afresh.

against, ku: *stand against the wall,* iminina ku cibumba. *be against somebody,* –pata (patile): *you are against me,* mwampata.

age, myaka: *what is your age,* muli ne myaka inga? *advanced age,* bukoloci; bukote; bukalamba. *come of age,* –kula (kukile), *reach the age of reason,* –salapuka (salapwike). *marriageable age,* cimo ca kûpa.

aggravate, –kusha (kushishe): *you aggravate your case,* mulekusha mulandu wenu.

agile. cf. active.

ago, papita: *two days ago,* papita inshiku shibili. *long ago,* kale. *very long ago,* kale na kale; kale fye. *not very long ago,* papita inshita inono fye.

agonize, –pumbuka (pumbwike).

agree, –sumina (sumine); v. rec. –suminishanya (suminishenye).

agreeable, –wama; –ba bwino: *it is agreeable,* cawama, or cili bwino. *cause an agreeable feeling,* v.i. –lowelela (lowelele).

agreement, cumfwano (fy); cipangano (fi). *come. to* –, –umfwana (umfwene), *fail to come to* –, –filwana (filwene).

agriculture, bulimi.

ah, interj. owe!

ahead, ku ntanshi: *he is ahead,* ali ku ntanshi. *go ahead,* –tangila (tangile).

aid, 1. n. afwilisho. 2. v.t. –afwa (afwile).

aim, 1. n. (of a journey), buyo. 2. v.t. *aim a gun,* –andike mfuti (andike) or –lungike mfuti (lungike).

air, 1. n. mwela; (in a tyre) mupu: *the tyre is flat,* takuli mupu mu mupeto; *let air out of tyre,* –pompolola (pompolwele); v. stat. –pompoloka (pompolweke). *stuffy air,* cipuki.

air, 2. v.t. (a) – *a room* –lekelo mwela ukwingila mu ŋanda. (b). – *blanket etc.,* –anika (anike).

air letter, kalata lya mu ndeke (ma–).

air mail, mêlu wa mu ndeke.

ajar, –penguka (pengwike), *the door is ajar,* cibi capenguka.

alas, interj. "owe!"

alarm, 1. warn of danger, –soka (sokele). 2. frighten, –tinya (tinishe).

alert, be on the –, –cebuka (cebwike); –shibuka (shibwike).

alien, mweni (bêni).

alike, –ba mumo; –pala (palile); –lingâna (lingêne): *we are alike,* tuba mumo / twapala / twalingâna. *make alike,* –pala-

nya (palenye); –linganya (lingenye).

alive, –ba no bumi; –ba bûmi: *he is alive,* ali no bumi or ali mûmi.

all, ...onse. *that is all,* epela.

allow, –suminisha (suminishe); –pêlo lusa (pêle); *he allows me,* ansuminisha or ampêlo lusa; –leka.

almighty, wa maka yonse.

almost, ni cikanga; –pana (pene); –swa (swile): *the lion almost killed me,* inkalamo yapene injipaye.

alms, bupe. *give alms to poor,* –kumbusuka balanda (kumbuswike).

alone, ...eka, cf. T. II.

along, go –, –konka (konkele): *go along the river,* konko mumana. *come along!* imp. isa! (isêni)! *along with,* pamo na.

aloud, talk –, –ikatishe shiwi (ikatishe).

alphabet, filembo fyonse.

already, apo pêne; kale: *it is already done,* capwa kale. *he returned already,* abwêla apo pêne.

also, na; na...o; kabili. *this book also,* ne citabo ici or citabo ici naco.

altar, alutâle (ba–).

alter, v.t. –lula (alwile); v.i. –aluka (alwike).

although, nangu; nelyo; nángula.

altitude, butali bwa câlo. *have a high altitude,* –sansuka (sanswike).

altogether (on the whole), pa kuloleshe milandu yonse pamo; pe na pe.

always, pe; pe na pe.

amaze, –sungusha (sungwishe). *be amazed,* –sunguka

(sungwike); –papa (pa-pile).

amazement, lupapo.

amazing, it is –, ca kusu-nguka; ca kupapa.

amend, –wamya (wemye).

amiable, –ba no mutembo.

amidst, pakati ka.

ammunition, cipolopolo (fi); cisongo (fi).

among, pakati ka; pa or pali.

amount, conse pamo: *what is the amount,* conse pamo ni shani?

ample, –fula (fulile).

amputate, –têta (têtele). *stump of amputated limb,* makunkutu. *person with amputated limb,* wa ma-kunkutu (ba).

amulet, lupimpi (m).

amuse, v.t. –angasha (ange-she). v.i. –angala (angele).

amusement, musamwe (mi).

ancestor, cikolwe (fi).

ancient, . . .kale: *ancient history,* milandu ya kale.

and, na.

anew, cipya cipya; see also *afresh.*

angel, malaika (ba–).

anger cipyu; cifukushi; bukali. *fit of anger,* cinse.

angle, itungi (ma); ikonta (ma). *be at an angle,* –ba na matungi.

angry, –fulwa (fulilwa); –kalipa (kalipe). *make angry,* –kalifya (kalifye). *become angry,* –sakatuka (sakâtwike).

animal, nama (n). *domestic animal,* citêkwa (fi). *ferocious animal,* ciswango (fi).

ankle, nkolokoso (n).

annihilate, –lofya (lofeeshe).

anniversary: *to day is the 1st aniversary of,* lêlo mwaka umo naupita apo...; (later on), êlo twaibukisho mwaka ilyo.

announce somebody, –sobe-la (sobele). *announce something,* –lundulula mu-landu (lundulwile). *an-nounce the death of some-body,* –bikula mfwa.

announcement (public –), mbila (m). *make a –,* –bila mbila (bilile).

annoy, –pimpila (pimpile); –afya (afishe); pamfya (pamfishe).

annual, . . .mwaka. *annual meeting,* cilonganino ca mwaka.

annually, cila mwaka.

anoint, –suba (subile).

another, . . .mbi.

answer, 1. n. casuko (fy); 2. v.i. –asuka (aswike). v. appl. –asukila (asukile): *you do not even answer me,* no kunjasuka iyo! *answer back,* –ankula (ankwile). *answer a call,* –itaba (itebe): *they call you, do answer,* bamwita, itabeni. *answer a letter,* –bwesha kalata (bwese-she).

ant, nyelele (n). *small ant,* kanyelele (tu). *white ant,* bubenshi. *winged ant,* cibe-ngele (fi); luswa (nswa); nakapelele (ba–). *collect winged ants,* –kole nswa (kolele). *red ant* or *army/ soldier ant,* lupashi (n).

antbear, nengo (n).

anthill (big kind), cûlu (fy); (small kind), ifwasa (ma).

anticipate, –bangilila (bangilile),

antipathy, lupato.

anus, mputi (m); musula (mi).

anxiety, isakamiko (ma).

anxious (afraid), –ba no mwenso; –tîna (tînine). *be anxious about*, –sakamana (sakamene). *be anxious to* (like very much), –fwaisha (fwaishe).

any, ...onse. *anybody*, muntu onse. *anything*, cintu conse. *anywhere*, mpânga yonse.

apart, be –, ...eka: *he sits apart*, aikala eka. *put apart*, –bîka ...eka: *put the cows apart*, bika ŋombe sheka. *put apart from*, –patula (patwile): *put the cows apart from the oxen*, patula ŋombe na bamutungu.

ape, 1. n. kolwe (ba–). 2. v.t. –kopa (kopele); –pashanya (pashenye).

apologize, –pâpâta (pâpête); *I apologize, please forgive me*, napâpâta, mumbeleleko luse.

apostasy, busangu.

apostate, musangu (ba).

apostatize, –sanguka (sangwike). v. appl. –sangukila (sangukile).

apostle, musole (ba); mutumishi (ba).

apparent, –moneka (moneke): *it is apparent that*, camoneka ukuti.

appear, –moneka (moneke).

appearance, mimonekele; ca kunse (fya); ca ku menso (fya).

appease, –talaliko mutima (talalike). *be appeased*, umutima nawikala. *become appeased*, –bwesho

mutima (bweseshe).

appetite, nsala: *I have a good appetite*, ndi ne nsala sâna.

applause, –tôta mapi (tôtele); –ombe ndupi (ombele).

application, make –, –fwaye ncito (fwaile).

apply for work, cf. application.

apply remedy, –bîkapo muti (bîkilepo). *apply ointment on a wound*, –shinga mafuta pa cilonda.

appoint, –sonta (sontele); lâsa (lâshile): *they appointed him to succeed Chitimukulu*, bamusonta wa kupyana pali Chitimukulu. *(Chitimukulu appointed "so and so" as governor of Chilinda*, Chitimukulu a lâsa kampanda mu Chilinda.

appoint as representative, –lâshika (lâshike): *you will be my representative*, ndemulâshika.

appoint as heir or successor, –pyanika (pyanike).

apprentice, musambilila (ba).

approach, v.t. –palamika (palamike). v.i. –palama (paleme).

April, Shinde.

apron (worn by women as underskirt), bukushi.

approval, nsambu.

approve, –suminisha (suminishe).

approximately, nga pali; kwati: *the distance is approx. 20 km* palêpa nga pali (or kwati) makilometre makumi yabili.

Arab. Mwarabu (ba); mulungwana (ba).

argue, –kansana (kansene); –bikana fikansa (bikene); –tintana (tintene).

argument, fikansa: *they have an argument,* bali ne fikansa.

arise, –moneka (moneke): *difficulty arose,* ubwafya (bwamoneke).

arm, 1. (limb), kuboko (ma). 2. (weapon), canso (fy).

armpit, kwapa (mâpa).

army, fita.

aroma, cena (fy).

around, mu mbali ya: *around the village,* mu mbali ya mushi. (see also encircle).

arrange (prepare), –pekanya (pekenye); (put in order). wamya (wemye); (put in line), –tantika (tantike); (settle a case), –putulo mulandu (putwile).

arrest, –kaka (kakile); –ikata (ikete).

arrive, –fika (fikile).

arrogance, cilumba; imiya.

arrow, mufwi (mi).

art, bafundi.

artery, mushipa wa mulopa (mi).

article (thing), cintu (fi).

articulate, –shimpe shiwi (shimpile); –lumbwisha (lumbwishe).

artisan, fundi (ba–).

as, 1. comparison, nga: *you are as poor as I am,* muli balanda nga ine. 2. cj. filya: *as it was formerly,* filya (or ifyo) cali kale. *as... thus,* ifyo... efyo. *as it was fomerly, thus it is now,* ifyo cali kale, efyo caba na nomba, *as for,*

...ena, cf. T. III, under "however"; *as from now on,* ukufuma nomba. *as if,* nga. *it looks as if,* caba nga. *as long as,* nshita yonse: *as long as I am here,* nshita yonse iyo naikala kuno. *as well as,* na...pamo: *Peter and Paul as well,* Petro pamo na Paulo.

ascend, –nina (ninine).

ashamed, –ba ne nsoni: *he is ashamed,* ali ne nsoni.

ashes, mito.

Ash-Wednesday, nshikunkulu ya mito.

aside, (it is expressed by the verb with which it stands), e.g. *pass aside* –taluka; –sela.

ask, –ipusha (ipwishe), v. appl. –ipushisha (ipushishe): *ask for me,* munjipushisheko. *ask for,* –lomba (lombele).

asleep, lâla (lêle).

ass, punda (ba–).

assault, 1. n. lubuli, 2. v.t. –lwisha (lwishishe): *they assaulted him,* bamulwishishe.

assemble, v.t. –longanya (longenye); –puminkanya (puminkenye). v.i. –longana (longene); –puminkana (puminkene).

assent, –sumina (sumine). v. appl. –suminisha (suminishe); –pokelela (pokelele): *do you assent,* bushe mulesumina? *I assented to the case,* nasuminisho mulandu or napokelelo mulandu.

assist, 1. (help), –afwa (afwile). 2. (attend), –sangwako (sangilweko).

assistance, cafwilisho.

assort, –sala (salile).

astonish, v.t. –sungusha (sungwishe); –pesha mâno (peseshe): *it astonishes me,* campesha mâno.

astonished, –sunguka (sungwike); –papa (papile): *I am astonished,* nasunguka or napapa. *it is astonishing,* ca kusunguka or ca kupapa.

astray, go –, –lube nshila (lubile). *lead –,* –lofya (lofeshe).

at, 1. ku or kuli; pa or pali: *at my home,* ku mwandi. *at 06.00 hours,* pali 06.00 hours. 2. kwa (with proper nouns). *at Mutale's,* kwa Mutale.

at once, apo pêne; nomba line.

atmosphere, lwelele, mwela.

atone, –futile (futile).

attach, v.t. –kambatika (kambatìke); v.i. –kambatila (kambatile).

attached to, (devoted), –temwa (temenwe): *he is attached to me,* antemwa.

attack, –tendeka (tendeke); –lwisha (lwishishe).

attempt, –esha (eseshe).

attend, 1. (be present), –sangwako (sangilweko). 2. (care for), –sakamana (sakamene).

attention, pay –, 1. (turn mind to), –twalako mano (tweleko); –tesha (teseshe); –teko mutima (tekele); –tekanya (tekenye). 2. (care for) –sakamana (sakamene). *call attention to by giving a sign,* –cebula (cebwile).

attentive, cf. pay attention.

attract, –koba, –kabela.

augment, –fusha (fushishe).

August, Kasakantobo; Ipukutú.

aunt, cf. T. V.

authority, maka; lusa. *have –,* –ba na maka. *abuse one's –,* –umyo bufumu (umishe).

authorize, –pêla maka or lusa (pêle): *I am authorized,* bampêle amaka.

avarice, kaso.

avaricious, ...kaso.

avenge, –landula (landwile).

average, cipimo ca pakati: *the average of 2 and 4 is 3,* icipimo ca pakati ka fibili na fine ni fitatu.

avoid, –taluka (talwike) –lâmba (lâmbile): *avoid this man,* taluka ku muntu uyu or lâmbo muntu uyu. If followed by a verb, it is translated by the neg. of the subjunctive, e.g. avoid to do, mwilacita, lit. (do not do).

await, –pemba (pembele); –linda (lindile).

awake, –shibûka (shibwike); –bûka mu tulo (bûke); –bûka mu tulo (bûkile). *be awake,* –lola (lolele): *I was awake all night.* nalola bushiku bonse.

awaken, –bûsha (bûshishe) mu tulo: *awaken him,* kamubûshe mu tulo.

aware, –ishiba (ishibe): *I am aware of it,* nacìshiba.

away, (can be translated by the neg.): *he is away,* talipo, lit. *he is not here,* cf. also: *off.*

awl, musumbo (mi).

axe, isembe (ma). *a nicely forged axe, ...*

used as a spade, ncinde (ba—).

— B —

babble, 1. (talk indistinctly), –longofyanya (longofyenye). 2. (let out secrets), –sosa fya mu nkâma (sosele).

babbler, bobo wa kanwa (ba–).

baby, kana (twana); kanya (tunya).

bachelor, mushimbe (ba).

back, 1. n. numa (n); musana (mi). 2. adv. ku numa.

backbite, –amba (ambile).

bacon, nama ya nkumba.

backward (s), 1. adv. bumfutete; buseneme. *go backwards,* –enda bumfutete. *fall –,* –wa buseneme. 2. adj. (dull), can be translated by the neg. of –cenjela: *he is –,* tacenjela, lit. *he is not clever.*

bad, ...bi. *be –,* bipa (bipile). *turn –,* (rot), –bola (bolele) of meat, fish, etc. –suka (sukile) of egg. *turn –* (morally), –sanguka (sangwike).

badge, cishibilo (fi).

badly, 1. (defectively), bubi; pipi (used with –nunka). *very –,* bubi bubi. 2. *very much –,* sâna: *I need –,* nimpamfiwa sâna.

bag, 1. (made of cloth), mufuko (mi). 2. (made of bark), lupu (ndupu).

baggage, cipe (fipe).

bake, –oca (ocele). v. pass. –ocewa (ocewe).

bald, –sebe pala (sebele);

–ba ne pala: *he is –,* asebe pala or ali ne pala.

baldness, ipala (ma).

ball, mupila (mi).

bamboo, lusengu (n).

banana, nkonde (n); also banana tree.

bandage, v.t. –kakako insalu (kakileko).

banish, –tamfya (tamfishe).

bank (of river), cituntu (fi); isense (ma).

banner, bendêla (mendêla or ba–).

banns, mbila (m). *publish –,* bile mbila (bilile).

banquet, malila.

baptism, lubatisho.

baptize, –batisha (batishe).

bar, 1. n. nkolonga (n). 2. v.t. –binda (bindile); –cilika (cilike).

bare, can be translated by the neg. of –fwala (fwele): *he is barefooted,* tafwele nsapato; lit. *he does not wear shoes.* It can also be translated by the neg. of –ba: *a bare place,* ncende umushilimo nangu cimo; lit. *a place where nothing is.* (see also naked).

bargain, –kabula (kabwile); –kabushanya (kabushenye).

bark, 1. n. cipâpa (fi). *cloth made of –,* cilundu (fi). *rope made of –,* lushishi (n). *piece of bark from tree used as a tray,* mukwa (mi). *pull of bark for making rope,* –kumpo lushishi (kumpile). *make rope from bark,* –fundo lushishi (fundile).

bark, 2. v.i. & t. –bosa (bosele); –kuwa (kuwile).

barn, butala (ma).

barrel, mutungi (mi).

barren, 1. of man & animal, –ba ŋumba. 2. of vegetation. can be translated by the neg. of –twala or the neg. of –ba na. *the tree is –*, umuti tautwala or umuti tawaba ne fitwala.

barricade, –konkomeka (konkomeke); –kolongela nkolonga (kolongele).

barter, 1. n. bukwebo (ma). 2. v.t. & i. –kabula (kabwile); –kabushanya (kabushenye).

basin, beseni (ma).

basket, 1. made of reeds, museke (mi). 2. made of bamboo, citundu (fi). *small –*, cipe (fipe), *winnowing –*, lupe (ndupe).

bastard, mwana wa mu bucende (bâna).

bat, kasûsu (tu). *fruit –*, mulima (mi).

bateleur (kind of vulture), mpungu (m).

bath, bafa (ma).

bathe, –owa (owele); (samba (sambile).

battle, 1. n. lubuli; bulwi. 2. v.i. –cito lubuli; lwa (lwile).

be, –ba. *let it be*, kacibe; nacibe.

be as if, –ba nga. *it is as if*, caba nga.

beach, lulamba

beacon, lupôpo (m).

bead, bulungu (ma).

beak, (bird's bill), mulomo wa cûni (mi).

beam, mwâlo (my).

bean, cilemba, s.; class 'mu/ba': *a good bean*, cilemba musuma. *many beans*, cilemba mwingi. pl. bacilemba may be used

when speaking of single grains, e.g. *3 beans*, bacilemba batatu. *green bean*, mutopoto (mi). *shell beans*, –puma cilemba (pumine); –tongola (tongwele).

bear, 1. (a child), –fyala (fyele). v. appl. –fyalila (fyâlile); –pâpa (pâpile). 2. (fruit), –twâla (twele). v. appl. –twalila (twalile). 3. (carry), –senda (sendele).

beard, mwefu (my). *grow a –*, –meno mwefu (menene).

beast, nama (n).

beat, –uma (umine); (of heart), –tunta (tuntile).

beating (chastisement), fikôti: *he got a –*, bamupêle fikôti.

beautiful, ...suma. *be –*, –wama (weme): *it is –*, cili cisuma or cawama.

beautify, –wamya (wemye).

beauty, busaka.

because, ico; pantu; cilya; ku mulandu wa.

become, –aluka (alwike); –sanguka (sangwike).

bed, busanshi (ma); musengele (mi). *make the –*, –anso busanshi (anshile). *go to bed*, –ya ku kulâla (ile). *rise from bed*, –bûka (bûkile).

bedroom, ŋanda ya kusendama.

bee, lushimu (n); (small kind), cipashi (fi). *queen bee*, nasununda (ba–). *bee hive*, cilunda (fi).

beer, bwalwa; *much beer*, bwalwa bwingi; fig. pl. mâlwa. *brew beer*, –longo bwalwa (longele). *work for beer*, –tumyo bwalwa (tumishe).

beetle, cishishi (fi). *boring beetle,* lupese (m). *dung-rolling beetle,* ntunka mafi (n).

before, 1. prep. pa ntanshi; *before the war,* pa ntanshi ya nkondo. 2. adv. pa kubala; ntanshi; –tala (talile) or –bala (balile): *before (first) tell me,* pa kubala unjebe (or) ntanshi unjebe (or) utale (or ubale) unjebe. 3. cj. (i), "previous to the time when" is expressed by the ta-la-a tense: *go before the rain comes,* kabiye mfula tailaisa. (ii) "rather than", is transcribed by "like more": *I would die before I lied,* kuti cawama nafwa ilyo nshilabepapo bufi.

beg, –lomba (lombele); –pula (pulile), *beg insistently,* –pâpata (pâpête). v. appl. –pâpâtila (pâpâtile).

beget, cf. bear.

beggar, mupushi (ba).

begin, –tampa (tampile); –tendeka (tendeke); –amba (ambile). *begin with,* –bangilila (bangilile): *begin with this work,* bangililo mulimo uyu.

beginning, citendekelo.

behalf, on behalf of, 1. pa malo ya. *on behalf of you,* pa malo yenu, 2. it can also be translated by the appl. extension: *I talk on behalf of you,* namulandila.

behave, –tekanya (tekenye); –têko mutima (têkele).

behaviour, micitile: myendele.

behead, –putulo mutwe (putwile).

behind, 1. prep. ku numa ya. *behind the house,* ku numa ya ŋanda. 2. adv. ku numa: *go behind,* kabiye ku numa.

behold, interj. lelo!

being, *human being,* muntu (ba).

belch, –byôla (byôlele).

belie, –bepesha (bepeshe).

belief, cisumino.

believe, –sumina (sumine).

bell, nyenjele (n). *ring the bell,* –lishe nyenjele (lishishe).

bellows, mûba (my).

belly, ifumo (ma); mu nda.

belong, 1. –ba mwine: *the book belongs to me,* ndi mwine citabo 2. it can also be translated by the pers. pr.: citabo candi, lit. *my book.* 3. Umwine citabo nine.

beloved, mutemwishi (ba); mutemwikwa (ba).

below, 1. prep. mwisamba or pe samba lya. *below the window,* mwisamba lye windo. 2. adv. mwisamba or pe samba: *he is below,* ali mwisamba.

belt, mushipi (mi).

bench, mbao ya kwikalilapo (m).

bend, 1. n. cinshoko (fi) 2. v.t. –peta (petele). *bend (incline),* v.t. inamika (inamike); v.i. –inama (ineme).

benediction, ibalaka (li); li-pâlo.

benefit, 1. (do good to) –wa mina. 2. (gain), –mwenamo; –lilamo. 3. (by) v.t. –wamina.

beseech, –pâpâta (pâpête).
beside (near), mupêpi or pêpi.
besides (in addition), pâmo na: *besides reading he also knows to write,* aishibo kusoma pâmo no kulemba.
besiege, –shinga (shingile).
best, –wamisha; –wama ukucila ...onse: *he is the best,* uyu awamisha or uyu awama ukucila bonse.
bet, 1. n. cipingano (fi). 2. v.i. –pinga (pingine); v. rec. –pingana (pingene).
betray, –sangukila (sangukile).
betroth, –kobekela (kobekele) (when man); –kobekelwa (kobekelwe) (when woman). *betroth definitely,* –imana (imene).
better, –wama ukucila; ...suma ukucila; –wamisha (wamishe).
between. 1. prep. pakati ka-2. adv. pakati.
beverage, cakunwa (fya); (kind of sweet –), lumembe.
bewail, –lôsha (lôseshe); –lile misôwa (lilile).
beware, tekanya (tekenye); –cenjela (cenjele). *beware there is a lion nearby,* tekanya nkalamo ili mupepi. *beware, he is cheating you,* cenjela, akucenjesha.
bewitch, –lowa (lowele); v. pass. –lowekwa (lowekwe).
beyond, 1. prep. peshilya ya: *beyond the hill,* peshilya lya lupili. 2. adv. peshilya or kwishilya: *he is beyond,* ali peshilya. *be beyond one's power,*

–añsha (anshishe).
Bible, Bibilia; Cipingo.
biceps, (of the arm), bombwe (ba–).
bicycle, ncinga (n). *ride a –,* –endela pa ncinga (endele). *pump a –,* –pompe ncinga (pompele). *mend a –,* –lungishe ncinga (lungishe).
bid, –eba (ebele). *I bid you to do this,* ndemweba ukucite ci.
bifurcation in road, masansa.
big, ...kulu; ...kalamba.
bile, ndusha (n).
bilharzia, mubongola.
bin, butala (ma).
bind, –kaka (kakile).
bird, cûni (fy). *little bird,* kôni (tùni). *birdlime,* bulimbo.
birth, kufyalwa. *the birth of Christ,* kufyalwa kwa kwa Kilistu. *give birth to the first born,* –beleka (beleke). *give birth,* fyala fyele).
bishop, shikofu (ba–).
bishopric, bushikofu.
bit, (a bit), panôno; panîni. *a little bit,* panônonôno; panîninîni.
bite, –suma (sumine). *– repeatedly,* –cimaula (cimawile).
bitter, –lula (lulile).
black, –fìta (fìtile). *very black,* –fìta fìtiti.
blacken, –fìsha (fìshishe).
blackish, –fìtuluka (fìtulwìke).
black-jack, kasokopyo (ba–). (ba–).
blacksmith, kafula (ba–).
bladder, cisu (fisu).
blade, cilimi: *the blade of*

the knife, cilimi ca mwèle.
blame, v.t. –kalipila (kalipile). *blame falsely* –bepesha (bepeshe).
blanket, bulangeti (ma).
blast furnace, ilungu (ma).
blaze, 1. n. lubingu (mingu
or mabingu). 2. v.i. –âka
(âkile).
bleed, v.i. –sûmo mulopa
(sûmine). v.t. –sumya (su-
mishe).
blend, v.t. –sansha (sanshishe).
bless, –balikila (balikile);
–pâla mate (pâlile) (fa-
vour) –senamina (senami-
ne).
blessing, ibalaka; lipalo.
blind. –pofula (pofwile).
blindfold, –shibatika menso
(shibatike).
blindness, bupofu.
blind person, mpofu (m).
blink (with eyes), –kapa-
kapa (kapakapile); –shi-
bashiba (shibashibe); (of
stars), –shibantukila (shibantukile).
blister, 1. n. citusha (fi).
2. v.t. –pya citusha (pile).
blood, mulopa (mi). *much
blood,* mulopa wingi or
milopa ingi. *pass blood,*
–sundo mulopa (sundile)
(sign of bilharzia). *excrete
blood,* –sûko mulopa (sû-
kile) (sign of dysentery).
bloodvessel, mushipa wa
mulopa (mi).
bloom, 1. of flowers. –satula
(satwile). 2. of trees, –balula (balwile).
blossom, 1. n. lutombo (n).
2.v.i. cf. *bloom.*
blow, 1. n. lupumo (m). 2.
v.i. –pûta (pûtile); (of
... ...–rupa (pupile).

blow the nose, –fyona
(fyonene).
blunder, v.i.–tena (tenene);
–luba (lubile).
blunt, –fûpa (fûpile): *the
axe is blunt.* isembe nali-
fûpa. *make blunt,* –fufya
(fûfishe).
board, n. ipulanga (ma);
itâbwa (ma).
boast, 1. n. mataki. 2. v.i.
–itakisha (itakishe).
boat, bwato (mâto).
boatsman, kashîka wa bwâto.
body, mubili (mi).
boggy, –tika (tikile). *this
place is boggy,* pano napa-
tika.
boil, 1. n. cipute (fi); mumena (ba–); cûlu (fy) *a
big boil.* 2. v.i. –bilauka
(bilawike); v.t. –bilaula
(bilawile); –ipika (ipike).
boil water, –kafya menshi
(kafishe). *boil water for
making mush,* –têkapo
bwâli (têkelepo).
bold, –pama (pamine).
bone, ifupa (ma). *bone cov-
ering the brain,* cipanga
(fi).
book, citabo (fi); ibûku
(ma).
boot, combo (fy).
border, n. mupaka (mi).
bore, –sumba (sumbile).
bore like a weevil, –pesa
(pesele). *bore a hole*
(pierce), –tula (tulile).
boredom, citendwe.
borer (tool), musumbo (mi).
boring beetle, lupese (m).
born, –fyalwa (fyelwe): *I
was born in ...* nafyalilwe
mu mwaka wa... *first
born,* ibêli (ma); *last born,*
kas... (b...).

borrow, -ashima (ashime);
-kongola (kongwele); -ko-
pa (kopele).

bosom, cêni (fy).

both, ...onse ...bili: *both
books,* fitabo fyonse fibili.

bother (worry), -sakamana
(sakamene); (annoy),
-afya (afishe).

bottle, musukupala (mi);
ibotôlo (ma).

bottom, isamba (ma). *at the
bottom,* pe samba lya.

bounce (a ball), -tama (mupila) (tamine).

bound (morally obliged),
-ba na: *we are bound to
obey,* tuli no kubêla.

boundary, mupaka (mi);
mupakwa (mi).

bounty, busuma.

bow, 1. n. (weapon), buta
(mata); 2. v.i. -inama
(ineme); -petama (pete-
me).

bowel, bula (mala).

bowl, mbale yafonka (m);
mbale yafongomana (m).

box, 1. n. mbokoshi (ma);
2. v.t. -fûta fifunshi (ûti-
le).

boy, mwaice mwaume (ba);
mwâna mwaume (one's
own male child). *house-
boy,* mulumendo wa ku-
bomba mu nanda.

bracelet (of ivory), ikôsa
(ma); (of grass), cindele
(fi); (of metal), cinkwi-
ngili (fi); (of copper), lusambo (n).

brag, 1. n. mataki (ma). 2. v.i.
-itakisha (itakishe).

brain, bongobongo (ba-).

bran, fisense.

branch, musambo (mi).
*branches cut for garden-
ing,* fisako; fibûla.

brave, -shipa (shipile); -pa-
ma (pamine).

bread, mukate (mi).

breadth, bukulu; bufumo.

break, v.t. -putula (putwile); v. stat. -putuka (putwike). *break into small
pieces,* -putaula (puta-
wile); -fungaula (funga-
wile). *break leg,* etc. -funa
(funine); v. stat. -funika
(funike). *break branch,*
etc., -kontola (kontwele);
v. stat. -kontoka (kontweke). *break dish,* etc., -lala
(lalile); -toba (tobele); v.
stat. lalika (lalike); -tobe-
ka (tobeke).

break off (chip), -mokola
(mokwele); v. stat. -mo-
koka (mokweke).

break up (dismantle), -pa-
ngulula (pangulwile); v.
stat. -panguluka (pangu-
lwike).

break a promise, -futuka
(futwike): *you refuse to
give me what you pro-
mised,* mwafutuka mu ku-
kanampêla ifyo mwanda-
ile.

breakfast, v.i. -ikula (ikwi-
le): *did you have your
breakfast,* bushe mwaciku-
la.

breast, ibêle (ma).

breastbone, nkombe (n).

breath, mupu; mupêmo; ci-
pêmo. *hold the,* -, -mino
mweo (minine).

breathe, -pêma (pêmene).

breed, -sanda (sandile).

brew beer, -longo bwalwa
(longele).

bribe, 1. n. mafisa kanwa.
2.v.t. -cita mafisa kanwa
(citile).

brick, itafwali (ma); njelwa

(n). *make* –, –tama matafwàli (tamine); –bumba matafwàli (bumbile).

brick kiln, cibili (fi); itanununa (ma).

bricklayer, kakùla wa njelwa (ba).

brickmould, cikombola (fi).

bride, nabwinga (ba–).

bridegroom, shibwinga (ba–). (ba–).

bridge, bulalo (a).

bride-price, mpango (m). *pay the* –, –leke mpango (lekele).

bright (shining), –bêka (bèkele); (clever), –limuka (limwike); –ba na mano; –cenjela (cenjele).

brim, 1. n. milomo. 2. *fill to the brim,* –isusha. 3. *full to to the brim,* ...isula.

bring, –lèta (lètele). – *in,* –ingisha (ingishe). – *near,* –palamika (palamike). – (*to*), –twala (twele).

broad, –lepa (lepele).

broaden, –lefya (lefeshe).

broken, cf. break, v. stat.

brook, kamana (tu).

broom, cêswa (fy); mukusao (mi) made of twigs.

brother, ndume; munyinane, etc., cf. T. V. *elder brother,* mukalamba, followed by poss. or *my* –, mukalamba wandi. *younger* –, mwaice, followed by poss. pr. *my* –, mwaice wandi.

brotherhood, bumunyina.

brother-in-law, bukwe(ba–).

bruise, 1. n. lùma (nùma). 2. v.t. –cena (cenene); –fwanta (fwantile).

brush, 1. n. cifuti (fi). 2. v.t. –fùta (fùtile), *tooth* –, muswaki (mi). *brush teeth,* –kusa mêno (kushile).

brutality, bunkalwe; butobatoba (ba).

brute, munkalwe (ba); mutobatoba (ba).

bubble, v.i. –selauka (selawike).

bucket, mbeketi (m).

bud, 1. n. lutombo (n). 2. v.i. –tombola (tombwele).

buffalo, mboo (m).

bug, cipu (fipu).

bugle, ipenga (ma).

build, –kùla (kùlile); –panga (pangile). *– a nest,* –pike cisansala (pikile).

bulky, lèpa mu bukulu (lêpele).

bull, cilume.

bullet, cipolopolo (fi); lusàshi (n).

bunch, cisangu (fi). *bunch of banana,* musemo (mi).

bundle, mwanshi (my); cango(fy).

burden, 1. n. cipe (fipe). 2. v.t. –twika (twikile).

burglar, mupùpu (ba).

burial place, nshinshi (n). *of Bemba Chiefs,* (Chitimukulu, Mwamba and Nkula) Mwalule.

burn, v.t. –oca (ocele); *burn this,* oce ci; v.i. –pya (pile): *I am burnt,* nàpya; àka (àkile): *the fire is burning,* mulilo waàka. *burn food,* –lungusha (lungwishe); v. stat. –lungula (lungwile): *food is burnt,* fyakulya fyalungula.

burrow, 1. n. (big kind) mwimba (mimba; (small kind) musombo (mi). 2. v.t. –imba (imbile).

burst, v.t. –lepula (lepwile); v.i. –lepuka (lepwike); –pùka (pùkile).

bury, –shika (shikile).

hush, mpanga (m). *bush where fire has passed,* mupya (mi).

bushbuck, cisongo (ba–).

business, mulimo (mi); ncito (n).

busy, –ba ne milimo: *I am busy,* ndi ne milimo. *be very busy,* –lwa ne milimo (lwile).

but, nomba; lelo. *but for* (however), ...ena: *but for these things,* ifi fyena. *but* (only), fye: *he is but a child,* ali mwaice fye, *but* (except), kano: *all but you,* bonse, kano imwe.

butcher, kakôma wa ŋombe (ba–); buca (ba–).

butter, mafuta ye shiba; mafuta ya mukaka.

butterfly, cipelebesha (fi).

buttock, litako (ma).

button, ipitawa (ma).

button hole, kapunda ke pitawa (tu).

buy, –shita (shitile).

buzz, –shîshîta (shîshîtile).

by, ku or kuli; na. *he was bitten by a snake,* asuminwe ku (ne) nsoka. *he was beaten by his father,* auminwe kuli wishi.

— C —

cabbage, kabeji.

cackle, –tetêla (tetêle).

calabash, nsupa (n).

calamity, bulanda.

calculate, –penda (pendele).

calf, ciponti ca ŋombe (fi). *calf* (of leg), kapafu (ba–).

call, 1. n. bwite. 2. v.t. –ita (itile).

call for help, 1. n. nkûta (n.) 2. v.t. –kûta (kûtile).

call out (names, etc.), –punda (pundile) mashina.

calm, –talala (talêle). 2. adv. tondolo; shilili.

calm down, v.t. –talaliko mutima ((talalike); v.i. –bwesho mutima (bweseshe): *he calmed down,* –abwesho mutima or umutima wakwe nawikala.

calmly 1. (noiseless), tondolo; shilili. 2. (slowly), bucebuce.

calumniate, –bepesha (bepeshe); –amba (ambile).

camel, ngamiya (n).

camera, kamela (ba–); ca kukopelamo (fya).

camp, 1. n. kampu (ma–); nsakwe. 2. v.i. –sake nsakwe (sakile).

camping place, ndo (n).

can, kuti; –ba na maka: *I can do this,* kuti nacite ci or ndi na maka ya kucite ci.

canal, mufôlo (mi); munyaŋgala (mi).

cancel, –pangulula (pangulwile.

cannot, –filwa (fililwe) –bula maka, tekuti: *I – do this,* nafilwa kuciteci or nabula maka ya kuciteci or tekuti nciteci. (short form: teti).

canoe, bwâto (mâto).

cap, kasote (tu).

capable, –linga (lingile); –fwa (fwile); *he is capable of doing it,* alingo kucite ci or afwile ukuciteci.

capital, musumba (mi).

capitulate, –cimba (cimbile).

capsize, v.t. –bunsha (bunshishe); v.i. –bunda (bundile).

captain, ntungulushi (n). kapitao.

captive, nkole (ba–).

carcass, citumbi (n).

card, kalata (ma–). *playing cards,* njuka (n).

care for, –sunga (sungile); –baka (bakile).

care about, –sakamana (sakamene). *take care* (behave), –tekanya (tekenye); *take care* interj. lelo!

careful, cf. take care.

carefully, bwino bwino; bucebuce.

careless, –pusauka (pusawike); –ba no busanku.

careless person, mupusaushi (ba); musanku (ba).

carelessness, bupusaushi; busanku.

carpenter, kabâsa (ba–)

carrier, wa cipe (ba fipe).

carry, –senda (sendele). *carry a load between two,* –pinga (pingile). *carry across water,* –abusha (abwishe), *carry in turns,* –senda kombokombo (se ndele. *carry on the back,* –pâpa (pâpele). *carry on the shoulder,* –sunsa (sunshile). *carry* (to), –twâla (twêle), v. appl. –twalila (twalile).

cart, iceleta (ma).

cartridge, cisongo (fi).

carve, –bâsa (bâshile).

case, (box) mbokoshi (m); (law suit), mulandu: *he has a case,* ali no mulandu. *study a case,* –shininkisho mulandu *(shini nkishe). alter a case,* –alulo mulandu (–alwile). *muddle up a case,* kanda-

wile). *interfere in a case,* –ampako mulandu (ampileko). *the case is insolvable,* mulandu wakosa. *settle a case,* –putulo mulandu (putwile). *in case,* cj. nga; kumfwa; kumona; nana, *in that case,* cj. lyêna; kwêna; nana.

cash, ndalama (n). *pay cash,* –libila apo pêne (lipile.)

cassava, kalundwe, cl. 1, s. *good –,* kalundwe musuma. *soaked cassava,* bwabi.

castor plant, munono (mi). *castor bean,* lumono (mono). *castor oil,* mafuta ya mono.

castrate, –tungula (tungwile). *castrated animal,* mutungu (n).

cat (domestic), côna (ba–). pushi (ba–); nyau (ba–). (wild), mpaka (m); *civet –,* mfungo (m).

catch, 1. (lay hold of), –ikata (ikete); 2. (– something thrown), –anka (ankile); (snatch), –sompola (sompwele); –fûba (fûbile). *fail to catch,* –pusa (pushile); –panya (panishe).

catechist, kafundisha (ba–); mwalimu (ba–).

caterpillar, cishimu (fi). *collect caterpillars,* –kole fishimu (kolele).

catfish, muta (mi).

Catholic, katolika (ba).

Catholic Church, ekeleshia katolika.

cattle, ŋombe (ŋ). *cattle shed,* itanga (ma) lya ŋombe; icinka (ma).

cause 1. (beginning), cishinte (fi) 2. (reason), mulandu (mi). 3. v.t. –lenga (lengele).

cautious, –cenjela (cenjele); –tekanya (tekenye).

cave, lucengo (n).

cavern, cf, cave.

cease, –leka (lekele).

celebrate, –cindika (cindike).

celibacy, bushimbe.

celibate, mushimbe (ba).

cement, shamende; sementi.

cemetery, nshinshi (n).

centipede, ciyongoli (fi).

central, ca pakati(fya).

certain, be –, –ishiba ca cine (ishibe), *make –,* –shininkisha (shininkishe).

certainly, ca cine, cine cine; naendi.

chaff, musungu (mi).

chain, munyololo (mi).

chair, mupando (mi).

chairman, shicilye (ba–).

chalk, côko (ma–); lupemba (m).

chalice, cikombe (fi).

chance, 1. n. (luck), ishuko; (occasion), nshita: *if I have a chance,* nga namone nshita. 2. v.i. –fika (fikile). *it chanced,* cafika fye. 3. adv. *by chance,* cafika fye.

change in silver, sha museke.

change, 1. n. (money returned as balance), ndalama ishashala. 2. v.t. –alula (alwile); –sangula (sangwile); –cinja (cinjile). v.i. –aluka (alwike); –sanguka (sangwile): *don't change your opinion,* mwiyaluka. *change direction,* v.t. –pindulula (pindulwile); v.i. –pinduluka (pindulwike), *change domicile,* v.i. –kûka (kû-

kile). *change place,* v.t. –sesha (seseshe); v.i. –sela (selele).

chapel, ŋanda ya kwa Lesa.

chapter (of a book), cipandwa (fi).

character, misango; mibêle: *myendele: how is his character?* misango, etc., yakwe yaba shani? *be of the same character,* –ba mumo.

charcoal, mufito (mi).

charge, 1. n. (load), cipe (fi); (price demanded). mutengo (mi). 2. v.t. (load somebody), –twika (twikile); (demand price), –lipilisha (lipilishe); (attack), –tendeka (tendeke). *the one-in-charge,* mukubwa (ba–). *the being-in-charge,* bumukubwa.

charitable, –ba no bupe: *he is charitable,* aba no bupe.

charity, citemwiko.

charm, 1. n. (beauty), busaka; (spell), bwanga. *charm for seeds,* cibyalilo (fi). 2. v.t. (throw a charm), –pando bwanga (pandile); –soko bwanga (sokele); –lowa (lowele). (remove a charm), –loolola (loolwele).

chase, v.t. –tamfya (tamfishe).

chat, 1. n. lyashi. 2. v.i. –pume lyashi (pumine).

cheap, –nako mutengo (nakile): *this hat is cheap,* mutengo wa cisote naunaka.

cheat, –cenjesha (cenjeshe); –bepa (bepele); (by copying), –kopa (kopele).

check, –lengula (lengwile);

–belenga (belengele).

cheek, isaya (ma).

cheer, v.t. –sansamusha (sansamwishe) ; v.i. –sansamuka (sansamwike).

cheerful, –ba ne nsansa.

cheerfulness, nsansa.

cheetah, cinseketa (fi).

chest, cifuba (fi).

chew, –sheta (shetele).

chicanery, bukakâshi.

chicken, mwana wa nkoko (ba).

chicken-pox, kabokoshi (tu).

chide, –kalipila (kalipile).

chief, mfumu (m or bashamfumu).

chieftainship, bufumu.

chief's quarters, isano.

child, 1. offspring –, mwana (bana) ; his/her –, mwane (ba–) ; *your* –, mwâno (ba–). 2. – boy or girl –, mwaice (baice). *bring up* –, kusho mwana (kushishe) ; –lelo mwana (lelele). *spoil a child,* –lemo mwana (lemene). *child whose upper teeth grow first,* cinkûla (fi). *favorite child,* kacele (ba–).

childhood, bwaice. first *childhood,* bunya.

childish, –ba nga kaice.

chill, v.t. –kasha (kashishe) : *rain chilled me,* mfula yankasha. *be chilled,* –kata (katile).

chimney, cipunda ca cushi (fi).

chin, kalefulefu (tu).

chip, v.t. 1. mokola (mokwele) ; v. stat. –mokoka (mokweke). 2. –kombola (kombwele) ; v. stat. –komboka (kombweke).

chisel, 1. n. cesulo (fy) ; mwengo (my). 2. v.t.

–fukula (fukwile).

choir (singers), baomba.

choke, v.t. –pwilisho mweo (pwilishe).

choose, –sala (salile).

chop. 1. (make a notch), –ceka (cekele). 2. (mince), –kaya (kaile). 3. (cut into small pieces), –putaula (putawile).

Christ, Kilishitu.

Christendom, bukilishityani.

Christian, mukilishityani (ba) ; mwina Kilishitu (bena).

Christmas, nshikunkulu ya kufyalwa kwa kwa Kilishitu.

Church, ekeleshia (ba–) ; chalici (ma–).

church (building), ŋanda ya Mulungu (ŋ or mayanda).

churn milk, —suka mukaka (sukile).

cinema, shinema (ba–) ; pikicala (ma–).

circle, cintengulusha (fi).

circumstances, *under these* –, apo cabe fi ; *under these* – *I accept,* apo cabe fi, kuti caba shani ; *under no* – *shall I accept this,* kuti caba shani, nakana fye. lit. *however it may be, I refuse only.*

cite, 1. (law) –lubulwisha. 2. (quote) –shimika.

citizen, mukaya (ba).

citizenship, bukaya.

city, musumba (mi).

civet cat, mfungo (m).

civil, ...bukaya. *civil war,* nkondo ya bukaya.

clan, mukôwa (mi) ; luko (nduko). *person of the same clan,* muntu (followed by pers. pr.) : *he is of my clan,* muntu wandl.

person of an opposite clan, munungwe (ba). *person of a clan or country.* mwina (bèna): *I belong to the clan of rain,* ndi mwîna mfula. *they are from the country of Tafuna,* bali bena Tafuna.

clap hands, –ombe ndupi (ombele).

clash, 1. n. lubuli. 2. –lwa (lwile): *it came finally to a clash,* basuka bálwa.

claw, 1. n. lwala (ngala). 2. v.t. –fôla (ôlele): *a leopard clawed him,* mbwili yamufôlele.

clay, ibumba (ma); iloba (ma). *white clay,* mpemba (m).

clean, 1. be clean, –bûta (bûtile). *a clean shirt,* ilaya lyabûta; –fûtuka (fûtwike): *the house is clean,* mu ŋanda namufûtuka. 2. *make clean,* –pukuta (pukwite). *clean the shoes,* pukute nsapato. –wamya (wenye): *make the table clean,* wamye tebulo.

clear (ground), –seba (sebele); –kungula (kungwile).

clear, 1. be clear (unspotted), –bûta (bûtile); (like water), lengama (lengeme): *the water is clear,* menshi nayalengama; (appear), –moneka (moneke): *it is clear that,* camoneka ukuti. 2. *make clear,* (water), –lengamika (lengamike).

clear up a case, –londololo mulandu. (londolwele). v. stat. –londoloka (londolwêke).

clear the table, –fumye

mbale pe têbulo; –teule fipe pe têbulo.

clearly, bwino bwino: *I told him clearly,* namwebele bwino bwino.

clerk, kalaliki (ba–).

clever, –ba na mâno; –cenjela (cenjele); –limuka (limwike).

cleverness, 1. skill, mâno; bufundi. 2. *deceit,* bucenjeshi.

climate, câlo (fy). *hot climate,* câlo cakaba (fy).

cling to, –konena (konene), –shangila (shangile).

cloak, isâba (ma).

clock, nkololo (n); nsa (n): *at 17.00 hours,* pali 17.00 hours.

close, v.t. –isala (isele). v. appl. isalila (isalile); *close the door,* isalèniko cibi. v. pass. –isalwa (isalilwe): *the door is closed,* cibi caisalwa 2. adv. pêpi (or mupêpi) na ku: *close to the village,* mupêpi na ku mushi. *close eyes,* –shibata (shibête).

clot, –tikama (tikeme).

cloth, nsalu (n). *ragged cloth,* lusamu (n).

clothe. 1. n. cakufwala (fya). 2. v.t. –fwika (fwikile); v.i. –fwâla (fwêle). 3. – oneself, –fwala.

cloud, ikumbi (ma). *cloud of dust,* etc. ntumba (n); lusuko (n).

cloudy, –kutika (kutîke); –bundama (bundeme): *the weather is cloudy to-day,* cakutika lelo or napabundama lelo. *cloudy weather,* cikutika.

club, mulanga (mi).

coal, malasha.

coast, lulamba.

coat (of animal), masako.

cobra (common), ngoshe (ba). *forest cobra,* mâmba. *water cobra,* mambalushi. also black mamba. *spitting cobra,* kafi (ba–).

cobweb, tandabube (ba–); bwile.

cock, mukolwe (ba–).

cockroach, lupemfu (m).

coco-nut, ngashi (n).

coddle, –tekelesha (tekeleshe); –tentemba (tentembe).

coerce, –patikisha (patikishe).

coffee, kofi.

coil, –nyongâna (nyongêne): *the snake coiled up,* nsoka yanyongâna.

coin, ikopala. (ma).

cold, 1. n. mpepo; also cold weather & common cold. *cold in the head,* cifine. *have a cold,* –kôla (kôlele). 2. *be cold,* –talala talele): *I want cold water,* ndefwaya menshi yatalala.

colic, mupindo. *suffer from* –. mu nda mulenyongana.

collapse, 1. (of man), –wa panshi (wile). 2. (of building), –bongoloka (bongolweke).

collar, nteneshi (n); mukoshi (mi).

colleague, cf. T. V.

collect, cf. assemble. – *money,* –sanshishe ndalama (sanshishe).

colour, ilangi (ma). *be of a variety of colours,* –balâla (balêle). *paint in different colours,* –balâlika (balalike).

column, luceshi (n).

comb, 1. n. cisakulo (fi). 2. v.t. –sakula (sakwile).

come, isa (ishile). – *about* (happen), –fika (fikile). – *across* (find), –sanga (sangile)); –kumana (kumene). – *after,* –konkapo (konkelepo). – *back,* –bwela (bwelele). – *between,* –cinga (cingile). – down, –ika (ikile). – *from,* –fuma (fumine); –tula (tulile): *where do you come from?* mwafuma kwi or mwatula kwi? – *here,* imp. isa kuno (isêni)! – *in,* –ingila (ingile). *come in!* interj. ingila (ingilêni)! – *near,* –palama (paleme). – *on!* interj. ale (alêni)! or (alwêni)! – *out,* –fuma (fumine). – *unexpectedly,* -pumikisha (pumikishe). – *upon,* cf. come across. – *with,* –konka (konkele).

comfort, v.t. –talaliko mutima (talalike).

command, 1. n. cebo (fy) 2. v.t. –pêle cebo (pêle).

commemorate, –ibukisha (ibukishe).

commence, cf. begin.

commerce, busulwishi; bunonshi.

common, ba ca ku ...nse: *it is common to all men,* cili ca ku bantu bonse.

commoner, mupabi (ba); muntunse (ba): wa fye (ba).

companion, cf. T. V.

compare, –palanya (palenye); –linganya (lingenye).

compassion, cilela. *feel –,* languluka (langulwike).

compel, –patika (patike).

compensate, –fûta mu kulinganya (fûtile).

compensation, mafuto. *ask for –,* –pindo mulandu (pindile).

compete, –cimfyanya (cimfyenye); –tangana (tangene).

complain, –isosha (isoseshe); –ilishanya (ilishenye).

complete, ...tuntulu; ...onse *it is complete,* cili cituntulu or conse.

completely, 1. ...onse nakalya: *he ate it –,* alile fyonse nakalya. 2. fye: *I forgot it –,* nalabá fye.

compliments, pay –, –tasha (tashishe).

compose, –panga (pangile). *compose a new song,* –shiko lwimbo (shikile). *be composed of,* –pangwa ku (pangilwe); –ba mo: *it is composed of,* icapangwa ku or icaba mo ni.

compound kompaundi (ma–).

compost, mufundo.

comrade, cf. T. V.

conceal, v.t. –fisa (fishile); –belamika (belamike); v.i. –fisama (fiseme); –belama (beleme).

conceive, –imita (imite).

concern, n. mulandu (mi); *it concerns you,* mulandu wenu.

concubinage, live in –, –tôlana mu cupo (tôlene).

concubine, mwinga (ba–).

concupiscence, lunkumbwa.

condition, cifwaikwa (fi). *on – that,* cikulu; kulila; kumfwa.

conduct, 1. n. cf. behaviour. 2. v.t. (lead), –ensha

(enseshe); v.i. cf. (behave).

confess, –lumbula (lumbwile).

confession, cilumbulo. *sacrament of –,* nsakalamenta ya cilapilo; cilumbulo.

confident, –sûbila (sûbile): *I am confident that,* ndesûbila ukuti,

confidential ca mu nkâma (fya).

confirm, –suminisha (suminishe).

confirmation, nkosho (as sacrament).

confluence, mawilo.

confuse, –fulunganya (fulungenye). *be confused,* –fulungana (fulungene): *I am confused,* mâno yandi yafulungana.

confusion, cimfulunganya; cimfundawila.

congeal, –tikama (tikeme).

congratulate, –tasha (tashishe).

congregation, cibungwe (fi).

connect, –kumbinkanya (kumbinkenye). v.stat. –kumbinkana (kumbinkene).

conquer, –tâsha (tâshishe); –cimfya (cimfishe).

conscience, mutima.

consent, –sumina (sumine): *do you consent?* bushe mwasumina? *consent to,* –pokeléla (pokelele); –suminina (suminine)): *did you consent* (take part in the case), bushe mwapokelele (or mwasuminine mulandu. *give mutual consent,* –suminishanya (sunishenye).

consequently, kanshi; e ico.

consider, –tontonkanya (tontonkenye): *I shall con-*

sider your application,
nkatontokanya pa kwipu-
sha kwênu.
consist, cf. composed.
console, –talaliko mutima
(talalike).
constable, polishi (ba-).
constipated, ifumo lyauma
ndi (lyaumine).
construct, –kûla (kûlile);
–panga (pangile).
consult, –bûsha (bûshishe).
–ipusha (ipwishe).
consume, –lya (lile)
consumption, (disease), nta-
nda bwanga.
contagious, . . .lwambu. *contagious* disease, bulwele
bwa lwambu.
contain, –ba mo: *this parcel
contains tobacco,* ici cipe
icabamo ni fwâka.
contaminate,   –ambukila
(ambukile); –ambukisha
(ambukishe), *get contam-
inated by a disease,* –ambulo bulwêle **(ambwile)**.
contempt, 1. n. musâlula
(mi); misûla. 2. v.t. –sâlula
(sâlwile). *show* –, –shuluka (shulwike).
content, –temwa (temwene):
are you –, bushe mwa-
temwa?
contents, ifyabamo (ify).
continue, –bikapo (bikilepo); –konkanya (konke-
nye); aku . . .a (eni). aku-
bombeni.
contract, cipangano (fi).
contradict, –bikapo fikansa
(bikilepo). –' *oneself,* –futuka (futwike).
contradicting, –lubâna (lubêne). *it is* –, calubâna.
contradictory person, wa
fikansa (ba).
contribute, –sangula (sa-

ngwile); –pêla (pêle). *they
– with money,* basangule
or (bapêle) ndalama.
control, –têka (têkele).
convenient, –linga (lingile):
it is – that, nacilinga
ukuti.
conversation, ilyashi (ma).
hold a –, –pume lyashi
(pumine). *keep a lively* –,
–kokeshe lyashi (koke-
she).
convert, –sangula (sangwile); –alula (alwile).
convict, –shinina (shinine). *he was convicted,* ba-
mushinina.
cook, 1. n. kûki (ba); kêpika (ba-). 2. v.t. –ipika (ipike). *be cooked,* –pya (pile): *food is ready* (cooked), fyakulya nafipya.
cool, –talala (talele); *the
weather is* –, kwatalala. –
off, –subuka (subwike):
hot water is cooling off,
amenshi yakaba yalesubu-
ka.
copper, mukuba.
copy, 1. n. cikope (fi). 2. v.t.
–kopa (kopele); –ambula
(ambwile).
cord, mwando (my). *twist
a* –, –pyato mwando (pya-
tile).
cork, nciliko (n).
cork screw, ncilwilo (n).
cormoran (water bird), nondo (n).
corner, ikônala (ma); itungi
(ma).
corpse, citumbi (fi); cala
(fy). *arrange a – for burial,* –onga (ongele).
correct, v.t. –wamya (wemye), –londa (londele). *be
–,* cf. accurate; right; true.
cost, 1. n. mutengo (mi). 2.

v.i. (it is transcribed by)
('mutengo'): *what does it
cost,* mutengo ni shani,
lit. *what is the price.*
cotton, tonge (ba-); also
cotton plant.
cough, 1. n. cifuba. 2. v.i.
–kóla (kólele).
council, cilye (fi).
councillor, wa mu cilye
(ba); cilolo (ba–); shicilye (ba–). – *of a chief,*
kabilo (ba–).
councellor, cf. adviser.
count –penda (pendele). –
on, –tetekela (tetekele);
countless, te fya kupenda.
country, mpânga (m).
courage, mute; kushipa. *be
courageous,* –shipa (shipile); – shipikisha (shipikishe).
court, 1. n. cilye (fi); kôti
(ma–). 2. v.t. –senga (sengele). *open court,* lwalâla.
bring somebody to court,
–biko muntu mu cilye (bi-
kile).
courtyard, lubansa (mânsa).
cousin, 1. (child of father's
sister or mother's brother),
mufyala (ba). 2. (child
of father's brother or
mother's sister), munyina
(ba–).
cover, 1. n. (lid), nkupiko
(n); (– of a book), nkupo
(n). 2. v.t. (cover with a
lid), –kupika (kupike);
(cover a book), –kupa
(kupile). (cover with
blanket, etc.), –fimba (fimbile).
covet, –kumbwa (kumbilwe).
cow, ŋombe.
coward, kûwe (ba–); wa
mwenso (ba).

cowshed, itanga (ma); icinka (ba).
crab, ŋanse (n).
crack, 1. n. (in wall), mulale
(mi); (in skin of heels),
liŋa (maŋa). 2. v.t. –lepula
(lepwile); v. stat. –lepuka
(lepwike); (– an egg), –lala
(lalile).
craft, bufundi.
craftsman, fundi (ba–).
craftmanship, bufundi.
cramp, n. ntontongolo (n).
*cramp with sensation of
"pins & needles",* cifungalashi (fi).
crane (crested –), ngôli
(n). (kind of crane-bird),
ikolongo (ma).
crash, v.t. –toba (tobele) v.i.
–onaika (onaike); –wa pa-
nshi (wile).
craving for meat, fish, etc.,
bukasha.
crawl, –amfula (amfwile).
craziness, bushilu.
crazy, –pena (penene).
create, –bumba (bumbile).
creator, kabumba.
creature, cibumbwa (fi).
creed, cisumino.
creep (like a child), –amfula (amfwile); (like a
hunter), –bendela (bende-
le).
cricket (burrowing insect),
–nyense (n).
criminal, cipondo (fi).
cripple, cîte (fîte); cilema
(fi).
crippled, –lemana (lemene).
crocodile, ŋwena (ŋ); ŋandu (used as term of to-
tem).
crooked, –kongama (kongeme).
crop, 1. n. fisabo. 2. v.t.
–sêpa (sêpele). *remaining*

crop of last year, ..comba; e.g. rest of last year's millet, male ya comba. *protect crop,* –amina (amine).

crop rotation, make –, –alule mbuto (alwile).

cross, 1. n. musalaba (mi). 2. v.t. (cross water), –abuka (abwike). *cross over a bridge,* , –abuka pa bulalo *be cross,* –fitwa (fitilwe); –fulwa (fulilwe). *be cross with,* –fuļilwa (fulilwe): *I am cross with you,* namufulilwa.

crossing place, câbu (fy).

crosswise, put –, âpindika (pindike).

crow, mwankole (ba–).

crowd, ibumba (ma); mpuka (m). *large crowd,* cinkupiti (fi).

crown, cisote ca mfumu (ff). *crown of flowers, thorns* etc., ŋana (ŋ).

crucifix, musalaba (mi).

crucify, –taņika (taņike) pa musalaba.

cruel, –luma (lumine); *he is cruel,* uyu uwaluma; –ba no bunkalwe.

cruelty, bunkalwe.

crumble, v.t. –bongolola (bongolwêle); –mokola (mokwele). v.i. –bongoloka (bongolweke); –mokoka (mokweke).

crush, v.t. –shina (shinine); –shôna (shônene); –ponda (pondele). cf. also crumble.

cry, –lila (lilile).

cry of welcome, kapundu (tu). *utter cries of welcome,* –aulo tupundu (awile).

cucumber, cibimbi (fi).

cultivate, –lima (limine).

cup, nkomaki (ba–).

cupboard, kabati, (ba–).

cure, v.t. –posha (poseshe); –undapa (undepe).

curl, 1. n. lupôto (m). 2. v.t. –luke mpôto.

curl up, v.t. –nyongânya (nyongênye); v.i. nyongâna (nyongêne): *the snake curls up,* nsoka yanyongâna.

current, mukuku (mi).

curse, 1. n. ntipu (n). 2. v.t. –tîpa (tipile); –lapisha (lapishe).

curtail, –cefya (cefeshe).

curve, 1. n. cinshoko (fi). 2. v.t. –kongamika (kongamike); v.i. –kongama (kongême).

cushion, musao (mi). *lay head on cushion,* –sailo mutwe pa musao (saile).

custom, musango (mi); cibelelo (fi); mibêle.

cut. 1. n. mulaba (mi). 2. v.t. –têta (têtele); v.i. –icena (icenene). – *by biting,* –ceta (cetele). – *hair,* –beo mushishi (bêle). – *off,* –putula (putwile). – *open* (operate), –tumbula (tumbwile). – *trees,* –tema (temene). – *up meat,* –tante nama (tantile).

— D —

daily, cila bushiku; nshiku shonse.

damage, –onaula (onawile); v. stat. –onaika (onaike).

damp, –bomba (bombele): *here it is damp,* kwabomba kuno or pano pali mutonshi.

dampness, mutonshi.

dance, 1. n. cîla (fi). **2.** v.i. –cinda (cindile). *dance for joy,* –anga (angile).

dandruff, nkuku (n).

danger, busanso.

dangerous, ...kali: *the lion is a – animal,* nkalamo ni nama ikali.

dare, –esha (eseshe); –pama.

dark, –fîta (fitile). *very –,* –fîta fititi *it is –* (at night), napafîta; (inside a room), namufîta.

darkness, mfîfi.

date, bushiku: *what date is it to-day,* lêlo bushiku nshi bwa mweshi.

daughter, mwâna mwana-kashi (bâna).

daughter-in-law, cf. T. V.

dawdle, –kokola (kokwele); –shingashinga (shingashingile).

dawn, 1. n. macâca. **2.** v.i. –ca (cêle). *it is dawning,* bwâca.

day, bushiku (n). *what day (of the week) is to-day?* lêlo bushikunshi? *every –,* cila bushiku: nshiku shonse. *all – long,* kasuba konse. *nowadays,* muno nshiku. *on an unexpected day,* bushiku bushilile kantu, *on such and such a day,* muli kantwa. *on which –,* bushiku nshi? pali cinga? *this very day,* lêlo line. *next or following day,* bushiku bwankonka. *day before yesterday & day after tomorrow,* bulya bushiku.

daybreak, macaca.

daylight, kasuba.

dead, –fwa (fwîle): *the cow*

is dead, ŋombe yâfwa. *pretend to be –,* –fwa bufi.

deaf, –koma matwi (komene): *are you deaf,* bushe mwalikoma matwi? *– person,* nkoma matwi (ba–). *deaf and dumb person,* cibulu (ba–).

deafen, –komya matwi (komeshe).

deal, v.t. **1.** (give out), –pèla (pêle). **2.** (occupy oneself with), –sakamana (sakamene): *I shall – with this matter,* nkasakamana mulandu uyu. *a great deal,* ...ingi; sana. *I have a great – to do,* ndi ne milimo ingi or ndi ne milimo sana.

dear, 1. (beloved), mute-mwishi (ba); mutemwîkwa (ba). **2.** (expensive), –koso mutengo: *this hat is –,* mutengo wa cisote îci untu wakosa.

death, mfwa. *lose somebody by –,* –fwilwa (fwililwe).

debate, 1. n. fikânsa mu kulondololo mulandu. **2.** v. rec. –bikana fikansa (bikêne).

debt, misha; nkongole; bukope. *pay debts,* –bwesha fya nkongole (bweseshe); –futa imisha (futile). *put off payment of debts,* –kokwesha misha (kokweshe).

decay, –bola (bolele).

decease, 1. n. mfwa. **2.** v.i. –fwa (fwîle).

deceit, bucenjeshi.

deceitful, –ba ne ndimi shibili.

December, Mupundu-milimo.

decide, –pingula (pingwile).

decision, ifyo bapingula.

what is the –, ifyo bapingula finshi? or ifyo bapingula ni shani?

declare, 1. (say), –sosa (sosele). 2. (make known in public), –bile mbila (bilile).

decorate, –sâmika (sâmike).

decorations cisâmo (fi). *take decorations off,* –sâmuna (sâmwine).

decorticate, –sokola (sokwele).

deep, ...tali (panshi); –shika (shikile): *a – pit,* mukanda utali (panshi may be added). *the river is deep,* mumana naushika.

defame, –sebânya (sebênye).

defeat, –cimfya (cimfishe); –ansha (anshishe).

defend, –pokako (pokeleko).

defend one's case, –lubulula (lubulwile).

defender, mpâlume (m).

defer, –tantalisha (tantalishe); –kokosha (kokweshe).

delay, v.t. –celesha (celeshe); linsha (linshishe). v.i. –kokola (kokwêle); –celwa (celelwe).

delete, –fûta (fûtile).

deliberately, ku mufulo.

delight, 1. n. nsansa (n). 2. v.t. –sansamusha (sansamwishe). *be delighted,* –sansamuka (sansamwike).

delirious, –sabaila (sabaile).

deliver, v.t. 1. (save), –pususha (puswishe); –lubula (lubwile). 2. (carry to), –twala (twele).

demand, –fwaya (fwaile); –lomba (lombele).

demolish, –onaula (onawile). v. stat. –onaika (onaike).

demon, shetâni (ba); ciwa (fiwa) cibanda (fi).

denounce, –seba (sebele).

deny, –kâna (kêne).

depart, –ya (ile). *– for good,* –ililila (ililile).

depend, –ba kuli: *it depends on you,* cili kuli imwe. *depend upon,* –ba mu minwe ya: *we depend upon him,* tuli mu minwe yakwe.

depth, butali panshi; kushika.

descend, –ika (ikile).

describe, –londolola (londolwele).

desert, 1. n. ciswebêbe (fi). 2. v.t. cf. abandon; leave.

deserter, musangu (ba).

deserve, –fwa (fwile): *he deserves a praise,* afwile bamutashe.

design, v.t. –lenga (lengele).

designer, kalenga (ba–).

desire, 1. (want), –fwaya (fwaile). 2. (covet), –kumbwa (kumbwilwe).

despise, cf. contempt.

despite, in – of. nelyo; nangu.

destroy, cf. demolish; annihilate; pull down.

destruction, bonaushi.

detach, –kakatula (kakatwîle). v. stat. –kakatuka (kakatwike).

detest, –pata (patile).

detour, 1. n. cinshoko (fi). 2. v.i. (make a –), –shoka (shokele); v. caus. –shosha (shoseshe).

develop (grow), –kula (kulile). *– a film,* –samba fílimu (sambile).

development, buyantanshi.

deviate, v.t. –petula (petwile); v.i. –petuka (petwike).

devil, cf. demon.

devour, –lya (lile); –mina (minine).

dew, mume (mime).

diarrhoea, shiki; kupolomya. *suffer from* –, –polomya (polwemye); –lwala shiki; –lwâla pa mutima.

die, –fwa (fwile); –leko mweo (lekele). – *a natural death*, –fwa mfwa Lesa. – *a martyr*. –fwila Lesa (fwilile). – *down* (of fire), –shima (shimine). – *in childbirth* (child being delivered), –fwe ncentu. – *in childbirth* (child not being delivered), –fwe ncila. – *of hunger*, fig. –fwe nsala. – *of thirst*, fig. –fwe cilaka. – *peacefully*, –fwa imfwa isuma. – *suddenly*, –shinsuka (shinswike).

differ, –ibela (ibelele). v. rec. –lekana (lekene); –pusana (pusene).

difference, bupusano.

different, cf. differ. *make* –, –pusanya (pusenye); –lekanya (lekenye).

difficult, –afya (afishe): *it is* –, calyafya.

difficulty, bwafya.

dig, –imba (imbile). *dig up*, –shula (shulile).

digest, v.t. –sungulula (sungulwile). v. stat. –sunguluka (sungulwike).

digit, ipendo (ma).

dignity, bucindami; mucinshi.

dilute, –sundula (sundwile); –songolola (songolwele).

diminish, –cefya (cefeshe).

dine, –lya (lile).

dining room, ŋanda ya kulìlamo.

dip, –tumpa (tumpile); –tumpika (tumpike). – *cattle*,

–sambe ŋombe (sambila).

direct, 1. (straight), v.t. –lungama (lungeme); v. caus. –lungika (lungike). 2. (lead), v.t. –tungulula (tungulwile).

direction, ntunga; lubali. *in what* –? ntunga nshi? lubali kwi? *change* –, v.t. –pinduluka (pindulwike).

dirt, ciko (fi); busâli.

dirty, –ba ne fiko; –lamba (lambile) (body or clothes); –sapa (sapile) (outside). *make* – (body or clothes), –lamfya (lamfishe); (outside), –safya (samfishe).

disadvantage, –bipile.

disagree, 1. dissent, –kanya (kenye). 2. differ, –pusana (pusene).

disappear, –loba (lobele). –ongoloka (ongolwêke); –tangâna (tangène).

disapprove, –kâna (kène).

disarrange, –fulunganya (fulungenye).

discontent, n. cifukushi; cikonko.

discourage, v.t. –nenuna (nenwine); –fûpula (fûpwile). *be discouraged*, –nenuka (nenwike); –cimba (cimbile); –lufyo mutima; fupuka, (fupwike).

discover, –sanga (sangile); *a place*, –sokola (sokwele).

discretion, mfundato. *be discreet*, –ba ne mfundato; –ŋika kanwa (ŋikile).

disdain, –fwita (fwitile); –sûla (sûlile).

disease, bulwele (ma). *lingering* –, ntanda-bwanga. *contagious*. –, bulwele bwa lwambu. *catch* a –, –ambulo bulwele (ambwile). *pass a – on* –ambukisho bulwele (ambukishe).

disgrace, –sebânya ·(sebênye).

disguise, –fisa (fishile).

disgust, 1. n. citendwe. 2. v.t. –tendusha (tendwishe). *be disgusted,* –tendwa (tendelwe).

dish, mbale yafonka; mbale yafongomana.

dishearten, –fûpula (fûpwile).

disinter, –shukula (shukwîle).

dislike, –pata (patile).

dislocate, –minya (minishe).

dismantle, –pangulula (pangulwile); –pangaula (pangawile).

dismiss, –tamfya (tamfishe).

disorder, cimfulunganya. cintobentobe, *in –,* pambilibili. *be in –,* –fulungana (fulungene). *put in –,* –fulunganya (fulungenye).

dispatch, –tuma (tumine).

dispensary, cipatâla (fi).

disperse, –salanganya (salangenye). *be dispersed,* –salangana (salangene).

dispersion, isunga.

displeased, –fulwa (fulilwe); –fitwa (fitilwe).

dispute, 1. n. fikansa. 2. v. rec. –citana fikansa (citêne); –tintana (tintene); –kansana (kansene); –afyanya (afyenye).

disregard, 1. n. musâlula (mi); misûla. 2. v.t. –sâlula (sâlwile); –sûla (sûlile).

disrespect, cf. disregard.

disrespectful, –ba ne misûla; –ba no musâlula.

dissension, lupato. *cause of –,* cimpatanya.

dissolve, v.t. –sungulula (sungulwile); v. stat. –sunguluka (sungulwike).

dissuade, –kânya (kênye).

distance, kulêpa. *what is the – from ... to,* ukulêpa ni shani ukufuma ku ... ukufika na ku or kwalepa shani ukufuma ku ... *keep distance,* –taluka (talwike). *put into* –talusha (talwishe).

distinguish, –lekanya (lekenye); –pusanya (pusenye).

distinguished (famous), –lumbuka (lumbwike).

distract, v.t. –pusaula (pusawile); v. stat. –pusauka (pusawike).

distribute, –akanya (akenye).

district, mpanga (m); câlo (fy).

ditch, mufôlo (mi).

dive, –ibila (ibile).

divide, –akana (akene).

divination, lubuko.

divine, 1. (pertaining to God), ...takatifu. 2. (foretell), –buka (bukile).

divinity, bumulungu.

divorce, v.t. –putule cûpo (putwile). v. i. –lekana mu cupo (lekene).

divulge, –ananya (anenye); –sokololo mulandu (sokolwele).

dizziness, lunshingwa.

do, –cita (citile). *– again,* –bwekeshapo (bwekeshepo). *– first,* –bangilila (bangilile). *do this first,* bangililo kuciteci. *– good/well,* –wamya (wemye). *you did well,* mwawamya. *well done,* interj. cawama; ci suma.

docile, –petama (peteme); –nakilila (nakilile); –ba no bupete.

docility, bupete; cumfwilo.

doctor, ndokotala (ba–); shiŋanga (ba–).

dog (domestic), mbwa (m); *small* –, kabwa (tubwa). *wild* –, ꞥumbulu (mi). *dog grass,* lunkoto. *set dog on,* –kuwishe mbwa pa (kuwishe).

doll, kalubi (tu).

domicile, bwikalo; cifulo (fi).

donkey, punda (ba–).

door, cibi (fibi): *open the door,* isulêniko cibi! *shut the door,* isalêniko cibi! *close with key,* –funga (fungile).

doorpost, ingwe (ma).

doorway, mwinshi (minshi).

dormitory, ŋanda ya kusendamano (ŋ or mayanda).

dorsal, longololo lwa numa; môngololo wa numa (my).

dot, 1. n. itoni⁻ (ma). 2. v.t. (with lime). –shiba (shibile).

double, 1. on two places, pabili. 2. *two,* …bili: *a double string,* myando ibili.

doubt, v.i. –twishika (twishike).

dove, cipêle (fi); nkunda (n).

dovecot, citele (fi).

down, panshi: *put it down,* bika panshi.

downstream, kwisamba lya mumana.

dowry, mpango (m). *pay the dowry,* –leko lupango (lekele); –leke mpango,

more used.

doze, –shipula (shipwile).

drag, –tinta (tintile); –kula (kulile). – *out of mud,* –tikulula (tikulwile); v. stat. –tikuluka (tikulwike).

draw (pull), –tinta (tintile).

draw a line, –shila cishilwa (shilile). *draw water,* –tapa menshi (tapile). *be a draw* (in sport), –filwâna (filwêne): *it was a draw,* bafilwâna.

draught, 1. (of drink), musa (mi). 2. (of wind), mwela.

dream, 1. n. cilôto (fi). 2. v.i. –lôta (lôtele).

dregs of beer, mashi.

dress, ndeleshi (n); ilaya lya banakashi (ma). 2. v.t. –fwika (fwikile); v.i. fwala (fwele).

drill, 1. n. musumbo (mi). 2. v.t. –pike coli (pikile).

drink, 1. n. cakunwa (fya). 2. v.i. –nwa (nwene).

drip, v.t. –tonya (toneshe). v.i. –tona (tonene).

drive, –ensha (enseshe); –tekenya (tekenye). *drive in,* –pôpa (pôpele) (with a hammer); –shimpa (shimpile) (by hand). *drive away,* –tamfya (tamfishe).

driver, talaifa (ba–); namutekenya (ba–).

drizzle. 1. n. bufumi. 2. v.i. mima (mimine).

drop, 1. n. itoni (ma). *a large* –, imata (ma). 2. v.t. (solid matter). –ponya (poneshe). v.i. –pona (ponene). *drop* (liquids) cf. drip.

dropsy, lusuku (n).

drought (in rainy season), cilala.

drown, v.t. –nwensha (nwe-nseshe). *get drowned,* nwêna (nwênene).

drowse, –shipula (shipwile).

drug, n. muti (mi); ndawa (n).

drum, n. ŋoma (ŋ). *beat a –,* –lishe ŋoma (lishishe). *fix a skin on –,* –bambe ŋoma (bambile).

drunk, be –, –kolwa (kolelwe). *make –,* –kolesho (muntu) kunwa bwalwa (koleseshe).

drunkard, mumwenshi (ba).

drunkeness, bunwenshi; kukolwa.

dry, be –, –ma (umine): *is the washing dry,* bushe ifyo mucapile fyauma. *dry up,* –kama (kamine): *the water is dried up,* menshi yakama. *put out to dry,* –anika (anike). *dry over fire,* –kanga (kangile).

duck (domestic), mbata (sha). (wild), coso (y).

duiker, mpombo (m). *blue –,* katimba (tu).

dumb person, cibulu (ba-).

dumbness, bucibulu.

dung, 1. (of cattle), citindi: mafi ya ŋombe. 2. (of other animals), mafi. 3. (of birds), itotoli (ma); citotoli (fi).

during, mu nshita ya; mu: *during the lesson,* mu nshita ya mafundisho. *during the harvest,* mu kusêpa.

dusk, lumonangala.

dust, 1. n. lukungu. 2. v.t. –fûto lukungu (fûtile).

duster, citambala ca kufûtilako (fi).

duty, ncito; mulimo: *it is your duty,* ni ncito yenu or mulimo wenu.

dwarf, kamuntu akepi (tubantu); ntuse (n).

dwell, cf. abide.

dying, –pumbuka pa kufwa (pumbwike); –naka (nakile).

dynamite, cisalatini (fi).

dysentery, cele. *suffer from –,* –sûko mulopa (sûkile); –polomyo mulopa (polwemye).

— E —

each, ...onse; cila. *each man,* muntu onse or cila muntu.

each one, ... mo ... mo: *each one received 10 ngwee,* bapoka 10 ngwee umo umo.

eager, –fwaisha (fwaishe).

eagle, kapumpe (ba-). *fish –,* cembe (ba-); nkwashi (n).

ear, kutwi (ma).

earache, mboboyo.

early, lucelo or kacelo. *very early,* kacelocelo or lucelocelo.

earn, –mwenamo (mwenenemo; –lipilwa (lipilwe): *what do you earn in a month,* ulipilwa shani pa mweshi.

earth, calo (fy); isonde. *on earth,* muno câlo; pano isonde; panonse.

earthquake, cinkukuma (fi).

East, kabanga.

Easter, Ipasaka.

Eastertide, mwaka we Pasaka.

easy, –anguka (angwike);

also *easy to do: it is easy,* cayanguka.

eat, –lya (lile). – *much,* –lisha (lishishe). – *well,* –ipakisha (ipakishe). – *unseasoned food,* –lya fyantalala.

eatable, cf. edible.

edge, (of a hole), milomo; (of a river), isense (ma); lulamba. (ma).

edible, –liwa (liliwe): *this mushroom is edible,* bôwa ubu bulaliwa.

educate, –funda (fundile).

education, kufunda; buleshi.

effort, maka. *with effort,* na maka. make effort, maka. *make effort,* –shipikisha (shipikishe); –shipa (shipile).

egg, lîni (mâni). *fried egg,* lîni lya kusalula. *scrambled egg,* lîni lya kukumbwa, *lay eggs,* –bikila mâni. *hatch* or *sit on eggs,* –lâlila mani (lâlile). *the egg is bad,* lini lyasuka.

eight, cine konse konse.

either, ...onse ...bili: *I like either,* (of two e.g. books), natemwa fyonse fibili.

either or, atemwa ...atemwa.

eland, nsefu (n).

elastic, –nyunsuluka (nyunsulwike).

elbow, nkonkoni (n).

elder, ...kalamba: *my elder brother,* mukalamba wandi.

elect, –sala (salile).

elegance, busaka.

elephant, nsofu (n).

elephantiasis, mubamba (mi).

elevate, v.t. –lundumanika (lundumanike); v. stat.

–lundumana (lundumene).

else (otherwise)), atemwa; (in addition), ...mbi. *somebody else,* umbi: *do you want something else,* bushe mulefwaya fimbi.

elsewhere, kumbi; pambi; mumbi. *quite elsewhere,* kumbi kumbi.

embellish, –waminisha (waminishe).

ember, musolilo (mi).

embrace, –fukatila (fukatile); –kumbatila (kumbatile).

emisary, nkombe; mutumishi.

employ, –pêlo mulimo (pêle): *who is your employer,* nani amupêle milimo.

empty, be –, –pwa (pwile). *it is empty,* capwa; tamuli. *make* –, fumya (fumishe)· –fukumuna (fukumwine).

encircle, –shinga (shingile); –bika mu côfi (bîkile); –ofya (ofeshe).

enclose, 1. (put into), –ingisha (ingishe). 2. (fence), –pindila (pindile).

enclosure, cf. fence.

encourage, –kosho mutima (koseshe); –koselesha (koseleshe).

end, 1. n. (local), mpela (m); lutwe (ndutwe). (time limit), kupwa. **2.** v.t. & i. –pwa (pwile). *at the end* (local), pa mpela; pa lutwe. (time limit), pa kupwa. *at the end,* 1. adv. (finally), pa kulekelesha. 2. aux. verb (finally), –suka (sukile). *end by,* –suka (sukile): *I shall end by knowing,* nkasuka njishiba. *place end to end,* –kumi-

nkanya (kuminkenye).
reach end, –pela (pelele).
enemy, mulwani (ba). *treat as –,* –cita ngo mulwani (citile).
energetic, –shipa (shipile).
energetically, maka maka.
energy, maka; bulamba. *do something with energy,* –cita bulamba; –cita na maka.
engage, 1. (give work), –pêlo mulimo (pêle); –lemba ku ncito (lembele). 2. (betroth), –kobekela (kobekele) (when man); –kobekelwa (kobekelwe) (when girl).
engine, injini (ma–).
enjoy, –shukila (shukile); –sekela (sekele).
enlarge, –kusha (kushishe).
enlighten, –panda mâno (pandile); –funda (fundile).
enmity, bulwani.
enough, –fula (fulile). *it is –,* cafula or fyafula.
enslave, –lofya (lofeshe); –cita musha (citile).
entangle, –fundikanya (fundikenye), v. stat. –fundikana (fundikene).
enter, –ingila (ingile).
entice, –pimpila (pimpile).
entire, …tuntulu; …onse.
entirely, …onse nakalya: *the millet is – finished,* male yalipwa yonse nakalya. It can also be translated by the aux. verb '-lala': *he stopped –,* alala alileka.
entrance, mwinshi (mi); mwingililo (fi).
entry, cf. entrance. *no entry here,* balibinda kuno or kwalibindwa kuno.
enumerate, –lumbula (lu-

mbwile); –tantawila (tantawile).
envelop, –pomba (pombele).
envelope, nkupo (n); enifulupu (ba–).
envious, –ba no mufimbila.
envoy, nkombe (n); mutumishi (ba).
envy, 1. n. mufimbila 2. v.t. –fimbila (fimbile).
epidemic, cikuko (fi).
epilepsy, kakoshi-musa; bushilu, *suffer from –,* –lwala shinsa (lwele).
epileptic fits, shinsa.
equal, –lingâna (lingêne). *make, –,* –linganya (lingenye).
erase, –fûta (fûtile).
erect, –imika (imike).
err, –luba (lubile).
error, cilubo (fi).
escape, –pusumuka (pusumwike); –fyuka (fyukile).
escort, shindika (shindike).
especially, pali bufi; ukucila.
esteem, 1. n. mucinshi. 2. v.t. –cindika (cindike).
eternal, …pe. *eternal life,* bumi bwa pe.
Eucharist, Lukalishitiya.
Europe, Bulaya.
European, musungu (ba).
European kind/language/ manners etc. cisungu (fi).
evangelist, mwalimu (ba–).
eve, cibelushi(fi).
even, be –, –lingâna (lingêne); –lungama (lungeme); papâtala (papâtêle): *make even,* –linganya (lingenye); –lungamika (lungamike); –papâtika (papâtike).
even, cj. nangu; nélyo; nangula.
evening, cungulo. *pass the*

evening, –isha (ishishe).

ever, –tala (talile). (followed by verb in a –a tense). *have you ever seen a lion*, bushe watala aumone nkalamo?

ever since, nshita yonse iyo: *ever since I have been here*. nshita yonse iyo naikala kuno. *for ever* (for good), –lala (lalile). *he has stopped lopping trees for ever*, alala alileko kutema. *for ever and ever*, nshiku fye pe.

ever so much, pakalamba; sâna sâna: *I thank you ever so much*, nasantika sâna sâna/pakalamba.

everlasting, ...pe; –belèlela (belèlèle). *everlasting life*, bumi bwa pe.

every, ...onse; cila. *every day*, nshiku shonse or cila bushiku.

everybody, onse or muntu onse.

everywhere, mpânga yonse; konsekonse; monse.

evidence, bunte. *give evidence*, –sosa mu mulandu (sosele) ; –ba kambone.

evil, bubi; cibi (fi).

evocation, lubuko (n).

evocator, kabuka (ba–); shiŋanga (ba–).

evoke spirits, –buka (bukile).

exact (accurate), –ba bwîno; (precise in time, answer, etc.), –lungika (lungike).

exactly (quite so), interj. na nomba; naendi; na kabushe; cine cine.

exaggerate, –lemyo mulandu (lemeshe).

exaggeration, makunka bulunda nkoloko.

examination, mashindano. *sit for –*, –shindana (shindene). *give an –*, –shindanya (shindenye).

examine, –lengula (lengwile).

example, cilangililo (fi) ; musango (mi): *follow his example*, konkelele misango yakwe.

excavate, –fonkola (fonkwele).

exceed, v.t. –cisha (cishishe) ; v.i. –cila (cilile).

excel, cf. exceed.

excellent, ...suma sâna –wama sâna (weme). *it is excellent*, cili cisuma sâna or cawama sâna.

except, 1. (exclude), –fumya (fumishe). 2. cj. kano: *I except you*, namufumya. *all except you*, bonse kano imwe iyo. *be an exception*, –ibèla (ibèlele): *he is an –*, uyu aibèla.

exchange, v.t. –kabula (kabwile) ; –cinja (cinjile) ; –kaula (kawile).

excrement, mafi; busâli.

excuse, 1. (lessen a blame), –cefyo mulandu (cefeshe). 2. (disregard a case), –sûla pa mulandu (sûlile). 3. (pardon), –belelo luse (belele). 4. (exempt), –fumya (fumishe).

exempt, –fumya (fumishe).

axemption from paying tax, kulesho musonko.

exhaust, v.t. –tembula (tembwile). v. stat. –tembuka (tembwike). –fumuna (fumwine). v. stat. –fumuka (fumwike).

exhort, –konkomesha (konkomeshe) ; –funda (fundile).

exhortation, ifunde (ma).

exhume, –shukula (shukwîle): *they exhume the body,* bashukule citumbi.

expect, –lolela (lolele).

expectoration, cikôla (fi).

expel, –tamfya (tamfishe).

expensive, –koso mutengo (kosele): *this hat is expensive,* mutengo wa cisote ici untu wakosa. *it is expensive,* umutengo wakosa; umutengo waluma.

experiment, v.i. –esha (eseshe).

expert, fundi (ba–), cibinda.

expiate, –fûtila (fûtile).

explain, –londolola (londolwele).

explode, v.t. –latula (latwile); v.i. –latuka (latwike).

explore, –lengula (lengwile).

extend, 1. (stretch out limbs), –tambalika (tambalike. 2. (reach at), –shinta (shintile).

extensible, –nyunsuluka (nyunsulwike).

external, ...kunse.

extinct, 1. (of fire), –shima (shimine). 2. (of family), –fwa (fwile).

extinguish, –shimya (shimishe).

extol, –lumbanya (lumbenye); –lumba (lumbile).

extract, 1. (tooth), –nukula (nukwile). 2. (thorn), –bangula (bangwile). – *by boiling,* –enga (engele).

extraordinary, (surprising), ca ku kusunguka (fya).

extreme unction, cisubo ca balwele.

extremity, lutwe (ndutwe).

eye, 1. n. lînso (mênso). *close* –. –shibata (shibete).

open –, –shibatuka (shibatwike). *cast* – *upon,* –pôsa mênso ku (pôsele). *turn* – *to,* –losha mênso ku (loseshe).

eye, 2. v.t. –tontomesha (tontomeshe). – *with hatred* or *envy,* –shuluka (shulwike).

eyebrow, cikumbi (fi).

eye-cataract, cibubi (fi).

eyelash, lukopyo (n).

eyelid, cipa ca linso (fi).

eyewitness, –mona ku menso: *I am an* –, namona ku menso; ndi kambone.

— F —

fable, mulumbe (mi); lushimi (n). *tell a fable,* –umo mulumme (umine).

fabricate, –panga (pangile).

face, 1. n. mpumi (m); ku menso. 2. v.t. –lolesha (loleshe).

facilitate, –angusha (angwishe).

fade, –fôta (fôtele); –bonsa (bonsele).

faeces, mafi.

faggot, cifinga (fi).

fail, –filwa (fililwe). *fail in strength,* –bula amaka (bulile): *I fail,* nabula maka or maka yandi yabula. – *to meet,* –pusa (pushile). v. rec. –pusana (pusêne). – *to catch,* –panya (panishe).

faint, –tembuka (tembwike); –fwa cipûpu (fwile); –fwa cipensepense, *fainting fit,* lupûma (ba–).

fair, 1. (beautiful), ...suma. 2. (blond), –butuluka: *he*

is fair-haired, imishishi naibutuluka. 3. (just), –lungika (lungike).
faith, cisumino.
faithful, ...cine cine; ... cishinka: *I remain Yours faithfully,* nine wênu wa cine cine or nine wênu pe. *He is –,* wa cishinka.
fake, v.t. cf. cheat.
fall, 1. n. (waterfall), cipôma (fi). 2. v.i. –pona (ponene); –wa (wile). *let fall,* –ponya (poneshe). *–of night,* –ila (ilile). *it is nightfall,* bwaila. *fall on all fours.* –wa bukupême. *– on the back,* –wa busenême. *– out* (as tool of handle), –sokoka (sokwêke). *–off* (whitewash, etc.). –komboka (kombwêke).
false, bufi. *it is false,* bufi fye.
falsehood, bufi. *say a falsehood,* –soso bufi (sosele).
fame, lulumbi.
family, lupwa (ndupwa). *family stock,* ishinte (ma).
famine, cipôwe (fi); nsala: *there is a famine,* kuli nsala or nsala yalipona; kuli cipowę.
famous, –lumbuka (lumbwike). *make –,* –lumbwisha (lumbwishe).
far, kutali; patali. *it is far,* kwalepa. *be far away,* –tantalila (tantalile).
farewell, bid –, –shalikapo (shalikepo).   *farewell!* (greeting), cf. T. VII.
farm, famu ma–).
farmer, mulimi ba).
   farther, ku ntanshi; pa ntanshi.
fast. 1. adv. lubilo. 2. v.i. –cefya cakulya (cefeshe).

fast-day, bushiku bwa kucefya cakulya.
fasten, –ikasha (ikeshe); –kaka (kakile).
fat, 1. n. mafuta. 2. be fat, –nona (nonene); –ina (inine): *the meat is fat,* inama nainona. *you are fat,* mwaina.
father, cf. T. V. *father of twins,* shimpundu (ba–).
father-in-law, cf. T. V.
fatten, –inya (inishe).
fault, cilubo (fi) (in writing etc.); mulandu (mi): *it is your fault,* mulandu wênu.
favour, v.t. –afwa (afwile): *do me a –,* mungafweko.
favourite, mubile (ba); kacele (ba–).
fear, 1. n. mwenso. 2. v.i. & t. –tîna (tînine); –ba no mwenso. *be seized by fear,* –ikatwa no mwenso. *reverential fear,* katina *show reverential fear,* –ba na katina.
fearless, –pama (pamine).
feast, malila.
feast-day, nshiku nkulu (n).
feather, isako (ma).
February, Kabengele kakalamba.
fecundate, –imisha (imishe).
fed up, –tendwa (tendelwe): *I am –,* nintendwa.
feeble, –bonsa (bonsele).
feed, –lisha (lishishe).
feel, –umfwa (umfwile): –tesha (teseshe). *feel like a blind man with a stick,* –pampanta (pampantile).
fell (cut down), –tema (temene):
fellow, mune (bane); cf. also T. V. (see also friend).
female, ...kota.
feminine, ...anakashi.

fence, 1. n. ilinga (ma); lubao (m); lusasa (n) made of reeds. 2. v.t. –pindila (pindile).
ferment, 1. n. nsashiko. 2.v. t. –sashika (sashike).
fern (kind of –), luputu (m).
ferocious, ...kali.
ferocity, bukali; bunkalwe.
ferry, 1. n. cikwepe. (fi). 2. v.t. –abusha (abwishe).
fertile, –funda (fundile). *the soil is fertile,* mushili wafunda.
fetch, –fwaya (fwaile). –bûla (bûlile).
fetish, kalubi (tu).
fever, mpepo.
few, ...mo ...mo. *a few men,* abantu bamo bamo. *be just a few,* –ba mpendwa. *be too few,* –cepa (cepele): *you are too few,* mwacepa.
fiancé, lumbwe (ba–).
fiancée, nkobekelwa (ba–)
field, ibala (ba); cilime (fi). (fi).
fierce, ...kali, ...nkalwe.
fig tree, mukunyu (mi).
fight, 1. n. lubuli; bulwi. 2. v.t. & i. –lwa (lwile): –cita lubuli. *provoke a fight,* –busho lubuli (bushishe)
file, 1. n. (tool), tâpa (ba–); (line), mulongo (mi). 2. v. t. –kûsa na tûpa (kûshile). *file up (line up),* –tantama mulongo (tanteme).
fill, v.t. –isusha (iswishe); –paka (pakile). *fill up a hole,* –shîka (shîkile). *fill up cracks in a wall,* –shibe milale (shibile).
filter, 1. n. nceemeko (n). 2. v.t. –cemeka (cemeke); –sansa (sanshile).

filth, ciko (fi); busâli.
filthy, –ba ne fiko.
finally, –suka (sukile) with verb in the same tense: *we finaly arrived,* twasuka twafika; adv. pa kulekelesha.
find, sanga (sangile).
fine, 1. n. mafuto ya kulipila. 2. v.t. –lipilisha (lipilishe). *pay fine,* –futa pa mulandu (futale); –leka mafuto (lekele).
fine, (handsome), ...suma.
fine (thin), –anguka (angwike).
finger, munwe (mi). *thumb,* cikumo (fi). *1st finger,* nkomfola musunga (n); cisonta bantu (fi). *2nd –,* munwe ukalamba. *3rd. –,* cikonka kantengesha (fi). *little finger,* kantengesha (tu).
kantengesha (tu).
finger nail, lwala (ngala).
finger ring, mbalaminwe (m).
finish, v.i. & t. –pwa (pwile); cf. also bula.
fire, mulilo (mi – ?) *in the open,* conto (fy). *light –,* –kosho mulilo (koseshe). *extinguish fire,* –shimyo mulilo (shimishe). *make a fireguard,* –babilile cipinda (babilile). *scatter fire,* –paso mulilo (pashile). *beat fire down with branches,* –kupo mulilo (kupile). *make – by friction,* –shiko mulilo (shikile). *blow on fire,* –puto mulilo (putile). *set – to,* –sonteka (sonteke).
firearms, canso (fy).
firebrand, cishishi ca mulilo (fi).

fireplace, lshiko (ma).
fire-poker, musolilo (mi).
firewood, lukuni (n). *fetch
–,* –têbe nkuni (tébele).
first, ...ntanshi. *at first,* pa
kubala; –bala .(balile) or
–tala (talile) followed by
a verb in the same tense:
first tell me, utale unjebe.
firstborn, ibêli (ma).
fish, 1. n. isabî. 2. v.t. –ipaye
sabi (ipeye). *many fish,*
isabi lingi. *many kinds of
fish,* masabi ayengi. *– with
a line,* –loba (lobele). *–
with a basket,* –ele sabi
(elele). *– with a net.* –sakile sabi (sakile). *take fish
out of a trap,* –fube sabi
(fubile). *kill fish with
"buba" plant,* –sungilo buba (sungile).
fish-bone, munga we sabi
(my).
fish-eagle, cembe (ba–);
nkwashi (n).
fish-hook, bulobo (ba).
fish-poison, buba.
fish trap, mono (my).
fisherman, mulondo (ba).
fist, ikôfi (ma) cifunshi
(fi). *close –,* leme kôfi (lemene). *hit with –,* –ume
cifunshi (umine).
fit, v.i. –linga (lingile);
–bêla (bêlele). *do not fit,*
–pata (patile).
five, fisâno.
fix, v.t. 1. (adhere), –kambatika (kambatike). 2. (fasten), –ikasha (ikeshe): *it
is fixed,* caikata. 3. (gaze),
lolekee...o (lolekeshe). 4.
...o), –shimpa (shi
...i. arrange, 6. cf.
...o,
...ag, bendêla (ba– or mendêla).

flag-staff, mulongoti (mi).
flame, lubingu (mabingu or
mingu).
flash, v.i. –byata (byatile).
flask, musukupala (mi).
flat, 1. (even), –papâtala
(papâtêle). 2. (punctured),
–pompoloka (pompolweke). 3. (straightened),
–ololoka (ololweke).
flatten, –papâtika (papâtitike).
flatter, –senga (sengele).
flatterer, mufukila kubili
(ba–).
flatulence, cisushi.
flavour, 1. n. cinushi (fi). 2.
v.t. –lunga (lungile).
flea, lupantila (m).
flee, –fyuka (fyukile); –butuka (butwike).
flesh, munofu (m).
flexible, –kondenkana (kondenkene). *make flexible,*
–kondenkanya (kondenkenye).
float, –elêla (elêle).
flog, –lapika (lapike).
flood, lyeshi. *be flooded,*
–bundwa (bundilwe).
floor, ica panshi (ifya). *on
the floor,* panshi, *put it on
floor,* bunga.
flour, bunga.
flow, –pita (pitile). *water
flows,* menshi yalapita.
flow (into), –wila (wilile);
–ita (itile). *flow out,* –pongoloka (pongolweke).
flow over (of river), –pôsa
(pôsele).
flower, 1. n. iluba (ma). 2.
v.i. cf. bloom.
fluff (soft short hair), ifufu
(ma).
flute, ...olilo (ba–).
fly, 1. n. lunshi (ba–). 2. v.i.
–pupuka (pupwike). *dragon fly,* mulengesha (ba–).

fly catcher, (kind of bird), mulongwe (ba-).

foam, ifulo (ma).

foe, mulwani (ba).

foetus, ifumo (ma).

fog, fubefube.

fold, –peta (petele). – *hands together,* –fumbate minwe (fumbete).

follow, –konka (konkele). *follow a spoor,* –lonsha (lonseshe).

following, –konkapo (ko-nkelepo); ...mbi: *the –* (man), ukonkapo; umbi.

folly, buwelewele.

fond of, 1. (desire much), –fwaisha (fwaishe). 2. (love), –temwa (teme-nwe).

food. 1. (in general), cilyo (fi). 2. (prepared food), cakulya (fy). *food for journey,* mpao. *unsalted –,* fyantalala *rest of –,* cimbala (fi).

fool 1. n. cipuba (fi); ci-welewele (fi); mpelwa mâno (ba-); cipumbu (fi). 2. v.t. –tumfya (tu-mfishe). *be a –,* –tumpa (tumpile); –ba cipuba, etc. cf. fool, 1. n.

foolish, cf. be a fool.

foolishness, buwelewele.

foot, lukasa (ma or n). *at the – of,* pe samba lya or mwi samba lya. *go on –,* –enda ku nkasa (endele).

football, mupila (mi).

footpath, nshila (n); kashi-la (tu).

footprints, makasa.

footsteps, 1. (traces), ma-kasa. 2. (manners), misa-ngo.

for, 1. prep. (a), ku; kuli: *he left – Kasama,* aile

ku Kasama. (b), it is most-ly translated by the appl. extension: *I work – you,* ndemubombela. (c), often it is not translated: *– the whole day,* kasuba konse. 2. cj. ico; pantu: *I am going, – there is no place,* ndeya, ico takuli ncende or ndeya, pantu...

forbid, –lesha (leseshe); v. pass. –leshiwa (leshiwe). *– entry,* cf. entry.

force, 1. n. maka. 2. cj. ico; pantu: *– patika (patike); v. int. (more used),* –patikisha (patikishe).

foreboding, lucêbu.

ford, cabu (fy).

forefather, cikolwe (fi).

forehead, mpumi (m).

foreign, ...eni.

foreigner, mweni (bêni); wa kunse (ba).

foreman, kapitao (ba-). *job of a –,* bukapitao.

forenoon, lucelo.

forest, mutengo (mi); mpa-nga (m). *thick –,* iteshi (ba).

forge, –fula (fulile).

forget, –laba (labile).

forgetful, –ba ne cilafi.

forgetfulness, cilafi. *out of –,* ku cilafi.

forgive, –belelo luse (bele-le).

fork, foloko (ba-). *– of a tree* or *branch,* mpanda (ma). *– of a pole,* lupanda (m).

form, 1. n. musango (mi). 2. v.t. –panga (pangile).

formerly, kale; pa ntanshi.

fornicate, –angala fyabipa (angele); –cito bupulu-mushi or bucende.

fornication, bupulumushi;

bucende.

forsake, –lekelesha (lekeleshe); –sha (shîle).

forsaken, adv. nsansalila: *they left him* –, bamusha nsansalila.

fortify, –kosha (koseshe).

fortnight, milungu ibili.

fortunate, –shuka (shukile); *he is* –, ashuka. *be fortunate in the possession of,* kushukila (shukile), (v.t.).

fortune, good –, ishuko; (ma); bad –, ishâmo (ma).

forward, 1. v.t. (send), –tu-–tuma (tumine). 2. adv. ku ntanshi.

foster, –tentemba (tentembe); –unga (sungile).

foster-father/mother, muleshi (ba).

foul, cf. bad; dirty; stink.

found, (recovered), –moneka (moneke); –londoka (londweke).

foundation, mufula (mi). *dig* –, –imbo mufula (imbile). *fill in* –, –isusho mufula (iswishe).

fountain, cishima (fi); kamfukwemfukwe (tu).

four, ...ne: *four men,* bantu bane.

fowl (hen), nkoko (n). *clean out* –, –tumbule nkoko (tumbwile).

fracture, v.t. –funa (funishe). v. stat. –funika (funike).

fraud, bucenjeshi.

free (set –), v.t. –lubula (lubwile). v. stat. –lubuka (lubwike).

freely, cabe: *I got it* –, nacipoka cabe.

freeze, –tikama (tikeme): *the water is frozen,* amenshi nayatikama.

frequent, (go habitually), is translated with the 'la-' tense.

frequently, libili libili.

fresh, 1. (raw), ...bishi 2. (new), –pya (pile), 3. (cold), –talala (talele).

Friday, (pali) Cisâno, also muli –.

friend, cibusa (ba–); mune (bane); munandi (ba), cf. T. V. muselwe (ba). *bosom* –, mubile (ba).

friendship, bucibusa. *make* –, –bîkana bucibusa (bîkene).

frighten, –tinya (tinishe); *you frighten me,* mwantînya, *be frightened,* –sûsuka (sùswike); –tina (tînine).

frightful, cakutîna (fy).

frog, cûla (ba–).

from, ku or kuli; kwa *from ... to,* ukufuma ku ... ukufika na ku.

front, mpumi (m). *in front,* pa ntanshi or ku –. *the one in front,* ...ntanshi.

frontier, mupaka (mi).

frost, mpepo.

froth, ifulo (ma).

frown, v.i. –tumbe nkanshi (tumbile).

fructify, –imisha (imishe).

fruit, citwalo (fi). *dried fruit,* mukoto (mi).

fry, v.t. –salula (salwile).

fulfil, cf. do; finish.

full, 1. (filled), –isula (iswile). *very* –, –isula pa: *the pot is very full,* umutondo nawisula pa. 2. (replete with food), –ikuta (ikwîte). 3. (whole) ...tuntulu. *a – week,* mulungu utuntulu.

fume, cushi. (fy).

fun, nseko; milangwe: *you

are full of fun, waba wa nseko; waba no twa milangwe.

funeral, cililo (fi).

funnel, mpakilo (m).

funny stories, imilandu ya nseko; mashiwi ya milangwe.

fur, masako ya nama.

furious, –sakâtuka (sakâtwike), –fulwa fulilwe).

furnace, ilungu (ma).

furnish (provide with), fwaila (fwaile).

furrow, mufôlo (mi); munyangala (mi). *small* –, mukolwa (mi).

further, ukucila; na nomba: *what do you want further?* mulefwaya nshi ukucila or mulefwaya nshi na nomba. *go further*, cf. go.

future, nshita ikesa. *in future*, ku ntanshi. or verb in the –akula, akala tenses.

— G —

gaiety, nsansa (n).

gain, v.t. –kwila (kwilile); –lya (lîle); –mwenamo (mwenenemo).

gale, cikûku ca mwêla.

gall, ndusha (n). *much* , ndusha shingi.

game, 1. (sport), cangalo (fy). 2. (animal), nama sha kulunga. *kill game*, –bamba (bambile).

game-pit, bucinga (ma).

gap, (gorge), mupokapoka (mi).

gape, –asama (aseme).

garden, malimino; ibala (ma). *old* –, cifwani (fi).

gardener, shimalimino (ba).

gargle, –sukusa (sukwise).

garment, cakufwala (fy); cifwalo (fi).

gate, mpongolo (m).

gather, v.t. –longanya (longenye). v.i. –longâna (longêne).

gathering, cilonganino (fi); ibungwe (ma).

gay, –ba ne nsansa.

gaze, –lolekesha (lolekeshe); –tontomesha menso (tontomeshe).

general ...onse. *a – famine*, nsala ya bonse.

generosity, bupe.

generous, wa bupe (ba).

gentile, musenshi (ba).

gentleman, munyamata (ba). muntu wa mibêle isuma (ba).

gentleness, cikûku.

genuflect, –tibila (tibile); –fuka kulu kumo (fukile).

germ, n. musonga (mi).

germinate, –mena (menene).

get, 1. (obtain), –poka (pokele). 2. cf. gain. *get away*, –fumapo (fuminepo). – *back*, –bwela (bwelele). – *down*, –ika (ikile). – *out*, –fumapo (fuminepo). – *up*, –ima (imine); – *from bed*, –bûka (bûkile).

ghost, mulungulwa (mi). *Holy Ghost*, Mweo Mutakatifu.

giant, cimuntu (fibantu).

giddiness, lunshingwa.

giddy, feel –, umfwo lunshingwa.

gift, bupe.

giraffe, ndyabuluba (n).

girdle, mushingo (mi).

girl, mwanakashi mwaice (banakashi baice).

give, pa (pele) or –pela (pêle). – *above measure*,

–ongeshapo (ongeshepo):
give away, –pêla (pêle);
–pôsa (pôsele). – *back,*
–bwesha (bweseshe). *give
generously,* –fumba (fu-
mbile). *give in,* –cimba
(cimbile). – *moderately,*
–nasha (nashishe). – *out,*
pôsa (pôsele). *give up,*
–leka (lekele).

gizzard, nondo (n).

glance, v.i. –ceba (cebele).

gland, *swollen* –, mutantamfula (mi).

glitter, –beka (bekele).

gloominess, cintefwila.

gloomy, –ba ne cintefwila.

glorify, –lumba (lumbile).

glory, malumbo. *sing glory
of,* –lumbânya (lumbênye).

glue, v.t. –kambatika (kambatike).

gluttony, bulili.

gnash teeth, –senganya mêno
(sengenye).

gnaw, –kokota (kokwete);
–celeketa (celekete);
mice gnaw, mpuku shilace-
leketa. – *off with teeth,*
–ceta (cetele); –cesaula
(cesawile). *gnaw a bone,*
–kolokota (kolokwete).

go, –ya (ile); –enda (endele). – *aimlessly,* –ya ciyeyeye. – *ahead,* –tangila
(tangile). – *aside,* –taluka
(talwike); –cinguka (ci-
ngwike); –funtuka (fu-
ntwike); –sela (selele). *go
astray,* –lube nshila (lubile). – *away,* –fuma (fumine). *go back,* –bwela (bwelele). – *beyond,* –cila (cilile). – *down,* –ika (ikile).
–*fast,* –endesha (endeshe).
go for a walk, –tandala (tandele), *go further,* cf. go

beyond. *go in,* –ingila
(ingile). *go in front,* –tangila (tangile). – *off the
road,* –pâsuka (pâswike).
– *on,* (continue), – konkanya (konkenye). – *on!*
interj. ale! (alêni!). – *out*
or *away,* –fuma (fumine).
– *out* (fire),–shima (shimine). – *round,* v.i. –shingauka (shingawike): *the
wheel goes round,* umupe-
to washingauka. *go round
something,* –libila (libile):
go round the house, libile
ŋanda. *go to,* –lola (lolele); –lungama (lungeme):
where do you go to? walola
kwi? or walungama kwi?
go to meet, –konkela (konkele). *go up,* –nina (ninine).

go, imper. kabiye! (kabiyeni!). *let go,* –leka (lekele).
(let us go, natuleya.

goat, mbushi (m). he-goat,
sâwe (ba–).

go-away bird, kûwe (ba–).

God, Lesa; Mulungu.

godchild, mwana wa luba-
tisho (bana ba –).

godfather, wishi wa luba-
tisho (ba–).

godmother, nyina wa luba-
tisho (ba–).

godparent, mwiminishi (be).

goitre, cibukulo (fi).

gold, goldi; cela ca paundi.

gong, lubembo (mêmbo).
strike the gong, –lisho lubembo (lishishe).

good,...suma. *be good,* –wamya (wemye).

good-bye greeting, kafikêni!
reply: shalenipo!

good-day, mwapolêni!
reply: mwapoleni!

good-enough, eyefilyako.
good-for-nothing, cinangwa (fi); canangwa (fy).
goose, ishipi (ma).
gooseberry (Cape –), lusongwa (n).
gorge, mupokapoka (mi); mukonko (mi); mupata (mi).
Gospel, Evangelyo.
gossip, 1. n. ilyashi (ma). 2. v.i. –pume lyashi (pumine).
gouge out, –tonkola (tonkwele).
gourd, nsupa (n); lukombo (n).
govern, –têka bantu (têkele).
government, kamfulumende (ba–); butekeshi. – *station,* ipoma (ma); boma (ma–).
governor, katêka wa calo (ba–).
gown, nkansu (n).
grace, busuma. (theology) nêma, bupe, bubîle. *sanctifying grace,* nêma ya kubûta. *actual grace,* nêma ya ku tûla.
graft, –alule mbuto (alwile).
grain, luseke (n); mbuto (m).
grain bin, butala (ma). *to store grain,* –tutila (tutile).
grand (great), ...kalamba; ...kulu.
grandchild, mwishikulu (bêshikulu).
grandfather, cf. T. V.
grandmother, cf. T. V.
grant, 1. (consent), –sumina (sumine). 2. (give), –pêla (pêle).
grasp, 1. (seize), –fumbata (fumbete). 2. (understand), –tesha (teseshe).
grass, cani (fy). *fine grass*

for thatching, lweo. *doggrass,* lunkoto. *course, tall* –, musanse (mi). *new – after burning,* mulemfwe (mi). *fetch* –, –fule cani (fulile). *slash grass,* –kumpe cani (kumpile).
grasshopper, kapâso (tu).
grateful, –santika (santike).
gratis, cabe.
gratuitously, cabe.
grave, cilindi (fi); luputa lwa muntu (m).
gravel, nsakalabwe (n).
graveyard, nshishi (n).
gravy, muto.
grease, 1. n. mafuta. 2. v.t. –suba (subile).
great, ...kalamba; ...kulu.
greatly, pakalamba.
greatness, bukalamba.
greediness, bulili.
green (colour), katapakatapa. *be green,* –ba katapakatapa; fita nga mabula.
green (not ripe), ...bishi.
greet, –posha (poseshe); celela (celele). *give the royal greeting,* –tôta panshi (tôtele). *refuse greeting,* –finda (findile).
greyish, –butuluka (butulwike).
grief, bulanda; bucushi (ma). *weep for,* –, –lilo bulanda (lilile).
grimace, isente (ma).
grin, –censa (censele); –ceneka (ceneke).
grind, –pela (pelele). *grind very fine,* –shutulwila (shutulwile). *grind badly,* –pununa (punwine). v. stat. –punuka (punwike).
grip, –manika (manike).
groan, –teta (tetele). *groan like a dying,* –ŋonta (ŋo-

ntele).

ground, panshi; also on the ground.

groundnut, lubalala (m). *crushed* –, cikonko. *cakes*

groundpea, lutoyo (n).

group, isese (ma); ibumba (ma). *walk in* –, –ende sese (endele).

grove, mushitu (mi).

grow, v.i. –kula (kulile) v.t. –lima (limine).

growl, –buluma (bulwime).

grudge, cikonko, cipyu. *hold a grudge,* –enda ne cikonko (endele).

gruel, musunga. *cook gruel,* –kumbo musunga (kumbile). *eat – with finger,* –komfolo musunga (komfwele).

grumble, –isosha (isoseshe); –ilishanya (ilishenye).

guard, –linda (lindile).

guardian, mulinshi (ba). *guardian angel,* malaika mulinshi (ba–). *– of goods,* mulinda fipe (ba–); shimalonda (ba–).

guava, ipêla (ma). *guava tree,* mupêla (mi).

guess, –elenganya (elengenye); –tunganya (tungenye).

guest, mweni (bêni).

guide, 1. n. ntungulushi (n). 2. v.t. –tungulula (tungulwile).

guilty, –ba no mulandu. *prove guilty,* –shinina (shinine). *plead guilty,* –sumina (sumîne).

guinea fowl, ikanga (ma).

gum, 1. (secretion of tree), cinyamuti (fi); namba (n). 2. (socket of teeth), ciponshi (fi).

gun, mfuti (nꞮ). *make a gun-* *shot,* –lishe mfuti (lishishe).

gunpowder, maluti.

— H —

habit, 1. (manner), mubêle (mi). 2. (dress), cakufwala (fy).

hail, 1. n. mfula ya mabwe. 2. v.i. –loka. mfula ya mabwe (lokele). 3. v.t. –posha (poseshe). 4. interj. mwapola (mwapoleni). 5. cf. come from.

hair, mushishi, (mi). *body hair,* ipipi (ma). *curled* –, mishishi yanyongana or mishishi ya mpolombo. *cut* –, –beo mushishi (bele). *cut all hair,* –beo lukuso. *hair of animal,* isako (ma). *ruffle hair,* –sakaliko mushishi (sakalike). *separate hair,* –uma sheti (umine). *uncombed* –, mishishi yafulubana. *white* –, lufwi (m).

half, pakati; lubali; afu.

halt, v.i. –iminina (iminine); v.t. –iminika (iminike).

halve (in width), –putula (putwile); (in length), –lepula (lepwile).

hammer, 1. n. nondo (n). 2. v.t. –pampamina (pampmine). *hammer in,* –popa (pôpele).

hammock, icila (ma).

hand, cisansa (fi); lupi (ndupi). *clap hands,* –ombe ndupi (ombele); –tôta mapi (tôtele). *close hand,* –fumbate minwe (fumbête). *open hand,* (fumbatule minwe (fumbatwile). *on the one –, on the other –*, lubali, lubali.

handcuff, nshimbi sha kalyati (n).

handful, lupi pa; ifuka (ma). *empty-handed,* iminwe mikutwa: *he comes empty-handed,* aisa iminwe mikutwa. *hand out,* –tambika (tambike). *hand round,* pokeleshanya (pokeleshenye).

handicap, v.t. cf. hinder.

handicraft, bufundi.

handkerchief, citambala ca kufyonenamo (fi).

handle, 1. n. mupini (mi). *put – to tool,* –kwika (kwikile). *remove – from tool,* –kwikula (kwikwile). *take tool out of its handle,* –sokola (sokwele). *fall out or fly out* (as tool from handle), –sokoka (sokweke).

handle, 2. v.t. cf. treat.

hang, v.t. –kobeka (kobeke).

hang oneself, –ikulika (ikulike): *he hanged himself,* aikulike.

happen, *it happened by chance,* cafika fye. *whatever may happen,* nelyo cikaba shani, *lit:* however it will be.

happiness, nsansa. *much happiness,* nsansa shingi.

happy, –ba ne nsansa; –sansamuka (sansamwike); –temwa (temenwe). *make happy,* –sansamusha (sansamwishe).

harbour, câbu (fy).

hard, 1. v.i. –kosa (kosele). *it is hard,* cakosa. *very hard,* –kosa ndi. *become hard* (congeal), –tikama

(tikeme). 2. adv. na maka: *work hard,* bomba na maka.

harden, –kosha (koseshe).

hard-headed, –koso mutwe (kosele).

hard-hearted, –uma ku mutima (umine). *a hard-hearted person,* munkalwe (ba).

hard-heartedness, bunkalwe; bulûlu.

hardly, 1. (with difficulty), kwempe: *he – escaped,* apusuka fye kwempe. 2. (scarcely), panôno fye: *he – did any work,* abomba panôno fye.

hardship, bwafya.

hare, kalulu (tu); kalulu (ba), (in native folklore).

hark, –umfwa (umfwile).

harlot, iule (maule); kêtwa (ba–).

harm, 1. n. bubi; lufyengo. 2. v.t –fyenga (fyengele).

harmful, –bîpila (bîpile).

harmonium, cinanda (fi). *play harmonium,* –lishe cinanda (lishishe).

harpoon, cibingu (fi).

harsh (cruel), ...kalwe.

harshness, bunkalwe.

hartebeest, nkonshi (n).

harvest, 1. n. kusêpa; *time of harvest,* nshita ya kusêpa. 2. v.t. –sêpa (sêpele).

haste, lubilo; *without –,* bucebuce; panôno panôno.

hasten, v.i. –anguka (angwike); –endesha (endeshe); –cincila (cincile). v.t. –cincisha (cincishe).

hat, cisote (fi).

hatch eggs, –tôta mani (tôtele); –lâlila mani (lâlile).

hate, –pata (patile).

hatred, lupatu. *cause of hatred,* cimpatanya (n).

have, –kwata (kwete); –ba na: *he has,* akwata or ali na.

hawk, pungwa (ba–). *Shikra hawk,* lukoshi (n).

hawker, musulwishi (ba); musulushi (ba).

he, cf. T. II.

head, mutwe (m.) *at the head of,* ku mitwe ya, *bend the –,* –iniko mutwe (ini- ke). *shake – with aston- ishment,* –pukunyo mutwe (pukwinye). *shake head in denial,* –kunto mutwe (ku- ntile). *lay head on cushion,* –sailo mutwe pa musao (saile). *light-headed,* –pu- sauka (pusawike). *thick- headed, ...* tumpa: *he is –,* alitumpa.

headman, kapitao (ba–). *– of a village,* mwinemushi (ba–).

heal, –posha (poseshe); –undapa (undepe).

health, mutende. *be in good health,* –endo mutende (endele); –ba ...tuntulu.

healthy, –ba mutende. *healthy person,* mûmi (bômi).

heap, mwina (mina). *put on a heap,* –tulika (tulike).

hear, –umfwa (umfwile).

heart, mutima (mi). *lose heart,* –nenuka (nenwîke). *v. caus.* –nenuna (nenwi- ne). *put one's heart into,* –biko mutima ku (bîkile). *heartless,* –uma ku mutima (umine). *heartless person,* munkalwe (ba).

hearth, ishiko (ma).

heat, 1. n. cikabilila; 2. v.t. –kafya (kafishe).

heathen, musenshi (ba).

heathendom, cisenshi.

heaven, mûlu.

heavy, –fina (finine).

hedge, ilinga (ma).

heel, citende ca lukasa ().

he-goat, sawe (ba–).

height, butali; cîmo.

heir, mpyani (m).

hell, mulilo wa pe; kwa shetani.

help, 1. n. cafwilisho. 2. v.t. –afwa (afwile); –pokako (pokeleko): *please, help me!* mungâfweko or mu- mpokeko, napâpâta. *help out,* –pokela (pokele).

helper, bukota; kâfwa (ba).

helpful, –tumike.

hemp, ibange (ma).

hemp smoker, kapêpa we bange (ba–).

hen, nkoko (n). *young hen starting to lay eggs,* musolo wa nkoko (mi).

hence, e ico; êco.

henceforth, ku ntanshi; ukufuma nomba.

her, 1. poss. pr. ...akwe: *her name,* ishina lyakwe. 2. pers. pr. mu, cf. T. II.

herald, kabila wa mbîla (ba–).

herd, 1. n. ibumba (ma). 2. v.t. –cema (cemene).

herdsman, kacema (ba–).

here, kuno; pano; apa; epo. *just here,* kuno kwine; pano pêne; apa pêne. *here I am,* interj. epo ndi; kalo- mbo; mukwai; kwaita! *here and there,* uko noku- mumomumo.

hereditary quality, cifyalilo (n); cifyalilwa (fi). *here- ditary disease,* bulwele bwa cifyalilo.

herein (in this point), mu

mulandu uyu; (in here), muno.

here outside, kunonse.

hereupon, elyo; ninshi; epa ku–

heron, nkôba (n). (egret).

herself, mwine.

hesitate, –twishika **(twishike).**

hey, interj. lelo; e!

hiccup, 1. n. muntekunteku; ntiku. 2. v.i. –tikule ntiku (tikwile).

hide, 1. n. mukupo (mi); mpapa (m). 2. v.t. –fisa (fishile); –belamika (belamike); v.i. –fisama (fisême); –belama (beleme). *bring out of hiding,* –sokolola (sokolwele); v. stat. –sokolola (sokolweke).

high, . . .tali. *be high,* –lepa (lepele). *it is* (too) *high,* kwalêpa. *be high above ground,* –sansuka (sanswike).

hill, lupili (m).

him, 1. poss. pr. . . .akwe: *the book belongs to him,* citabo cakwe. 2. pers. pr. mu, cf. T. II.

himself, mwine: *he told me himself,* anjebele mwine.

hinder, –fufya (fufishe): *he – my work,* amufyo mulimo. – *work by talking,* –konga (kongele).

hindrance, cilesha.

hip, lutungu (n).

hippo-fly, cipobe (fi).

hippopotamus, mfubu (m).

hire, –ashima (ashime).

his, . . .akwe.

history, ancient –, milandu ya kale; modern –, milandu ya nomba.

hit, –uma (umine); –puma (pumine); –tobo lupi (to-

bele).

hit and kill, –koma (komene).

hither, kuno.

hive, (in tree), cilunda (fi).

hoarse, –kome shiwi (komene): *my voice is –,* ishiwi lyandi lyakoma. *be cured from hoarseness,* –komoke shiwi (komweke).

hoe, 1. n. lukasu (n). 2. v.t. –shima (shimine).

hold, –ikata (ikete). *hold tight,* –ikatisha (ikatishe). – *back* (delay), –kashakasha (kashakeshe). *lay – of,* –obola (obwele).

hole, 1. n. (for animals), bwendo; (in ground), cilindi (fi); (through any object), cipunda (fi). hole (made in mush for relish), lukondwa (n). *make a – in mush for relish,* –lemo lukondwa (lemene). *stop a –,* –cilika (cilike). *remove earth from a –,* –fukulo mushili (fukwile).

hole, 2. v.t. (the ground), –imbe cilindi (imbile); (cloth etc.), –tula (tulile).

holiday, bushiku bwa kutusha: *to-day is a holiday,* lêlo . bushiku bwa kutusha or takuli isukulu lêlo.

holiness, butakatifu.

hollow, 1. n. lupako (m). 2. v.t. –fonsha (fonseshe); –fukula (fukwile). *be –,* –fonka (fonkele). *a – plate,* mbale yafonka.

holy, . . .takatifu.

homage, mucinshi. *pay homage to,* –cindika (cindike); –tasha (tashishe).

home, cifulo.

homesick, –fuluka **(fulwike).**

honest, ...cishinka: *he is honest,* uyu wa cishinka.

honesty, bucinshika.

honey, buci. *pure honey,* luto lwa buci. *collect –,* –pando buci (pandile).

honeybird, lûni (ŋûni).

honeycomb, cipêpe (fi). *honeycomb full of honey* lupuma (m).

honeyfly, kabulubulu (tu).

honour, cf. homage.

honourable, –cindama (cindeme), –pûlama (pûleme). *– person,* mucindami (ba); (mukankala (ba). *have a – position,* –ikalo bukata (ikele).

honourableness, bukata.

hoof, lubondo (mondo); cibondo (fi).

hook, 1. n. bulobo (ma); ndobâni (n). 2. v.t. (catch with –), –loba (lobele).

hoot, –sopesha (sopeshe).

hop, –toboka (tobweke); –toloka (tolweke); –tomboka (tombweke).

hope, 1. n. cisubilo. 2. v.i. –sûbila (sùbile). *put hope into,* –tetekela (tetekele); also –cetekela.

horn, lusengo (n).

hornet, ilonda (ma).

horse, mfwalashi (m); kabalwe (ba–).

hospital, cipatâla (fi).

horsefly, cipobe (fi).

host, kasunga (ba–).

hostile, ...lwani.

hostility, bulwani.

hot, –kaba (kabile): *it is hot to-day,* kwakaba lêlo. make hot, –kafya (kafishe).

hotel, otela (ba–).

hour, nsa (n). *half an hour,* nsa afu; nsa pakati.

hourly, cila nsa.

house, ŋanda (ŋ or mayaanda). *brick house,* ŋanda ya njelwa. *storeyed house,* ŋanda ya ntunti or lupuŋgu. *deserted house,* cipompa (fi). *house in which somebody died,* ŋanda ya ndililwa.

how, 1. adv. shani? musango nshi? *how do you do it,* ulecita shani or musango nshi? 2. cj. ifyo; te pa: *how hot it is to-day,* ifyo kukabile lêlo or te pa kukaba lêlo.

however, 1. nomba; nge fyo: *you say they understand each other, however I have just seen them quarrelling,* iwe auti baleumfwana, nomba or ngefyo ine nabamona baleumana. 2. ...êna. *the trees however,* miti yêna. cf. also T. III.

how much/many, ...nga? *how many men,* bantu banga?

howl, –kûwa (kûwile).

hum, –tâta (tâtile).

human being, muntu (ba).

humanity, bumuntu.

humble, v.t. –cefya (cefeshe; v.t –icefya (icefeshe); –fûka (fûkile).

humiliate, cf. humble, v.t.

hump, ntengele (n).

hundred, mwanda (my).

hunger, nsala; cipôwe.

hungry, –ba ne nsala; nsala yakalipa, *very –,* –fwa ku nsala (fwile).

hunt, 1. n. (with gun etc.), bulunshi; (ritual hunt), ibanda (ma). 2. v.t. (with gun etc.), –lunga (lungile); (with nets), –sowa (sowele); (make a ritual –),

–sowe banda (sowele).

hunter, (with gun etc.), kalunga (ba–); mulunshi (ba); (with nets), kasôwa (ba–); (with dog), mulenga (ba–).

hurricane, cikûku ca mwêla (fi).

hurry up, v.i. –endesha (endeshe); –cincila (cincile); anguka (angwîke). v. caus. –cincisha (cincishe); –angusha (angwishe). *be in a hurry,* –pamfiwa (pamfiwe).

hurt, 1. v.i. –kalipa (kalipe); –tanta (tantile); *the legs hurt,* môlu yakalipa or ciletanta mu môlu. 2. v. caus. –kalifya (kalifye). 3. v.t. –cena (cenene).

husband, cf. T. V. *husband of,* muka (ba–): *the husband of Mutale,* muka Mutale.

husk, 1. n. cipâpa (fi). 2. v.t. –sokola (sokwele).

hut, ŋanda (ŋ or mayanda). *hut for spirits,* lufuba (m). *– in the gardens,* mitanda. *– made of poles,* ŋanda ya filu. *– with walls made of branches,* nsakwe (n). *– with walls made of grass,* cisakuta (fi). *round hut,* ŋanda ya mushiki. *conical hut,* tûti (ba–). *rectangular hut,* itembe (ma). *small – for children,* itanda (ma). *small hut for children to play house-keeping,* mutundu (mi); mansansa.

hyena, cimbwi (ba–).

hymn, lwimbo (nyimbo).

hypocrite, wa ndimi shibili (ba); wa bufi (ba).

— I —

I, ine or ne. cf. also T. II. *I myself,* ne mwine.

ice, menshi makâsa; menshi yakambantana.

idea, muntontonkanya (mi).

identification card, citupa (fi). *– mark,* cishibilo (fi).

idiot, ciwelewele (fi); cipuba (fi); cipumbu (fi); mpelwa mâno (ba).

idle, –nanana (naŋene).

idleness, bulamu; bunaŋani.

idol, kalubi (tu).

i.e. ekutila; nimukuti.

if, nga.

ignore, (pay no attention), –sûla (sûlile): *don't pay attention,* sûla fye.

iguana, (water –), nsamba (n).

ill, –lwala (lwele).

illness, bulwele.

ill-treat, –cito lucu (citile).

ill-treatment, lucu.

illustrate, v.t. –langa (langile); –londolola (londolwele).

illustrious, –lumbuka (lumbwike).

image, nsalamu (n).

imagination, muntontonkanya; mwelenganya.

imagine, –tontonkanya (tontonkenye); elenganya (–elengenye).

imitate, –pashanya (pashenye).

immediately, apo pêne; nombaline; ndakai.

immerse, –tumpa (tumpile); –tumpika (tumpike); –abika (abike).

immodest, bulungani.

immorality, bupulumushi.

immortal, ...pe, –belêlela

(belêlêle).

impala (kind of antelope), mpala (m).

inpartial –linganya (lingenye); –ba no mulinganya.

impartiality, mulinganya.

impatient, –ba ne cipyu; –fulwa (fulilwe).

impediment, cilesha (). – *of marriage,* mushinga (mi).

impertinent, –ba no musâlula.

implement (tool), cibombelo (fi).

implore, –papâta (papête). v. appl. –papâtila (papâtile).

important, ...kalamba; ... kulu: *an – matter,* mulandu ukalamba/ukulu.

importunity, mukosela.

impossible, –ansha (anshishe): *it is –,* cayansha.

impotency, bucibola.

impotent man, cibola (ba).

impoverished (soil), –fumuka (fumwike): *the soil is –,* mushili naufumuka.

imprison, –kaka (kakile); funga mu cifungo (fungile).

improve, –wamya (wemye); – *your ways,* mulewamya misango yenu. – *a country,* –ĩmye câlo (imishe).

in, mu or muli; pa or pali: *in water,* mu menshi; *in an hour,* pa nsa imo *in here,* muno.

inadvertently, ku cilafĩ.

inattention, bupusaushi.

incapable, –filwa (fililwe); *I am incapable,* nafilwa.

incence, 1. n. bubâni. 2. v.t. –fukilisha (fukilishe).

incision, 1. (for remedy), lulembo (nêmbo); *make incision,* –kome nêmbo

(komene). 2. traditional incision cf. tattoo.

incite to fight, –songo lubuli (songele); (urge), –cincisha (cincishe).

incitement for good, kucincisha; – *for bad,* ntunko (n).

incline, (head), –iniko mutwe (inike); (body), –inama (ineme). *be inclined to,* umutima walola ku: *he is inclined to steal,* umutima wakwe walola ku bupûpu.

include, –ingisha (ingishe).

incomplete, –bulila (bulile).

incomprehensible, –lubana (lubene): *it is –,* calubana.

increase (enlarge), v.t. lunda; –sandulula (sandulwile); v. stat. –sanduluka (sandulwîke).

incredible, te ca kusumina iyô.

increment, bulundo. – *in wages,* bulundo bwa mpiya.

indeed, interj. mwandi; nakabushe; naendi.

independent (self-governing), –itêka mwine (itêkele).

indigenous, ...kaya.

indiscreet person, bobo wa kanwa; mukwakwa (ba).

indiscretion, bukwakwa.

individually, ...mo ... mo: *you must come –,* muleisa umo umo.

indocile person, cintomfwa (ba–).

infancy, bunya.

infant, kanya (tu); kana (twana).

infect, v.t. –ambukila (ambukîle).

infection, lwambu.

infectious, ... lwambu.
infectious disease, bulwele
bwa lwambu.
infinite, ... pe; ... onse:
God is infinite, Mulungu
wa pe; *God is - in his
power,* Mulungu mwine
wa maka yonse.
infirm, –bonsa (bonsele);
–lwalilila (lwalilile). *infirm person,* ntenda (n).
inflammation, fundwefu-
ndwe.
inform, –ebako (ebeleko):
I inform you, ndemwe-
bako; –ishibisha (ishibi-
she). *- of danger,* –soka
(sokele).
inhabitant, umwikala calo
(abe).
inherit, –pyana (pyene),
v. caus. –pyanika (pya-
nike).
inheritance, bupyani.
inhospitable person, ushi-
sekelela babiye (aba);
munkalwe (ba).
ink, inki. *blot of ink,* imata
(ma).
injure, v.t. –cena (cenene);
–fwanta (fwantile).
injustice, lufyengo.
innocence, bukaele.
innocent, neg. of –ba no
mulandu: *he is –,* taba no
mulandu. *- person,* wa
kaele (ba).
innumerable, te fya kupe-
nda: *- times,* imiku te ya
kupenda.
inquire, –bûsha (bûshishe);
–ipusha (ipwishe).
insane, –pena (penene).
insect, cishîshi (fi).
any insect that stings,
cisumi (fi).
inside, mukati or pakati.
inside the stomach, mu

nda.
insist, –bwekeshapo mashiwi (bwekeshepo); –pa-
mfya (pamfishe).
insolence, musâlula; misûla;
mupukila (mi).
insolent, –ba no musâlula;
–ba no mulomo. *insolent
person,* wa mulomo; mu-
kakashi (ba).
inspect, –lengula (lengwile); –londa (londele).
instantly, nombaline; ndakai.
instead, mu ncende ya.
instinct, mutima (mi).
instruct, –funda (fundile);
–langa (langile).
instruction, mafundisho.
instrument (tool), cibo-
mbelo (fi); (musical –),
cilimba (fi); isese (ma).
insufficient, –cepa (cepele):
it is insufficient, cacepa.
insult, 1. n. lusele (n).
2. v.t. –tuke nsele (tukile).
intact, ... tuntulu.
intellect, mâno.
intelligence, mâno.
intelligent, wa mâno; –ba
na mâno; –cenjela (cenje-
le). *not intelligent,* –bulwa
mâno (bulilwe); –tumpa
(tumpile).
intend, –fwaya (fwaile):
what do you intend to do?
cinshi mulefwayo kucita?
intentionally, ku mufulo;
ku kutemwa.
intercede, –pâpâtila (pâpâtile); –soselako (soselako).
intercessor, bukota; ndubulwila (ba–).
interpret (language), –pilibula mashiwi (pilibwile);
alula (alwile). (dream),
–longola (longwele).
interpreter (of language).

kapilibula (ba-); kalondo-
lwela (ba-).
interrupt (talking), –cilinganya (cilingenye).
(work), –fufyo mulimo
(fufishe).
interweave, –pikula (pikwile).
intestine, bula (mala).
intimidate, –tìnya (tinishe).
into, mu; mukati.
intone (a song), –bûlo lwimbo (bûlile).
intoxicate, v.t. –kolesho
muntu kunwa bwalwa.
v.i. –kola (kolele).
introduce, –ingisha (ingishe); –ishibisha (ishibi-
she).
intrude in other one's
matters, –ampula mu mi-
landu ya bêne (ampwile).
inundated, –bundwa (bundilwe).
inundation, lyeshi.
invent, –panga (pangile);
–sanga (sangile). – a new
song, –shiko lwimbo (shi-
kile).
invite, –ita (itile); –kûta
(kûtile).
invitation, bwite.
invoke spirits, –pàla mipashi (pàlile).
involuntarily, ku cilafi; ku
kukana ishiba.
involve in a case, –biko
muntu mu mulandu;
–ampulo muntu mu mula-
ndu.
iron, 1. n. cêla (fy). 2. v.t.
(– cloth), –cisa (cishile);
-olola (olwele). *sheet-
iron*, ilata (ma).
irrigate, –tapilila (tapilile).
irritable, wa cau (ba); wa
cipyu (ba) *irritate*, (person) –kalifya (kalifye) (as

sore) –tapata (tapete).
is, –li, –ba; e; ni. *it is not*,
te. *it is so*, interj. nifyo
fine. *it is not so*, interj. te
ifyo iyo. *it is not that*
(what you mean), interj.
ico teco. *is that so?* interj.
bushe? batini? mwa? *there
is or there are; there was
or there were*, pali.
island, cishi (fi).
itch, 1. n. lupele (m). 2. v.i.
–baba (babile).
its, 1. ...akwe with nouns
of class 'mu/ba': *the cat
and its tail*, cona no mucila wakwe. 2. with all
other classes it is tran-
scribed by 'of it' and has
the suffix 'ko': *the leopard
and the tail of it*, mbwili
no mucila waiko.
ivory, lino lya   **nsofu**
(mêno).

— J —

jackal, mumbwe (ba-).
jail, cifungo (fi).
jam (squeeze), –fenenkesha
(fenenkeshe).
January, Kabengele kanono.
jaw, mubango wa kanwa
(mi); mucendwa (mi);
ncendwa (n).
jealous, –ba no mufimbila.
jealousy, mufimbila; bufuba.
jeer at, –wêla (wêlele).
Jesus, Yesu.
jigger, ibundu (ma).
job, ncito (n); mulimo
(mi). *apply for a job*,
–fwaye ncito (fwaile).
look in vain for a job,
–ambakala (ambakele).
get a –, –lembwa ku ncito

(lembelwe), *leave a –*,
–leko mulimo (lekele).
join, 1. (connect), –kumbinkanya (kumbinkenye).
v. stat. –kumbinkana (ku-
mbinkene); –lundikanya
(lundikenye). 2. (follow
somebody), –konka (ko-
nkele). 3. (become mem-
ber of), –ingila mu
(ingile); –lembwa ku
(lembelwe).
joint (knuckle), lupingu
(m); *mulundo (mi).*
joke, 1. n. milangwe; nseko.
2. v.i. –sose milangwe. *be
fond of –,* –ba ne nseko.
jostle, –tensha (tenseshe);
–sunka (sunkile).
journey, lwendo (nyendo);
bulendo.
joy, nsansa (n).
joyful, ...nsansa: *he is
joyful,* ali ne nsansa.
judge, 1. n. kaputula wa
milandu (ba–); kapingula
(ba–). 2. v.t. –putula
mulandu (putwile); –pi-
ngula (pingwile).
judgement, bupingushi; cipingulo (fi).
juice, menshi: *lemon juice,*
menshi ya ndimu.
July, Cikungulupepo.
jump, 1. n. ibaka (ma);
ibimbili (ma) 2. v.i.
–ime baka (imine); –tolo-
ka (tolweke); –tomboka
(tombweke). *jump aside,*
–cilimuka (cilimwike).
– over, –ciluka (cilwike).
June, Kapepo kakalamba.
just, 1. v.i. –linganya
(lingenye). 2. adv. nombaline. *just now,* nombaline
fye. *– the same,* ...mo
...ine: *it is –,* cimo cine.
justify oneself, –iwaminisha

(iwaminishe). *– one's
action,* –ipokako (ipoke-
leko).

— K —

keen (eager), –fwaisha
(fwaishe).
keep, 1. (hold), –ikata
(ikete). 2. (care for),
–baka (bakile); –sunga
(sungile). 3. (observe),
–konka (konkele). *keep
away,* v.t. –talusha (talwishe); v.i. –taluka (talwike). *– off,* same as keep
away. *– on,* cf. go on;
persevere. *– out,* v.t. –sha
kunse (shile); v.i. –shala
kunse (shele).
kettle, ikètulo (ma).
key, lufungulo (m).
khaki, kaki.
kick. 1. n. munshele (mi);
cipaka (fi). 2. v.t. –nya-
ntilo munshele (nyantile);
–panta (pantile). *kick
aside,* –kumuna (kumwi-
ne).
kidney, lufyo (m).
kill, –ipaya (ipeye). v. appl.
–ipaila (ipaile). *kill by
hanging,* –kulika (kulike).
– game, –bamba (bambi-
le).
killed, –ipaiwa (ipaiwe).
kiln, cibili (fi); itanuna
(ma). *build up a kiln,*
–pange cibili (pangile).
break up a –, –bongolole
cibili (bongolwele).
kind, 1. n. (class, manner),
musango (mi): *what kind?*
musango nshi? 2. adj.
...suma: *a kind man,*
umuntu musuma. 3. v.i.

(be), –wama (weme):
you are kind, mwawama.
be – enough to, kuti: *be
kind enough to help me*,
kuti mwangafwako.
kindle, -sanika (sanike);
–sonkelesho mulilo (so-
nkeleshe).
kindness, busuma; cilela;
cikuku.
king, mfumu (mfumu or
bashamfumu).
kingdom, bufumu.
kiss, –shintiko mulomo ku
(shintike).
kitchen, icikini (ma); ŋanda
ya kwipikilamo.
kite, black – (bird), pungwa
(ba-).
klipspringer, cibushimabwe
(ii).
knapsack, côla (fy).
knead, –kanda (kandile).
knee, ikufi (ma).
kneel (on both knees),
–fukama (fukeme); (on
one knee), –fukama kulu
kumo.
kneeling position, bufuke-
me.
knife, mwele (my).
knit, –pikula (pikwile).
knock, –konkonsha (konkonseshe). – *against*, –ipununa (ipunwine), v.g. a
toc. *knock down*, –futula
(futwile); –wisha (wishi-
she).
knot, cifundo (fi). *knot in
reed*, lupingu (m).
know, –ishiba (ishibe). v.
pass. –ishibikwa (ishibi-
kwe); –ishibwa (ishi-
bwe). – *by heart*, –ishiba
ku mutwe. – *for certain*,
–ishiba ca cine. *let know*,
–ishibisha (ishibishe).
make known, –alasha (ale-

she); –sokolola (soko-
lwele). *be well known*,
(famous), –lumbuka (lu-
mbwike). *I do not know*,
nshaishiba; nshishibe;
katwishi.
knowledge, mano.
to the knowledge of all,
pa menso ya bantu bonse.
knuckle, lupingu (m).
kraai, icinka (ma); itanga
(ma).
kudu antelope, nsansala (n).

— L —

label, 1. n. kalata we shina
(ma-). 2. v.t. –lembako
ishina (lembeleko).
labour, v.i. –bomba na maka
(bombele).
lack, v.i. –bula (bulile):
strength is lacking, amaka
yabula.
lad, kalume (ba-).
ladder, mutanto (mi).
lady, lôna(ba-).
lair, mutundu (mi).
lake, bemba (ba-).
lamb, mwana wa mpanga.
lame, –lemana (lemene).
lame person, cilema (fi);
cite (fite).
lament, –lilila (lilile).
lamp, lampi (ma-).
lance, lifumo (ma).
land, 1. n. calo (fy). 2. v.i.
(of plane), –ika (ikile);
(ship), –fika ku câbu: *the
plane is landing*, ndeke
ileika; *the ship is landing*,
bwato bulefika ku câbu.
dry land, ciswebebe (fi).
language, lulimi (ndimi).
use abusive –, –tuke nsele
(tukile).

lap, cèni (fy); còfi (fy).
lard, mafuta.
large, ...kulu.
be large, –lèpa (lêpele).
largeness, .bukulu.
larva, bube.
larynx, cikolomino (fi).
lash, bwembya.
last, be –, ...pa kulekelesha *last long*, –kokola
(kokwele). *make last*,
–kokweshe (kokweshe):
*make food last by ration-
ing*, –kokwesha cakulya.
at last, pa kulekelesha.
cf. also 'finally' *up to the
last*, kale na kêpi: *they
died up to the last*, bafwile
kale na kêpi.
late, –celwa (celelwe): *you
are late*, mwacelwa.
lately, papita nshita inôno;
tapalapite nshiku.
later on, ku ntanshi; pa
numa or ku numa.
lath, lubango (mango);
ilonde (ma).
latrine, cimbusu (fi).
go to latrine, –ya kunse
(ile).
laugh, –seka (sekele). v.
caus. –sekesha (sekeshe).
– without reason, –seka
ciseke seke.
laughter, nseko. *cause a –*,
–kokeshe nseko (kokeshe).
burst out into laughter,
–wa ku nseko (wîle). *roar
with –*, –uma kunseko.
lavatory, cimbusu (fi).
lavishly, ubusa: *sow lavishly*, **-tando busa** (tandile).
law, cêbo (fy).
lawsuit, mulandu (mi). *the
in-laws*, buko (mako).
lay, –bìka (bìkile). *lay
across*, –cilinganya (cili-

ngenye); –pindika (pindî-
ke). *lay hold of*, –ikata
(ikete). *lay out* (spread),
–ansa (anshile); –lambalika (lambalike). *lay the
table*, –anse tebulo (anshile).
lazy, ...naŋani; –naŋana
(naŋene). *lazy person*,
munaŋani; wa bulamu.
laziness, bulamu; bunaŋani.
lead, 1. n. mutofwe (mi);
2. v.t. –tungulula (tungulwile).
leader, ntungulushi (n);
katungulula (ba–).
leadership, butungulushi.
leaf, ibùla (ma). *make leaf
into a drinking cup*, –leme
bùla (lemene). *leaves used
as relish*, cimpapila (of
beans); katapa (of cas-
sava; cibwabwa (of pu-
mpkin); mulembwe (of
different plants, pupwe,
cinsanki, etc.).
leak, v.i. –sùma (sùmine);
–tona (tonène).
lean, 1. adj. (thin), –onda
(ondele). 2. v.t. –shintilisha (shintilishe); v.i.
–shintilila (shintilile): *do
not lean against the wall*,
mwishintilila ku cibu-
mba.
leap, n. & v. cf jump.
learn, –sambilila (sambilile). *– by heart*, –sambilila ku mutwe.
learned man, muntu wa
mâno (ba).
lease, –kopesha no kulipilisha (kopeshe).
least, 1. adj. (smallest),
...nônonôno. 2. adv. (at
least), cine cine; mba:
there are at least two men,
baliko bantu babili cine

cine or baliko bantu babili mba.

leather, mpapa.

leave, 1. n. lifi (ma-). 2. v.t. –sha (shile); v.i. –ya (ile); –fuma (fumine); coka (cokele) (abusive). *leave for a journey,* –ima ulwendo (imine). *leave for good,* –ililila (ililile). *take leave,* –shalikapo (shalikepo).

lechwe antelope, nja (n).

left, to the –, ku kuso. *be – over,* –shaka (shele).

left-handed, –ba no kuso.

leg, mukonso (mi), *hindleg,* kulu (môlu). *foreleg,* kuboko(ma). *leg of a kill,* mwendo (my).

legend, mulumbe (mi); lushimi (n).

lemon, ndimu (n).

lend, –ashima (ashîme); –kopesha (kopeshe).

length, butali.

lengthen, –lefya (lefeshe).

Lent, nshita ya kwaleshima.

lentil, ilanda.

leopard, mbwili (m).

leper, wa fibashi (ba).

leprosy, fibashi.

less, –cepa (cepele): *cloth is less expensive now,* insalu yacepo mutengo nomba.

lessen, 1. (in length), –cefya (cefeshe). 2. (in weight), –angusha (angwishe).

lesson, ifunde (ma).

lest, atemwa; epali: *write it down, lest you forget,* lemba epali walaba.

let, –leka (lekele). *let it be,* interj. leka; cili fye; nacibe. – *alone,* –leka. – *me alone,* interj. abwe! leka!; ndeka mbe ne mwine. *let*

down, –isha (ishishe). – *fall,* –ponya (poneshe). – *let go,* cf. release. – *in,* cf. open; admit. – *loose,* cf. release.

letter, kalata (ma-). *air letter,* kalata wa mu ndeke. *answer a letter* –bwesha kalata (bweseshe); –asuka kalata (aswike). *send a letter by hand,* –laisha kalata (laishe).

letter of alphabet, cilembo (fi).

level, v.t. –linganya (lingenye); v.i. –lingâna (lingène); –papâtala (papâtele).

liar, wa bufi (ba).

liberate, –lubula (lubwîle).

license, lasenshi (ma-).

lick, –myanga (myangile).

lid, nkupiko (n). *cover with lid,* –kupika (kupîke). *take off lid,* –kupukula (kupukwile).

lie, 1. n. bufi. 2. v.i. –bepo bufi (bepele). *tell a lie,* –bepa (bepele). *retract a lie,* –bwesho bufi (bweseshe).

lie across, –pindama (pindeme). *lie down,* –sendama (sendeme); –lâla (lêle), *lie flat on the ground.* –lambalala (lambalêle). – *in wait,* –lalilila (lalilile). *lie on the back,* –lâla buseneme. *lie on the stomach,* –lâla ubukupeme.

life, bumi. *eternal life,* bumi bwa pe.

lift, –imya (imishe); –sansula (sanswîle).

light, 1. n. laiti (ma-); cengelo (fy). 2. v.t. (light a lamp), –sanika lampi (sanîke); (– fire), –kosho

mulilo (koseshe). 3. adj.
(light in weight), –anguka
(angwike); (– in colour),
–bùta (bùtile).
lighten, 1. (reduce weight),
–angusha (angwishe); 2.
(flash), –byata (byatile).
lightning, mwele wa mfula
(my): *it is* –, mwele wa
mfula ulebyata.
like, 1. adj. (similar), –pala
(palile). v. rec. –palana
(palene); v. caus. palanya
(palenye). 2. adv. efyo;
fino: he is like that, efyo
aba; *he is like me,* ali fino
ndi. 3. v.t. (love), –temwa
(temenwe). 4. cj. (as),
nga filya.
likely (perhaps), nalimo,
nakalimo, namponga. *very
likely,* ukuba.
likeness, cipasho.
limb, mwendo (my). *stump
of amputated limbi,*
makunkutu.
lime, mpemba.
limit, mpela (m).
limp, –sunta (suntile).
line, 1. (row), mulongo
(mi). 2. (a drawn line),
cishilwa (fi). *draw a line,*
–shila cishilwa (shilile).
be in straight –, tololo: *the
line is straight,* mulongo
tololo. *be in line with,*
–lungatana (lungatene). *be
out of line,* –tantuka
(tantwike). *break up a
line,* –tantula (tantwile).
line up, v.t. –tantamika
(tantamìke); v.i. –tantama
(tanteme). *put in line
with,* –lungatanika (lungatanike). *put in one line,*
–lungika (lungike). *set
out of line,* same as break
up a line.

linger, –kokola (kokwele).
ikashakasha (ikashake-
she).
link up, –kumbinkanya (kumbinkenye); v. stat. –ku-
mbinkana (kumbinkêne).
be linked up, –ikatana
(ikatêne): *this matter is
linked up with the other,*
mulandu uyu waikatana
no ubiye.
lion, nkalamo (n). *maneater
lion,* nkalamo **yalubûka**
(nkalamo shalubûka); ci-
sanguka (fi).
lip, mulomo (mi).
liquid, be –, –songoloka
(songolweke). *make* –,
songolola (songolwêle).
lisp, –bulubusa (bulubushile).
listen, –umfwa (umfwîle);
–tesha (teseshe). *one who
does not listen,* munshu-
mfwa (ba–). *– attentively,*
–kutika (kutike).
litany, malumbo, mishika-
kulo.
little, 1. adj. ...nôno;
...nìni. *be little,* –cêpa
(cêpele). 2. adv. panôno;
panìni. *very little,* panônonôno; paninininì. *not a
little,* nelyo panôno.
little by little, panôno panôno; buce buce.
live, 1. (be alive), –ba no
bumi. 2. cf. abide. *live in
good understanding,* –ikala
busaka pamo; –umfwâna
(umfwêne).
lively, –luma (lumine):
he is lively, uyu aluma.
liver, libu (mabu).
lizard, mulinso (ba–). *blue-
headed lizard,* kolyokolyo
(ba–). *iguana* –, cf. iguana;
monitor.

load, 1. n. cipe (fipe). **2.** v.t. –twika (twikile). *load a gun,* –sokele mfuti (soke-le).

loaf, 1. n. mukate (mi). **2.** v.i –talatanta (talata-ntile).

loafer, ntalatanshi (n).

loam, mushili we lambo.

loan, 1. n. bukope. **2.** v.t. –kopesha (kopeshe).

lock, 1. n. loko (ma–). **2.** v.t. –funga (fungile).

locust, makanta, s. class 'mu/ba': – *are coming,* makanta aisa.

log, mulando (mi). *hollowed log used as mortar,* cinkolobondo (fi).

loin, musana (mi).

loiter, –elepeta (elepete) –enda cendeende (ende-le –).

long, ...tali. *be long,* lepa (lepele). nshi. *as long as,* cj. nshita yonse iyo; *cf. as.*

long ago, kale. *not long ago,* papite nshita inôno fye. *very long ago,* kale na kale; kale fye.

long for, 1. cf. homesick. **2.** cf. covet.

longing for meat/fish, etc. bukasha.

look, v.i. –lolesha (loleshe). *look after, 1.* cf. care for. **2.** cf. supervise. *look all around,* –cebaceba (ceba-cebe). *look as if,* –ba nga. *look at,* cf. admire. *look carefully,* –lolekesha (loleke-she). – *fixedly,* –tonto-mesha menso (tontome-she). *look for,* –fwaya (fwaile). *look forward to,* –fwaisha (fwaishe). *look in,* cf. visit. *look into,* cf. examine. – *like,* –moneka

nga (moneke). *look on,* cf. admire, *look out,* cf. watch. *look out for,* cf. wait for. *look over,* cf. inspect. *look up,* –sansula menso (sanswile).

looking glass, cilola (fi); mulolâni (mi).

loose, 1. (as something tied), –kakuka (kakwike). **2.** (as axe in handle). –sokona (sokwene); –kwi-kuka (kwikwike).

loosen, 1. (something tied), –kakula (kakwile). **2.** (axe in handle), –sokonya (sokoneshe); –kwikula (kwikwile).

lop, –tema (temene).

lose, –lufya (lufishe).

loss, be at a –, –kutumana (kutumêne).

lost, –luba (lubile).

lot, 1. n. (much), bwingi. **2.** adj. ...ingi.

loud, –kafya (kafishe).

louder, speak –, –ikatishe shiwi (ikatishe).

louse, nda (nda). *catch a louse,* –sala inda (salile).

love, 1. n. citemwiko. **2.** v.t. –temwa (temenwe). **v.** appl. –temwana (temwa-nene). v. pass. –temwikwa (temwikwe).

low, –ipipa (ipipe).

lower, –isha (ishishe).

loyal, ...cishinka: *loyal people,* abantu abacishi-nka.

loyalty, cishinka.

lucifer, shetani mukalamba.

luck, good –, ishuko (ma); bad –, ishâmo (ma). *have bad –,* –shama (sheme).

lucky, –shùka (shùkile).

luggage, cipe (fi). *pack*

luggage, –longe fipe (lo-ngele).

lukewarm, ...cifulefule: *lukewarm water,* menshi ya cifulefule.

lump, lutoshi (n).

lungs, pwapwa (ba–).

lunatic, ishilu (ma).

lust, lunkumbwa.

— M —

machine, mashini (ba–).

machine-gun, mfuti ya ci-waya (m).

mad, –pena (penene). *mad person,* ishilu (ma).

madam, lôna (ba); mama (ba–). *madam, interj.* mu-kwai!

madness, bushilu; bucipena.

maggot, mutiti (mi).

maid, mukashana (ba).

maidenhood, bukashana.

mail, mêlu. *air mail,* mêlu wa mu ndeke. *surface mail,* mêlu wa panshi.

mailman, wa mêlu (ba –).

maimed, –lemana (lemene).

maize, nyanje. *break off a maize cob,* –kobole nyanje (kobwele).

make, 1. (do), –cita (citile). 2. (manufacture), –panga (pangile).

malaria, bulwele bwa mpe-po; malelya.

male, 1. n. cilume (fi). 2. adj. (of man), ...aume; (of animal), ...lume.

malice, mufulo; mumbo.

maliciously, ku mufulo; ku mumbo.

man, mwaume (ba).

manager, mushika (ba–).

mane, mwansa (my).

mango, iyembe (maembe/ mayembe).

manhood, bwaume.

manifest, 1. (be clear), –moneka (moneke). 2. (show plainly), –londolola (londolwele); –langa (la-ngile).

mankind, bwina bantu.

manner, cf. kind, n.; be-haviour. *in what manner, musango nshi? in such a manner,* musango wa kuti. *good manners,* mucinshi; mibêle isuma. *bad manners,* butûtu; (morally –), bûlungani. *– of behaving,* myendele. *– of doing,* micitile. *– of sitting,* mika-lile. *– of talking,* mila-ndile.

manslayer, cipondo (fi); cisanguka (ba–) (when going about in a lion skin).

mantle, isâba (ma).

manure, 1. n. cf. dung. 2. v.t. –fundika (fundike).

many, ...ingi. *be many,* –fula (fulile); *we are many,* tuli bengi/twafula.

marabou stork, mukanga (mi); cipampa (ba–).

March, Kutumpu.

march, –enda (endele).

mark, 1. n. (sign) cishibilo (fi); (results), itoni (ma). 2. v.t. –bîkapo cishibilo (bîkilepo). *mark out a road,* –sake nshila (saki-le).

marriage, cupo (fy). *– cere-mony,* bwinga. *give in –,* –ufya (ufishe).

marrow, 1. (of bone), bu-fyompo. 2. (gourd), mu-ngu (my).

marry, v.i. –upa (upile)

when man; –upwa (ûpi-
lwe) when girl. v.t. –ufya
– (ufishe).
marsh, tefwetefwe.
martyr, malitili (ba–).
die a martyr, –fwila Lesa
(fwilile); –fwa bumalitili
(fwile).
marvel, cisungusho (fi).
marvellous, ca kusunguka
(fya –).
Mass, minsa *attend* –,
–umfwe minsa (umfwile).
serve at –, –(tumike minsa) (tumike).
massage, v.t. –cina (cinine).
master, bwana (ba–).
masticate, –sheta (shetele).
mat, butanda (ma). *coarse
mat,* cisani (fi). *make a
mat,* –paso butanda (pashile); –luke cisani (lukile).
match, 1. (football –), mupila wa kucimfyanya. 2.
(safety –), cibiliti (fi);
mulilo (mi); macishi.
strike a match, –fwalula
macishi (fwalwile).
matchbox (when empty),
cifwambo (fi).
mate, 1. n. mune (bane) 2.
v.t. (animals) –tamfye nko-
ta (tamfishe) when male;
–tamfiwa (tamfiwe) when
female.
material (writing –), ifile-
mbelo.
matter, cf. thing; affair.
what is the –? cinshi?
what does it –, interj. lelo
mulandu; *it does not* –,
te mulandu iyô; cili fye;
kabe; nacibe. *no matter
how/what,* cj. nelyo/na-
ngu … shani: *no matter
what will happen,* nelyo
cikaba shani …
mature, –kula (kulile).

May, Kapepo kanono.
may, kuti: *may I go?* bushe
kuti naya. *may be,* nalimo;
nakalimo; nampo **nga.**
me, n/m, cf. T. II.
meagre, cf. lean; little.
meal, 1. (food), cakulya
(fy). 2. (flour), bunga.
mean, 1. adj. (stingy), wa
kaso. 2. v.i. cf. think; say;
–losha mashiwi (loseshe);
mashiwi yalola: *what do
you mean,* cinshi mwato-
ntonkanya or mwasosa/
mwalosha **mashiwi** kwi/
mashiwi yenu yalola kwi/
that means, e kutila; ni
mukuti.
meanness, kaso; butani.
meanwhile, mu nshita.
measure, 1. n. cipimo (fi).
2. v.t. –pima (pimine).
measure against an equal,
–linganya (lingenye).
measure correct, –linga
(lingile).
meat, nama (n). *lean meat,*
munofu (mi). *fat* –, mafuta. *piece of* – *without bone,*
mutante (mi).
medal, nsalamu (n).
mediator, ndubulwila (ba–).
medicine, muti (mi); ndawa (n).
medicine-man, shinanga
(ba–).
meek, –temba (tembele);
–nakilila (nakilile).
meekness, mutembo.
meet, v.i. –kumana (kumêne); –monana (mo-
nêne); v.t. –kumanya
(kumenye). *fail to meet,*
–pusa (pushile. *go to
meet,* –konkela (konke-
lele).
meeting, cilonganino (fi).
melancholy, cintefwila; bu-

landa.

melt, v.t. –sungulula (sungulwîle). v. stat. –sungululuka (sungulwîke).

memorial, ca cibukisho (fya).

memory, cibukisho.

menace, –pangila (pangile): *he menaced to kill me,* ampangila ukunjipaya.

mend, wamya (wemye): –menda (mendele). *mend iron things,* –lungisha (lungishe). – *clothings,* –tútula (tútwîle).

menstruation, have –, –ba ku mweshi. *first* –, cisungu; *have* –, –wa cisungu (wîle).

mention, –eba (ebele): *I – it to him,* ndemwebo mulandu. *don't – it,* te mulandu.

marchant, kashitisha (ba–).

merciful, wa luse. *be merciful,* –ba no luse.

mercy, luse. *have mercy,* –belelo luse: *have – on me,* mumbele leko luse.

merely, fye.

merit, v.t. 1. (gain), –kwîla (kwilile). 2. (deserve), –fwile: *he merits to be praised,* afwile bamutasha.

merry, –sansamuka (sansamwîke).

mess, cimfulunganya: *what a mess,* te pa cimfulunganya.

message, mashiwi: mbila. *I have a message,* ndi na mashiwi.

messenger, mashinjela (ba–); kapaso (ba–); nkombe (n).

metal, cêla (fy).

method, musango (mi).

midday, kasuba pakati.

middle, pakati. *in the middle of,* pakati ka.

midnight, bushiku pakati.

midwife, nacimbusa (ba–).

migrate, –kúka (kúkile).

mild (kind,) wa cikúku; wa cilela.

mildness, cikúku; cilela.

mile, mailoshi (ba–).

milk, 1. n. mukaka. 2. v.t. –kame shiba (kamine).

milky way, cipinda bushiku.

mill, 1. n. cikayo (fi). 2. v.t. –kaya (kaile).

millet, male. *germinated* –, mumena (mi). – *of last year,* male ya comba. – *field,* bukula (ma); *old* –, cifwani (fi).

mince, –kaya (kaile); –pela (pelele).

mind, 1. n. mâno. 2. v.t. (care about), –sakamana (sakamêne). 3. interj. lelo! *don't mind,* te mulandu; mwisakamana. *keep in* – –sunga 'mu mutima (sungile). *change* –, aluka (alwîke); –futuka (futwîke).

mine, n. mukôti (mi). *mines in Zambia and Rhodesia,* kalâle.

mine, pers. pr. ...andi: *it is mine,* candi.

mingle, v.t. 1. (different things), –sakanya (sakenye); –tobenkanya (tobenkenye). v.i. –sakâna (sakêne); tobenkana (tobenkene). 2. (same things), –sansha (sanshi she): *mix beans with other beans,* sansha cilemba na cilemba mubive.

miracle, cisungusho (fi); cipesha mâno (fi).

mirror, mulolani (mi);

cilola (fi).
misbehave, –pusauka (pusawike).
misbehaviour, kupusauka.
miscarry, –pòse fumo (pò-
sele); –pulumune fumo.
mischievous, –belebensa
(belebensele).
miser, mutani (ba); wa
butani (ba); mupapa (ba).
misery, bulanda.
misfortune, ishâmo (ma).
mislay, –lufya (lufishe).
miss, v.t. 1. (fail to catch),
–panya (panishe). 2. (fail
to meet), –pusa (pushile).
missing, –bulila (bulile);
–shala (shele): there is
something –, pabulila or
kwashala.
mist, fubefube.
mistake, 1. n. cilubo (fi).
2. v.t. –lêbela (lêbele):
you – me for another,
mwandêbela. be mistaken,
–luba (lubile).
mix, cf. mingle, blend.
mix-up, n. cimfundawila.
moan, –teta (tetele).
mob, ibungwe (ma).
mock, –seka (sekele);
–wêla (wêlele).
model, cilangililo (fi).
moderate, 1. v.i. –naka
(nakile). 2. v.t. –nasha
(nashishe).
modern, ...pya; ...nomba.
moist, –bomba (bombele).
moisten, –bomfya (bomfe-
she).
moisture, mutonshi.
mole, mfuko (m).
molest, –pamfya (pamfi-
she); –afya (afishe);
–cûsha (cûshishe).
moment, kashita (tu): wait
a moment, linda panôno.
at this moment, nombaline;

ndakai. not at this –, nomba telyo; te homba iyo.
at that –, lilya line.
Monday, muli Cimo; pali
Cimo.
money, lupiya (mpiya); ndalama (n).
mongoose, ipulu (ma).
monition, mashiwi: listen to
my monition, muleumfwa
mashiwi yandi.
monitor (kind of lizard),
mbulu (m).
monkey, kolwe (ba–). blue
–, nsange (ba–).
monster, cingulungulu (fi).
month, mweshi (my).
monthly, cîla mweshi.
moody, –fuka (fukile).
moon, mweshi. full moon,
mweshi waba uwashingu-
luka; cibosa-nkulungwe.
new –, mweshi wamoneka;
cipâpa ca mweshi.
more, 1. v.i. –cila (cilile):
it is –, cacilapo. 2. adv.
ukucila. all the –, nakanga;
nakansha; pali bufi. moreover, kabili.
morning, lucèlo; also in
the morning.
morrow, bushiku bwako-
nka.
mortal, 1. (of man), mwina
kufwa (bena –). 2. (of
things) cina kufwa (fi).
mortar, 1. (for pounding),
ibende (ma); cinkolobo-
ndo (fi). 2. (for building),
ndaka. make – (for build-
ing), –kande ndâka (ka-
ndile).
mosquito, muŋwiŋwi (ba–).
– net, candaluwa (fy).
most, ...ingi cikanga
...onse: most people, ba-
ntu bengi cikanga bonse.
mostly, miku ingi fye; ci-

kanga pe.

mother, cf. T. V. *mother of twins,* nampundu (ba–).

mother-in-law, cf. T. V.

motorcar, motoka (ba–).

motorcycle, mpumpumpu (ba–).

motorcar road, musebo wa motoka (mi).

mould, 1. n. cikombola (fi). **2.** v.t. bumba (bumbile).

moulder, nakabumba (ba–).

mouldy, –fufuma (fufwime).

mound (round), luputa (m); (long), molwa (ba–). *level* –, –pase mputa or molwa (pashile).

mount, –nina (ninine).

mountain lupili (m). *mountain chain,* mpili.

mourn, –lôsha (loseshe); –lile misowa (lilile).

mournful, –languluka (langulwike).

mourning, musôwa (mi). *person in* –, mfwilwa (m).

mouse, mpuku (m). *– with a bushy tail,* sekeseke (ba–).

moustache, mwefu (my).

mouth, kanwa (tu). *open* –, –asama (aseme). *shut* –, –isala kanwa (isele).

move, v.t. –sesha (seseshe); v.i. –sela (selele). (put out of way), v.t. –cingula (cingwile); –talusha (talwishe). v.i. cf. go aside. *move over,* (nearer or further). v.t. –sengelesha (sengeleshe); v.i. –sengelela (sengelele). *move on,* –enda (endele).

movies, shinema (ba–).

much, 1. adj. ...ingi. *be much,* –fula (fulile). **2.** adv. sâna; pakalamba. *very*

much, sâna sâna; sâna fye; cibi; nganshi. *how much,* **1.** inter. pr. ...nga? **2.** adv. ifyo (in what degree). *as much as,* **1.** (comparison), –lingâna; pamo nga: *I am as poor as you,* twalingâna mu bulanda, or ndi mulanda pamo nga iwe. **2.** adv. apo. *take as much as you like,* bùla apo utemenwe.

mud, 1. n. matipa; iloba (ma). **2.** v.t. –masa (mashile): *mud the wall,* masa cibumba.

muddle, –fulunganya (fulungenye). *muddle up a case,* –lufyanyo mulandu (lufyenye). *muddle up water,* –fundawila menshi (fundawile).

muddy, –fundauka (fundawike): *the water is* –, menshi nayafundauka.

multiply, 1. (increase), –fusha (fushishe); **2.** (math.), –mikula (mikwile).

mumble, –ŋwiŋwinsa (ŋwiŋwinshile).

mump, (sullen), v.i. –fûka (fûkile).

mumps, sakatila.

munch, –sheta (shetele).

murder, musoka (mi).

murderer, wa misoka (ba); cipondo (fi).

murmur, –isosha (isoseshe); –ilishanya (ilishenye).

muscle, munofu (mi).

mush, bwâli. *heat water for making* –, –têkapo bwali (têkelepo). *make* –, –nayo bwali (naile). *eat – with relish,* –tobelo bwali (tobele). *eat – without relish,*

-kutula (kutwile).

mushroom, bôwa. *different
kinds of mushroom*, môwa.
must, –ba na: *you must go*,
muli no kuya. It can also
be translated with the –le
tense: *you must go*, muleya.
mute, cf. dumb & hoarse.
mutilate, –têta makunkutu
(têtele).
mutilated person, wa makunkutu (ba).
my, ...andi: *my book*, citabo candi.
myself, ne mwine.
mystery, bwile, cipesha mano.

— N —

nail, 1. n. musomali (mi);
lusunga (n). 2. v.t.
–pampaminako musomali
(pampamineko). *finger –*,
lwala (ngala).
naked, bwamba; also nakedness. *be –*, –ba bwamba.
name, 1. n. ishina (ma).
v.t. (give a –), –inike
shina (inike). *name given
at birth*, ishina lya mutoto.
*Mr./Miss/Mrs. what's his/
her name*, kampanda
(ba–); ntwanikane (ba–);
ntweno (ba–). *use bad
names*, –tuke nsele (tukile).
name, 2. v.t. (mention),
–lumbula (lumbwile).
nap, –shipula (shipwile).
nape, ikoshi (ma).
napkin, citambala (fi).
narrate, –shimika (shimike); –shimikila (shimi-
kile).

narrow, –ipipa (ipipe).
nasty, ...bi; –bîpa (bîpile).
nation, mushobo (mi).
native, mukaya (ba).
nausea, musêlu.
navel, mutoto (mi).
near, adv. & prep, pêpi;
mupêpi. *near to*, pêpi or
mupêpi na ku.
nearby, mu mbali; lubali
lwa.
nearly, ni cikanga; –pana
(pene): *he nearly died*,
nicikanga afwe or apene
afwe.
neat (person), ...busaka;
(place), –fûtuka (fûtwi-
ke).
neatly, busaka busaka.
neatness, busaka.
necessary, –fwaikwa (fwaikwe): *what is necessary
to*, icifwaikwa ku...
neck, mukoshi (mi).
need, 1. cf. necessary. 2. cf.
must. 3. (be in need),
–bula (bulile); –kabila
(kabile); –pamfiwa (pa-
mfiwe). *I am in need of
money*, nabule or nakabile
ndalama or nimpamfiwa
ukumone ndalama.
needle, nshindano (n);
kêla (twêla).
neglect, –lekelesha (lekeleshe); –pôsa (pôsele).
negligence, busanku; mulêle.
negligent, –ba no busanku;
wa mulêle.
neighbour, mwina mupalamano.
neither ... nor, nangu ... nangu; nelyo ... nelyo.
nerve, lushipa (n).
nephew, mwipwa mwaume
(bêpwa baume).
nest, cisansâla (fi).

net, isumbu (ma). *make a net,* –pike sumbu (pikile). *set –,* –tea masumbu (têle). *remove net.* –andula masumbu (andwile). *mosquito –,* candaluwa (fy).

never, nangu limo: *he never came,* taishile nangu limo; it can also be translated with the aux. v. –tala (lalile): *I have never seen a lion,* nshatala njimone nkalamo.

nevertheless, nge fyo.

new, . . .pya.

next, –konkapo (konkelepo).

nib, nibu (ba–).

nice, suma. *be nice,* –wama (weme).

nicely, bwino. *very nicely,* bwino bwino.

niece, mwipwa mwanakashi (bêpwa banakashi).

night, bushiku (n). *midnight,* bushiku pakati.

night-blindness, kafîfi.

nightfall, bwaila.

nightjar, lumbâsa (ba–).

no, iyô.

noble, . . .kankala. *be noble,* –cindama (cindeme).

nobody, nangu umo.

noise, congo. *what a noise,* te pa congo! *stop making noise,* interj. congo; leke congo (lekeni); talala (talalêni)!

noisy, . . .congo. *be noisy,* kafya (kafishe).

nominate, –sonta (sontele).

none, nangu . . .mo. *none who could,* nangu umo wa kuti.

nonsense, 1. n. cilandelande. 2. interj. abwe! *talk nonsense,* –landa cilandelande (landile); –sabaila (saba-

ile).

noon, kasuba pakati.

north, kapinda ka ku kuso.

nose, môna (myona); also *nostrils.* blow the nose, –fyona (fyonene). *speak through the –,* –sosela mu myona (sosele).

not. 1. (with verb), shi; ta. cf. T. II, 2. 2. (with rel. pr.), shi; sha. cf T. IV, Note 2. *it is not,* te. cf. 'not' with pers. pr. T. II, 1, & with dem. pr. T. III.

not at all, interj. nakalya; alai; awi se.

not a little, nangu panono; nelyo panono.

notch, 1. n. ifwa (ma); lukomo (n). 2. v.t. –ceka (cekele). *notch tree to show the trail,* –komo lukomo (komene).

note, 1. n. (sign), cishibilo (fi). 2. v.t. cf. pay attention to; notice; write; observe.

nothing, nangu cimo; nelyo cimo. *there is nothing that could,* takuli ca kuti. *there is nothing left,* takuli.

notice, 1. n. cishibisho (fi). v.t. (give notice), –ishibisha (ishibishe); –eba libêla (ebele). cf. also perceive.

notify, cf. make known; report; inform; give notice.

notwithstanding, nelyo.

not yet, it is expressed by the ta-la-a tense: *he has not yet arrived,* talaisa na nomba.

nought, shifulu.

nourish, cf. feed.

nourishment, cakulya (fy).

November, Cinshikubili;

mwanganamfula.

now, nomba. *just now*, nombaline; ndakai; apo pêne. *up to now*, ukufika nomba.

nowadays, shino nshiku; mu nshita ya nomba; muno nshiku.

nowhere, nangu kumo.

nude, cf. naked.

number, 1. n. ipendo (ma). 2. v.t. –penda (pendele). *in such a number*, filya. *in great –*, fumfwe; cinkupiti. *in small –*, mpendwa.

numerous, . . . ingi; –sêka (sêkele); –fula (fulile).

nurse, 1. n. kasunga (ba–); muleshi (ba). 2. v.t. –tênsha (tênseshe).

nut, lubalala (m).

— O —

oar, nkafi (n).

oath, cilapo (fi); mulapo (mi). *take an oath*, –lape cilapo (lapile). *oath breaking*, –onaule cilapo (onawile).

obedience, bupete; cumfwîla; kubêla.

obey, –bêla (bêlele); –konka mashiwi (konkele).

object, 1. n. cf. thing; cf. purpose. 2. v.i. –bîkapo fikansa (bîkilepo).

obligation, 1. n. cf. duty; cf. agreement. *be under an –*, –patikwa (patikwe); –kakwa (kakilwe); cf. must. *put under an –*, –patika (patike).

oblige, –patika (patîke).

obliging, –nakilila (nakilile); –petama (peteme).

obscene, cf. bad.

obscure cf. dark.

obscurity, cf. darkness.

observe, 1. cf. obey; 2. cf. see. 3. cf. examine; 4. cf. say.

obstacle, cilesha (fi). *raise an –*, cilinganya (cilingenye).

obstinate, –koso mutwe (kosele).

obtain, cf. get; cf. gain.

occasion, nshita: *if I have –*, nga namone nshita. *on that –*, mu nshita lilya.

occasionally, mu nshita mu nshita.

occur, –fikila (fikile): *it occured*, cafikile.

ocean, bemba mukalamba (ba–).

October, Lusuba lukalamba.

odour, cinunshi; cinunko; cena (fy).

of, prep, cf. T. I.

off, 1. adv. it is translated with the verb, cf. break off; cut off; fall off; go off; shake off. 2. prep. ukufuma ku: *2 km off the town*, bakilo mita babili ukufuma ku musumba. *be off duty*, –tûsha (tûshishe).

offence, (disrespect), musâlula (mi); misûla.

offend, cf. contempt. *offend against*, –pulamo (pulilemo).

offer, 1. (– a sacrifice), –tûle cita (tûlile). 2. (give), –pêla (pêle).

offering, cita (fita).

office, ofishi (ma–).

often, libili libili; miku ingi; ilingi; miku ne miku. *how often?* miku inga? linga?

oh, interj. yangu.

oil, 1. n. mafuta. 2. v.t. –suba mafuta (subile).

old, ... kote; –kota (kotele): *you are old,* muli bakote or namukota. *how old are you?* muli ne myaka inga? *old person,* mukote (ba); mukoloci (ba).

omen, (good), malyo; (bad), mupamba (mi).. *meet with a bad* –, –tôlo mupamba (tôlele).

omit, –leka (lekele).

on, pa or pali.

once, 1. (one time), muku umo; limo. 2. (formerly), kale. – *and again,* miku imo imo. *at* –, apo pêne; nombaline; ndakai. – *for all,* muku umo fye. – *in a while,* limolimo. – *more,* kabili; nakabili. – *upon a time,* 1. (formerly), kale. 2. (for opening a story), patile akantu.

one, num. ...mo; muntu (someone): *one says,* muntu asosa. – *after another* or *one by one,* ...mo ...mo: *come* –, isêni umo umo. – *another,* cf. reciprocal extension in grammar. *one, another,* ...mo, ...mbi: *one says this, another that,* umo asose fi, umbi asose fyo.

oneself, mwine (bêne).

onions, kanyense (tu).

only, fye. cf. alone. *only if,* kano.

ooze, –sûma (sûmine).

open, v.t. –isula (iswile): *open the door,* isulêniko cibi. *be open,* –isuka (iswîke): *the door is* –, cibi caisuka. *be wide open,* 1. v.i. –cenama (ceneme). 2. adv. buse-nême. – *the mouth,* –asama (aseme). – *a book,* –kupukule citabo (kupukwîle). – *the eyes,* –lolesha (loleshe). – *up a hole,* –cilula (cilwile). *in the* –, pa kasuba.

opening, kanwa (tu).

openly, pa menso ya bonse.

operate, –tumbula (tumbwîle).

opinion, what is your –, muleti shani pa; cili shani kuli imwe. *be of the same opinion,* –wila kumo (wilile).

opportunity, nshita.

oppose, –kânya (kênye).

or, atemwa.

orally, ku kanwa.

orange, icungwa (ma). *wild orange like fruit,* linkolobwe (ma).

order, 1. n. (neatness), busaka. *put in* –, –wamya (wemye); –bîko busaka (bikile). *be out of order,* –fwa (fwile): *the clock is out of* –, nkoloko naifwa.

order, 2. n. (law), cebo (fy). *give an* –, –pêle cebo (pêle).

order, 3. n. (row), mulongo (mi). *set in* –, –tantika (tantike).

order, 4. v.t. (buy), –shita (shitile). *in order to,* cj. pakuti.

orderly, kasunga (ba–); muleshi (ba).

ordinary, fye; e filyako: – *days,* nshiku sha fye. *he is an* – *worker,* alabomba e filyako.

oribi (small gazelle), kasele (tu).

orient, kabanga.

origin, cishinte (fi).

originate, –tula (tulile);
–fuma (fumine).
ornament, cisâmo (fi).
orphan, kashîmo (ba–).
other, ...mbi.
otherwise, atemwa. (in
another way), musango
umbi.
otter, mukobe (mi). (a big
kind), mumpanda (ba–).
ought, –fwile: *he – to obey,*
afwile ukubêla.
our, ...êsu.
ourselves, ifwe bêne or
fwe bêne.
out, 1. adv. kunse or panse.
2. interj. kunse! panse!
go out, –ya panse: *he went
out,* aya panse. (of fire),
–shima (shimine): *the fire
goes out,* mulilo washima.
be out, is translated by
neg. of –ba: *he is out,*
talipo, lit. *he is not here.*
keep out, –sha kunse.
out of, prep. ku or kuli.
come out of, –fuma ku.
outdo, –cisha (cishishe).
outrun, –tanga (tangile).
outside, panse; kunse.
outwit, –cenjesha (cenje-
she).
over, pa mûlu wa. *over the
tree,* pa mûlu wa muti.
overburden, –finya (fini-
she).
overcome, –ansha (anshi-
she); –cimfya (cimfishe).
overhaul, –sangule (cintu)
cipya (sangwile).
overflow, –pôsa (pôsele):
the river overflows, mumana walipôsa.
overhear, –pula mashiwi
(pulile).
overlook, –laba (labila).
over again, cipya cipya.
over there, kulya; palya.

owe, –ba ne misha: *you
owe me,* muli ne misha
kuli ine.
owl, cipululu (fi). *barn
owl,* swelele (ba–).
own, –kwata (kete). *out of
his own,* ku maka yakwe;
pa mutwe wakwe.
owner, mwine (bêne): *the
owner of the book,* mwine
citabo.
oyster, lwili (njili).
ox, mutungu (ba–).

— P —

pace, n. lutampulo (n).
pack, 1. n. cifunda (fi).
2. v.t. (– luggage), –longe
fipe (longele); (put in),
–paka (pakile): *put the
millet in the bag,* paka
male mu mufuko.
packet, cifunda (fi). *empty
packet,* cifwambo (fi).
pact, cumfwano (fy).
paddle, 1. n. nkafi (n).
2. v.t. –shîko bwato (shîkile).
pagan, musenshi (ba).
paganism, cisenshi.
page of a king, kalume wa
mfumu (ba–). *page of a
book,* ibûla (ma).
pail, mbeketi (ma–).
pain, 1. n. bukali (physical);
bucushi; bulanda (moral).
2. v.t. –kalipa (kalipe);
–tanta (tantile). cf. hurt.
afflict pain, –cûsha (cûshishe). *cause sharp pain,*
–soma (somene).
painful, cf. pain, v.i.
paint, 1. n. ilangi (ma)
2. v.t. –lenga (lengele).
paint in different colours,

-balâlika (balâlike).

painter, kalenga (ba-).

pair, ...bili: *a pair of shoes*, nsapato shibili.

palate, camfu (fy).

pallet, mwiko (mìko).

palm (of hand), lupi (ndupi).

palmtree, some kinds are: cibale (fi); kambili (tu); kancindu (tu); kakoma (tu).

palpitate, -tunta (tuntile).

pan, pani (ma-).

pant, -asâsa (asâshile); -pemekêsa (pemekêse).

papacy, bupâpa.

paper, ipêpala (ma).

parable, ipinda (ma). *tell a parable*, -ume pinda (umine).

parallel, -lungatana (lungatêne). *make* -, lungatanika (lungatanike).

paralysed, -lemana (lemene).

paralysis, bulebe.

parcel, cifunda (fi).

pardon, 1. n. luse. 2. v.t. -belelo luse (belele): *I ask your pardon*, napapata mumbelelê uluse.

parent, mufyashi (ba).

parenthood, bufyashi.

parents-in-law, buko (ma).

parrot, (small kind), mucence (ba-); (big kind), icela mpundu (ma).

part, 1. n. cipande (fi); cipandwa (fi). 2. v.t. cf. divide. (leave one another). -lekana (lekene).

partial, -ba no mucisha cinani.

partiality, mucisha cinani.

particularly, pali bufi; nakansha.

partition in a house, mupu-

tule (mi).

partly...partly, lubali... lubali.

pass, -pita (pitile). *pass away*, cf. die. *pass blood*, -sundo mulopa (sundile). - *by*, -pita (pitile). - *round*, -sengeleshanya (sengeleshenye). - *water*, -sunda (sundile).

passion, bucûshi (ma).

passport, pasu (ma-).

past, 1. adj. ...kale. *in the past*, mu nshita ya kale. 2. prep. (later) papita; ku numa or ku ntanshi: *two days past*, papite nshiku shibili; ku numa (or ku ntanshi) ya nshiku shibili.

paste, musunga.

pastime, mulesha citendwe.

patch, 1. n. cikamba (fi). 2. v.t. -bîkapo cikamba (bîkilepo).

path, nshila (n). *small path*, nshila ya tondo. - *made by game*, mukondo (mi). *make out a - for those who follow*, -sake nshila (sakile).

patience, 1. (endurance of pain), kushipikisha mu kucûla. 2. cf. perseverance.

patient (bear pain), -shipikisha mu kucûla (shipikishe). 2. cf. persevere.

patrol, fita. *send patrols*, -soke fita (sokele).

pave, -kubatila (kubatile).

paw, lukasa (ma).

pawpaw, ipapao (ma).

pay, 1. n. malipilo. 2. v.t. -lipila (lipile). *receive* -, -fole mpiya (folele); -lipilwa (lipilwe).

pea, ntongwe. *ground pea*, lutoyo (n). *dig out pea*, -fuke ntoyo (fukile).

peanut, lubalala (m). *peanut butter,* cikonko. *make sauce with peanuts,* –sashile ntwîlo (sashile).

peace, cibote.

peaceful, –talala (talele).

peck, –sompa (sompele); –kompa (kompele); –soba (sobele).

peculiar, –belebensa (belebensele).

pedal, 1. n. cinyantilo ca ncinga (fi). 2. v.t. –cofa (cofeshe).

peel, –pala (palile).

peep, –lengela (lengele).

peer, –bêbêta (bêbête).

peg, 1. n. lupôpo (m). 2. v.t. –ikasha ne mpôpo (ikeshe).

pell-mell, cimfulunganya; cintobentobe.

pen, nibu (ba–).

penalty, mafuto; kupanikwa; kukalipilwa.

penance, mafuto. *do penance,* –futa pa mulandu (futile). *sacrament of –,* nsakalamenta ya cilapilo; cilumbulo.

pencil, pensulo (ba–). *slate pencil,* côko wa seleti (ba–).

penetrate, –ingila (ingile).

penny, peni (ba–); ikôbili (ma); ipesa (ma).

people, bantu. *people of* (a contry or clan, etc.), mwina (bêna): *the people of Makasa,* bêna Makasa.

pepper, mpilipili.

perceive, –umfwa (mfwîle). –mona (mwene).

perfect, (complete), ...tuntulu; (nice), ...suma sâna; –wama sâna; –ba ...pwililika.

perfection, bukumanisho.

perforate, –tulaula (tula-

wile); –pongola (pongwele). v. stat. –pongoka (pongweke).

perhaps, nalimo; nakalimo; nampo nga.

period, nshita.

perish, –onaika (onaike); –fwa (fwile).

perjury, cilapo ca bufi. (fi). *commit perjury,* –lapo bufi (lapile).

permission, lusa. *ask permission,* –lombo lusa (lombele). *give –,* –pêlo lusa (pêle); –suminisha (suminishe). *obtain permission,* –poko lusa (pokele).

perpetual, ...pe; –belêlela (belêlêle).

persecute, –cûsha (cûshishe).

perseverance, mute; mukubi.

perseverantly, mute mute.

persevere, –shipikisha (shipikishe).

person, mwine (bêne); cf. also people.

perspiration, ibe (mabe).

perspire, –piba mabe (pibile).

persuade, –cimfya (cimfishe).

pester, –pamfya (pamfishe); –pimpila (pimpile).

pestle, mwinshi (mî).

perversity, bupulumushi; bulungani.

pet, –tentemba (tentembe); –tekelesha (tekeleshe).

petrol, petulo.

photograph, 1. n. cikope (fi). 2. v.t. –kopa (kopele).

piano, cinanda (fi). *play piano,* –lishe cinanda (lishishe).

pick, 1. n. cimbo (fi). 2. v.t. –swa (swile); –saba (sabile). – *up,* –tôla (tôlele);

–sompa (sompele).

picture, nsalamu (n); pikicala (ma–).

piece, cipande (fi); cipandwa (fi).

pierce, –tula (tulile). v. stat. –tulika (tulike); –cima (cimine).

pig (domestic), nkumba (n); (wild), kapôli (ba–); ngulube (n).

pigeon, nkunda (n).

pigmy, kantele mafwasa (tu).

pile, 1. n. mwina (mîna). 2. v.t. –tûlika (tûlike).

pillar, luceshi (n).

pillow, musao (mi). *rest head on pillow,* –sailo mutwe pa musao (saile).

pilot, n. 1. namutekenya (ba–). 2. v.t. –tekenya (tekenye).

pimple, lufine (m); kapumba (tu).

pincers, lumano (mano).

pinch, –shina (shinine); –fenenkesha (fenenkeshe).

pineapple, cinanashi (fi).

pioneer, solwesolwe (ba–).

pipe, paipi (ma–). *pipe made from a calabash,* cinkuli (fi).

pit, mukanda (mi). *game pit,* bucinga (ma).

pity, 1. n. luse. 2. v.t. –kwato luse (kwete); –ba no luse; –languluka (langulwike). v. appl. –langulukila (langulukile). *have pity and help,* –sengulwila (sengulwile).

place, 1. n. ncende. *– where roads part* masansa. *– where branches were cut for gardening,* citemene (fi). *– where things of any kind meet,* bukumanino. *–*

where bushfire passed, mupya (mi). *appointed – of meeting,* makumanino. *at this –,* pano pêne. *in the – of,* pa mâlo ya. *on two places,* pabili. *sleeping* or *camping – on journey,* ndo (ndo); bulo (malo).

place, 2. v.t. (put), –bîka (bîkile); –têka (têkele). *place high up,* –sâmika (sâmîke). *make –,* v.i. –sèla (sèlele); v.t. –sesha (seseshe). *take the place of,* –selela pali (selele); –ikala pa malo ya (ikele). *change place,* –teluka (telwike).

plague, cikuko (fi).

plain, 1. n. nika (n). 2. adj. cf. be even & flat.

plait, 1. n. citabataba (fi). 2. v.t. –luke citabataba (lukile).

plan, v.i. –panga (pangile); –tontonkanya (tontonkenye).

plane, v.t. –bâsa (bâshile); –pala (palile); –engula (engwile). *aeroplane,* ndeke (n).

plank, ipulanga (ma); itâbwa (ma); mbao (m).

plant, 1. n. câni (fy). *plant for making fishpoison,* buba.

plant, 2. v.t. –byala (byele).

plaster, v.t. –masa (mashile). *take plaster away,* –masula (maswile).

plate, mbale (m).

platform, cintamba (fi). *– for smoking meat/fish,* bulambo (ma). *– above fireplace,* lwino (nyino).

play, 1. n. cangalo (fy). 2. v.t. –angala (angele). *play a musical instrument,*

-lisha (lishishe). – *cards,* -teye njuka (têle). – *football,* -to mupila (tele). – *with something,* -angasha (angeshe).

plead guilty, -sumina (sumine).

please, 1. v.t. -sansamusha (sansamwishe). 2. interj. napapâta. *be pleased,* -temwa (temenwe): *are you pleased,* bushe mwatemwa?

pleasure, nsansa. *much –,* nsansa shingi.

pleasant, ... suma; -wama (weme).

plenty, 1. n. bwingi. 2. adj. ... ingi. 3. *be plenty,* -fula (fulile).

pleurisy, kabali.

pliable, -kondenkana (kondenkene). v. caus. -kondekanya (kondekenye).

pliers, lumano (mano).

plough, 1. n. lukasu lwa ŋombe. 2. v.t. -lima ne ŋombe (limine).

pluck (fruits), -saba (sabile); -swa (swile); (feathers), -sesa (sesele).. *pluck out,* cf. pull out.

plug, v.t. -cilika (cilike).

plum, lufungo (m).

plunder, -tapa (tapile) (fyuma).

plunge, v.t. -tumpa (tumpile); v.i. -ibila (ibile).

pneumonia, kabali.

pocket, itumba (ma).

point (sharpen), -songola (songwele). v. stat. -songoka (songweke). *point out,* -sonta (sontele). *be on the – of,* -ba mu or pa; -swa: *he is on the – of dying,* ali pa (or mu) kufwa; alaswa afwe.

poison, busungu; cinkolwankolwa (fi). – *put in food or drink,* bwanga. – *used in trials,* mwafi.

poisonous, -ba no busungu.

pole, cilu (fi); cimuti (fi). *tentpole,* mulongoti (mi).

police, polishi (ba-).

polish, -pukuta (pukwite); -pukusa (pukwise); -pûpûta (pûpûtile).

polite, -fûka (fûkile); -lango mucinshi (langile).

politeness, mucinshi.

pollen, muluba (mi).

pollute, -lamfya (lamfishe).

polygamist, wa mpali (ba). *become a –,* -palika (palike); upe mpali.

polygamy, mpali.

pond, cishiba (fi).

pool, same as pond.

poor ... landa. *poor person,* mulanda (ba); mupîna (ba).

pop off (as a cork), -fyontoka (fyontwêke).

Pope, Pâpa (ba-).

porcupine, cinungi (fi).

porridge, musunga. *make –,* -kumbo musunga (kumbile).

port, câbu (fy).

portion out, -akanya (akênye).

possess, -kwata (kwete). *be possessed,* -wilwa ku (wililwe); -obelwa (obelelwe). *possessed person,* ngulu (n).

possible, kuti: *it is – that he is coming,* kuti aisa.

possibly, nalimo; nakalimo.

post, v.t. -poshita (poshite): *go and post the letter,* kaposhite kalata.

poster, cipampila (fi).

postpone, cf. defer.

pot (iron –), mupika (mi). (clay – for cooking), nongo (n); (for keeping water), mutondo (mi); (small clay –), kapalwilo (tu); kanweno (tu).

potash. fishikisa. *potash for snuff,* nungo (n).

potato, cilashi (fi). *sweet potato,* cumbu (fy). *pieces of dried potato,* nsemwa (n).

potter (woman), nakabumba (ba–).

pound, 1. n. (money and weight), paundi (ba–). 2. v.t. twa (twile); –ponda (pondele).

pour out (liquid), –itila (itile); (solid), –fukumuna (fukumwine).

poverty, bulanda; bupîna.

powder, bunga. *crush to powder,* –shona (shonene); –shina (shinine). *red* –, nkula. *gun powder,* maluti.

power, maka. *be beyond one's* –, –ansha (anshishe): *it is beyond my power,* canyansha.

praise, 1. n. malumbo. 2. v.t. –lumba (lumbile); –tasha (tashishe).

pray, –sálika (sálike). v. appl. –sálikila (sálikile); v. rec. –sálikishanya (sálikishenye). pepa (pepele); ipepo.

prayer, isáli (ma).

praying mantis, kakonkote (tu).

preach, –funda (fundile).

precede (in rank), –cilila (cilile); (go in front), –tangila (tangile).

precept, cebo (fy).

precious, ca mutengo·

precipitous, –lundumana (lundumene).

precise, –ba bwino.

predecessor, mutanshi (ba).

prefer, –temwapo ukucila (temenwepo); –temwisha (temwishe).

preference, show –, –sôbolola (sôbolwele); give –, cishanya (cishenye).

pregnancy, ifumo. *advanced* –, ifumo lyakula; *be in* –, –ba pa bukulu.

pregnant, –ba ne fumo. imita (imite). *render* –, –imisha (imishe).

preliminary, ... ntanshi. *preliminary notes,* ishiwi lya ntanshi.

prepare, –pekanya (pekenye). v. appl. –pekanisha (pekanishe). – *in advance,* –teya (têle).

prescribe (order), pêle cêbo (pêle); –eba (ebele).

presence, in –of, pa menso ya.

present, 1. n. (gift), bupe. (time), nshita ya nomba. *make a present,* –leko bupe (lekele). *at present, mu* nshita ya nomba.

present, 2. v.i. –sangwako (sangilweko): *I am* –, intrj. kalombo; epo ndi; mukwai; kwaita.

presently, nombaline; apo pêne; ndakai.

president, katungulula (ba–); mukalamba (ba); katêka (ba–).

press against, –tininkisha (tininkishe). – *in,* –shindaila (shindaile). – *out,* –tina (tinine).

pretence, malêle: *he is late under some, –,* acelwa mu malêle.

pretend, –cila nga: *he pretends to sleep,* acita ngo ulelâla.

pretext, mambepa.

pretty, ...suma. *be pretty,* –wama (weme). *make –,* –waminisha (waminishe); –wamya (wemye).

prevent, –lesha (leseshe) – *from work,* –fufyo mulimo (fufishe).

previous, ... ntanshi.

price, mutengo (mi). *fix a price,* –pango mutengo (pangile). *lower the price,* –nasho mutengo (nashishe). *raise the –,* –niniko mutengo (ninike), also –kosho (koseshe) or –umyo (umishe) mutengo. *what is the –,* umutengo ni shani? *it is of moderate price,* umutengo wanaka. *it is expensive,* mutengo wakosa.

pride, cilumba.

priest, mupatili (ba); shimapepo (ba–).

priesthood, bupatilisho; bushimapepo.

prison, cifungo (fi).

prisoner, nkole (ba–); *make a prisoner,* –ikata (ikete).

privilege, bukata.

probably, cf. perhaps.

proclamation, mbila. *make a –,* bile mbîla (bilile).

produce, cf. grow, v.t.; cause, v.t.

profession, ncito (n); mulimo (mi).

profit, make –, –mwenamo (mwenenemo): *he made a good profit,* amwenenemo ndalama shingi.

profusely, busa.

prohibit, cf. forbid.

progress, buyantanshi.

prolific. –sanda (sandile).

promise, 1. n. cilayo (fi). *mutual promise,* cilayano (fi). *break a –,* –onaule cilayo (onawile).

promise, 2. v.t. –laya (laile).

pronounce, –lumbula (lumbwile). *pronounce distinctly,* –lumbwisha (lumbwishe); –sosesha (soseshe). *pronounce indistinctly)* –sosela mu masaya (sosele). *pronounce incorrectly,* –benda (bendele).

proof, cishinino (fi).

prophesy (as an evoker of spirits), –sesema (seseme); –sobela (sobele).

prophet, kasobela (ba–); munabii (ba); kasesema (ba–).

prosperity, bukankala.

prosperous, –ba mukankala.

prostitute, kêtwa (ba–); iule (maule).

protect, –sunga (sungile); –bîka ku mubili (bîkile). *– crops from animals or birds,* –amina (amîne). *– against sun or wind* etc. –cinga (cingile).

protector, mwiminishi (bêminishi).

prove, –shininkisha (shininkishe). *prove guilty,* –shinina (shinine).

proverb, ipinda (ma). *tell a –,* –ume pinda (umine).

provide, –fwaila (fwaile): *could you provide me with the following goods...,* kuti mwamfwaile fintu ifi... 2. cf. prepare.

provided that, cikulu; kumfwa; kulila: *provided that you do this work,* cikulu/kumfwa/kulila mulebombe ncito ii.

provocation, lubuli.

provocative, ... lubuli·

provoke, –tendeka (tendeke); –busho lubuli (bushishe).

provokingly, lubuli lubuli.

pseudo, wa bufi (ba).

public, ... bonse. *public holiday,* holiday wa bonse or bushiku bwa kutusha kuli bonse.

publish (news), –salanganya mashiwi (salangenye). (– a secret), –alasha fya nkâma (aleshe); –sokolola fya nkâma (sokolwele).

pudding, pudingi.

pull, –tinta (tintile); –kula (kulile). *pull down,* –toba (tobele). *pull off* (leaves), –pululula (pululwîle). *pull out* (feathers), –sesa (sesele). (a nail), –pôpolola (pôpolwele). (a plant), –limbula (limbwile). (a pole), –shimpula (shimpwile). (an axe, etc.), –sokomona (sokomwene). (a sword), –somona (somwene). (a tooth), –nukula (nukwîle). (a thorn or jigger), –bangula (bangwîle).

pull out of mud, (a man), –kofolola (kofolwele); (a car), –tikulula (tikulwile).

pulse, 1. n. mutunta. 2. v.i. cf. palpitate.

pump, 1. n. pompi (ma–); 2. v.t.–pompa (pompele).

pumpkin, cipushi (fi). (kind of –), mungu (my).

punch, v·t. –fûta fifunshi (fûtile).

punctual, –lungika mu nshita (lungîke); it can also be translated by the neg. of –celwa: *be punctual,* mulefika mu nshita or mwilacelwa iyô.

puncture, v.t. –tula (tulile); v. stat. –tulika (tulîke).

punish, –pânika (pânike).

pupil, musambilila (ba); we sukulu (bêsukulu). *pupil of eye,* mboni ya linso.

purchase, –shita (shitile).

pure (100%), nkonko:· *he is a – Mubemba,* Mubemba nkonko; cf. also absolute.

purgatory, mutwala.

purify, –wamya (wemye).

purpose, mulandu: *what is the purpose of the journey,* mulandu wa lwendo mulandu nshi?

purr, –buluma (bulwîme).

pursue, –tamfya (tamfishe).

pus, mafina.

push away, –sunka (sunkile). *push on,* –tunkilisha (tunkilishe). – *out,* –tamfya (tamfishe).

put, –bîka (bîkile); –têka (têkele). – *apart,* cf. apart. – *aside,* –têka (têkele); (– for future use), –sunga (sungile). – *back,* cf. retard. – *crosswise,* –pindika (pindike). – *down,* –bîka panshi. – *near,* –palamika (palamîke). – *one another,* –palamanya (palamenye). – *off,* cf. defer & delay. – *on,* cf. clothe. – *out,* cf. extinguish. *put outside,* –bîka kunse. *put upright,* –imika (imike).

puzzle, –sungusha (sungwishe).

pygmy, cf. pigmy.
python, lusato (n).

— Q —

quack doctor, mucapi (ba-).
quagmire tefwetefwe.
quality, musango (mi). *of good* –, ... mpomfu. *cloth* –, nsalu ya mpomfu. *inherited* –, cishilano (fi).
quantity, bwingi. *in large* – cinkupiti; misasatwe; fumfwe. *in small quantity*, mpendwa.
quarrel, 1. n. lubuli; fikansa. v.i. –cito lubuli (citile; –umana (umene); –cita fikansa; –afyanya (afyenye); –tintana (tintene). – *with*, –umana (umenye). *incite to a* –, –songo lubuli (songele). *start a* –, –busho lubuli (bushishe). *cause a* –, –kokesho lubuli (kokeshe). *stop a* –, –lamununa (lamunwine).
quarrelsome, wa lubuli; wa fikansa; wa cau. *quarrelsome person*, mukakashi (ba).
queen, mfumu yanakashi (bashamfumu banakashi). *queen bee*, nasununda (ba-).
queer, –belebensa (belebensele).
question, 1. n. cipusho (fi). 2. v.t. –ipusha (ipwishe).
quick, cf. hurry up.
quickly, bwangu; lubilo. *very* –, bwangu bwangu.
quiet, 1. adv. tondolo; shilili. 2. v.i. –talala (talele); –têko mutima.

quieten down, –fumuka (fumwike).
quietly, buccbuce: *work quietly*, mulebomba buccbuce.
quinine, kwinini.
quite, sâna: *it is quite good*, cisuma sâna.
quite so, interj. ifyo fine! nififine! mwandini!

— R —

rabbit, kalulu (tu); also kalulu (ba-) when used in folklore.
race, 1. n. (species), bwina human race, bwina bantu
race, 2. v.i. cf. compete.
rafter, lusonta (n).
rag, lusâmu (n); ciboshi (fi). *be in rags*, –fwale nsamu (fwele); –sapula (sapwile).
rage, cinse. *be in a rage*, –ba ne cinse; –fulwa sâna (fulilwe).
railway, shitima wa panshi (ba-). – *line*, nyanji (n).
rain, 1. n. mfula. 2. v.i. –loka (lokele). *rain is coming*, mfula naitêka. *it rains*, ileloka. *the rain has stopped*, mfula yakalika.
rainbow, mukolamfula (mi).
rainy day, mufumbi (mi)
raise (lift), –imya (imishe). *raise the eyes*, –sansula menso (sanswile) *be raised like bread*, –tutumuka (tutumwike).
rake, lêki (ba-).
ram, sukusuku (ba-).
ram down, –shindaila (shi-

ndaile).
rapid, mukuku (mi).
rapidity, lubilo.
rapidly, lubilo.
rare, –cepa (cepele) –kana sêka.
rascal, mpulumushi (ba–).
rat, kwindi (ba–). *cane rat,* nsenshi (n).
rather, (has no immediate translation. Can be translated for kucila: *I would rather leave than,* kuti natemwo kufuma ukucila...)
rations, iposo. *rations for journey,* mpao.
rattle, –kulukunta (kulukuntile).
ravine, mupata (mi).
raw. ...bishi.
razor, lubêlo (m).
reach, –fika (fikile). *reach end,* –pela (pelele); –shinta (shintile).
read, –soma (somene); –belenga (belengele)·
ready, –ipekanya (ipekenye).
real, ...ine ...ine: *he is a real man,* uyu mwaume wine wine.
realize, cf. succeed and understand.
really, 1. adv. cine cine. 2. interj. mwa!
reap, –sêpa (sêpele).
reappear, –loboka (lobweke).
reason, 1. n. mulandu. *there is no – to,* tapali mulandu wa. *with greater reason,* nakansha; nakanga. *have reached the age of –,* –cenjela (cenjele); –salapuka (salapwike).
reason, 2. v.i. cf. think; v.t. cf. persuade.

reasonable (of sound judgement), wa mano; cf. also moderate.
rebuke, –kalipila (kalipîle); –ebaula (ebawile).
receipt, lishîti (ba–).
receive, –poka (pokele) *receive wages,* –fole mpiya (folele). *– visitor kindly,* –sekelela mweni (sekelele).
recent, ...nomba: *this case is recent,* mulandu uyu wa nomba.
recently, nombaline; mu nshita ya nomba.
reckon, –penda (pendele).
recognize, –ishiba (ishibe).
recommend, –landila (landile). lit. talk in favour of.
reconcile people, –ampanya bantu (ampenye).
recover from illness, –polelela (polelele).
recruit, –kûta (kûtile).
red, –kashika (kashike). *very red,* –kashika ce; –kashikisha (kashikishe).
redeem, –pususha (puswishe); –lubula (lubwile).
redemption, bulubushi; cilubula.
redish, –kashikila (kashikile).
reduce, –cefya (cefeshe). *reduce to powder,* –shina (shinine).
reed, itete (ma). *reed for drinking,* mutete (mi). *poisoned reed,* munwêna (mi).
reedbuck, mfwi (m).
refrain (of a song), ipinda (ma). *take up a –,* –poke pinda (pokele).
refuge, ibutukilo.
refuse (to do), –kâna (kêne); (to give), –tana

(tanine). *one who refuses all he is asked,* mukâni (ba). *- a gift,* –fwita (fwitile). *- greeting or answer,* –finda (findile).

regard (look upon), –tamba (tambile). *as regards,* pa mulandu wa. *kind regards to,* muposhe.

regiment, mpuka.

regret, –lapila (lapile): *it is with deep – that...,* tuli no bulanda sana ukuti...

reign, 1. n. bufumu. 2. v.t. –têka bantu (têkele).

reject, cf· refuse.

rejoice, –sansamuka (sansamwike).

relate, –shimika (shimike).

relative (kinsman), bululu (ba–); muntu (ba) followed by poss. pr.: *he is my relative,* muntu wandi.

relax, –pêma (pêmene); –tûsha (tûshishe).

release (spring), –fwampula (fwampwîle); –futula (futwile). (a snare or gun), –teulula (teulwîle). (a prisoner), –kakula (kakwile).

relic (of a deceased chief), benye (ba–).

relieve from work, –inusha (inwishe). *relieve one another,* –komboshanya (komboshenye).

religion, ipepo (ma).

relish, munani; citobelo. *eat –,* –tobela (tobele). *eat – without mush,* –shinko munani (shinkile).

rely on, –tetekela (tetekêle); also –cetekela; –sûbila (sûbile) kuli.

remain, –shala (shêle)); –linda (lindile). *remain*

for ever, –belêlela (belêlele).

remainder, Math, icashala (ify).

remark, v.i. cf. say & see.

remedy, muti (mi); ndawa (n). *concoct –,* pando muti (pandile).

remember v.i. –ibukisha (ibukishe); –ibusha (ibwishe).

remembrance, cibukisho. *– day,* bushiku bwa kwibukisha.

remind, v.t. –ibukisha (ibukishe): *do remind me,* kuti mwanjibukisha.

remnant, cishala (fi).

remove, (take away), –fumya (fumishe); –andula (andwile); –teula tewile. *– things spread out,* anuna (anwine). *remove cover,* –fimbula (fimbwile).

renew, –cita cipya cipya.

renounce, –kâna (kêne)·

renown, lulumbi.

renowned, be –, –lumbuka (lumbwike). *make –,* lumbwisha (lumbwishe).

repair, –wamya (wemye); –lunda (lundile). *repair an engine,* etc., –lungisha (lungishe).

repeat, (once or twice), –bwekesha (bwekeshe) (often), –kosha cimo cine (koseshe).

repent, –languluka (langulwike).

replace, cf. succeed and substitute.

reply, 1. n. câsuko (fy); v.i. –asuka (aswike). v. appl, –âsukila (âsukile).

report, 1. n. lipôti (ba–). 2. v.t. –shimika (shimike); –fisha mashiwi (fishishe).

have something to report,
–ba na mashiwi. – *a case,*
–lisho mulandu.

repose, –tùsha (tùshishe).

represent, –ikala pa malo
(ikele).

representative, waikala pa
mâlo (ba); nkombe (n).

reprimand, cf. rebuke.

reproach, cf. rebuke.

reprove, cf. rebuke·

repulse, –tamfya (tamfishe).

request, v.t. cf. demand &
ask permission.

require, cf. demand & need.

rescue, –pususha (puswishe); –pokako (pokeleko).

resemblance, cipasho.

resemble, –pala (palile).
v. rec. –palana (palene);
–lingâna (lingene).

resent, –enda ne cikonko
(endele).

resentment, cikonko.

reserve, –sunga (sungile).

reset, –lundila (lundile).

reside, –ikala (ikele).

residence, bwikalo; cifulo
(fi). *change* –, –kûka
(kûkile).

resign, –leko mulimo.

resist, –kâna (kêne); –lwa
(lwile).

respect, 1· n. mucinshi. 2.
v.t. –cindika (cindike).
pay –, –pakata (pakete);
–tôtela (tôtele).

respectability, bucindami;
bukata; bukankala.

respectable, –cindama (cindême); –pulama (pule-
me). – *person,* mucindami
(ba).

respiration, mupêmo.

respire, –pêma (pêmene).

responsible person, cibinda
(ba–).

rest, v.i. –tûsha (tùshishe);

–pèma (pêmene).

resthut, nsaka (n).

restless, –salakata (sala-
kête).

restore, cf. give back and
substitute.

resume, –tampa kabili
(tampile).

resurrect, –shukuka ku
bafwa (shukwike).

resurrection, kushukuka.

retain, –ikata (ikete).

retaliate, –linganya (lingenye).

retard, –celesha (celeshe).

retire, cf. go away.

retire from work, –leko
mulimo (lekele); –leko
kubomba.

retract, –bwela kunuma
(bwêlele). – *a lie,* –bwesho bufi (bweseshe). – *a
statement,* –futuka (futwîke): *you* –, mwafutuka pa
fyo musosele.

retreat, –bwêla (bwelele).

return, –bwêla (bwêlele);
–bwekelapo (bwekelepo);
v.t. –bwesha (bweseshe).

reveal, –sokolola (soko-
lwêle). – *a secret,* –sosa
fya mu nkâma (sosele).

revenge, 1. n. cilandushi.
2. v.t. –landula (landwîle).

revile, –sâlula (sâlwile);
–tukana (tukene).

reviling, musâlula; misûla;
miponto; lusele.

revolt, mpasase (m)·

reward, cilambu (fi); malipilo. v.t. –lipa (lipile).

rheumatism, suffer from –,
–lwalo musana (lwele).

rhinoceros, cipembele (ba–).

rib, lubafu (m).

rice, mupunge. *decorticate*
–, –sokole mupunge (so-
kwêle).

rich, ...kankala. *rich person,* mukankala (ba).

riches, fyuma.

rid, (a country of a dangerous animal), –salipa (salipe).

ride, –endela pa: *he is riding a horse,* aendela pa mfwalashi.

riddle, 1. n. bwile. 2. v.i. –côleka (côlêke). *solve a riddle,* –pikululo bwile (pikulwîle).

rifle, mfuti (m).

right, 1. n. nsambu; maka: *he has the right to,* ali na maka ya. *human rights,* nsambu sha bantungwa.

right, 2. v.i. be right, –lungika (lungîke). *set –,* –lungamika (lungamîke).

right, 3. adj. kulyo. *the right arm,* kuboko kwa kulyo. *to the –,* ku kulyo.

right, 4. interj. cisuma; cawama.

rigid, –talama (taleme).

ring, 1. n. mbalaminwe (m); lingi (ba–). 2. v.t. –lisha (lishishe).

ringworm, cisesea (fi).

rinse, –sukusa (sukwise).

ripe, –pya (pile). *put aside to ripen,* –fumbika (fumbike).

rise (get up), –ima (imine); (– from bed), –bûka (bûkile); (of sun), –tula (tulile): *the sun rises,* kasuba katula: (start out), –ima (imine).

rise early, –celela (celele).

rise from death, –shukuka (shukwîke).

risk, v.i. –esha (eseshe): *do not risk that,* te ca kwesha iyô.

river, mumana (mi).

river-bed, mulimba (mi). *dry –,* mukonko (mi).

road, musêbo (mi). *motorcar –,* musêbo wa motoka.

roam, –endauka (–endawîke); –talantanta (talantantile).

roan antelope, mpelembe (m).

roar, –buluma (bulwîme); –lila (lilile).

roast, –salula (salwîle); –ôca (ôcele). *roast on a platform,* –kanga (kangile). *– groundnuts,* –babe mbalala (babile).

rob, –iba (ibile).

robber, mupûpu (ba).

robbery, bupûpu.

robe, nkansu (n).

rock, ibwe (ma).

rod, bwembya (membya). *flexible –* lubango (mango).

rogue, mubîfi (ba).

roll, v.t. –kunkulusha (kunkulwishe); v.i. –kunkuluka (kunkulwike). *roll over and over,* –kunkulukila (kunkulukile). *roll up,* –ansula (answile).

roof, 1. n. mutenge (mi). 2. v.t. –pâlika mutenge (pâlike). *flat roof,* cimpangilile (fi).

roof-pole, lusonta (n). *top of a roof,* nsonshi (n).

room, muputule (mi); cf. also place.

root, 1. n. mushila (mi). 2. v.t. –nukula (nukwîle). *take root,* –limbuka (limbwîke).

root-stock, cishinte (fi).

rope, mwando (my). *make a rope,* –pyato mwando (pyatile). *rope made of bark,* lushishi (n). *rope*

made of hide, lushinga (n).
rosary, kolôna (ba–). *say the –,* –salika pali kolona.
rot, –bola (bolele).
rotate, v.i. –shingauka (shingawîke); –shinguluka (shingulwîke); v.t. –shingulusha (shingulwishe).
round, –bulungana (bulungêne). *make –,* –bulunga (bulungile).
round about, go –, –shoka (shokele). v. caus. –shosha (shoseshe).
row, mulongo (mi). *line up in a –,* –tantama mu mulongo (tanteme). *walk in a –,* –endo mulongo (endele).
rub, –cina (cinine). *rub aqainst,* –senganya (sengenye). *– in,* –shinga (shingile). *– off* (dirt), –kûsa (kûshile). *– out,* –fûta (fûtile). *– with oil,* –sûba (sûbile).
rubber, mupila (mi).
rubbish, (worthless), ca fye (fy) ; cinangwa (fi) ; (waste matter), cisoso (fi).
rubbish heap, cishala (fi).
rude, –pontela (pontele).
ruin, v.t. –lofya (lofeshe). *fall in –,* –bongóloka (bongolweke).
rule, 1. n. cebo (fy). 2. v.t. –têka bantu (têkele).
rumble, –kulukunta (kulukuntile).
rumour, ilyashi (ma).
run, –butuka (butwike). *run about,* –pinta (pintile). *run after,* –tamfya (tamfishe). *– away,* –fyuka (fyukile); –butuka (butwike) ; –fulumuka (fulumwîke), *run away from,* –tâba (tâbile). *– down* (dribble), –konkoloka (konkolweke). *run*

rust, ngalâwa (n).
rustic person, mutûtu (ba).
rusticity, butûtu.
rusty, –ba ne ngalâwa.

— S —

sable antelope, kanshilye (ba–).
sabre, lupanga (m).
sack, 1. n. isâka (ma)· 2. v.t. cf. dismiss & plunder.
sacrament, nsakalamenta (n).
sacred, ...takatifu.
sacrifice, 1. n. cîta 2. v.t. –leke cîta (lekele).
sad, –languluka (langulwike). *very sad,* –lilishîka (lilishîke). *it is sad,* ca bulanda.
sadness, cililishi; bulanda.
safe, –pusuka (puswîke): *I am safe,* napusuka.
safety pin, pini (ba–); kanapini (tu).
saint, mutakatifu (ba).
salary, malipilo.
saliva, mate.
salt, 1. n. mucele· 2. v.t. *–* lungo mucele (lungile): *make –,* –engo mucele (engele). *be too salty,* –kauka (kawike).
salute, v.t. –posha (poseshe); –celela (celele). *give the royal salute,* –tôta panshi (totele).
salvation, ipusukilo.
same, ...mo ...inc. *it is*

the same, cimo cine. *just the –,* ...mo na ...mo. *it is –,* cimo na cimo.
sample, cilangililo (fi).
sanction, 1. n. cf. penalty. 2. v.t. cf. authorize; –kosha ne cèbo (koseshe).
sanctity, butakatifu·
sand, musenga (mi); musensenga (mi); mucanga (mi).
sandal, ndyato (n).
sap, menshi.
sash, mushipi (mi).
satan, shetani (ba–).
satiate, v.t. –tùsha (tùshishe); v.i. –ipakisha (ipakishe).
satisfactory, ...linga (lingile). *it is –,* nacilinga.
satisfied (be full), –ikuta (ikwite); (content), –temwa (temenwe).
satisfy, cf. satiate.
saturate, –bomfya sâna (bomfeshe).
Saturday, Cibelushi (fi).
sauce, muto; ntwilo (when made of pounded groundnuts). *make sauce,* –sashila (sashile).
savage person, mutûtu (ba).
savageness, bututu.
save, 1. v·t. cf. redeem & rescue. 2. prep. and cj. kâno. *save* (put aside for later use), bika (bikile).
Saviour, mulubushi.
savour, cf. flavour, n.
saw, 1. n. so (ba–). 2. v.t. –lepula (lepwile).
sawyer, fundi wa kulepule mbao (ba–).
say, –sosa (sosele); –eba (ebele); –tìla (tîle); –ti: *he says,* asosa ati or aeba ati or atìla ati or ati. *have something to say* (report),

–ba na mashiwi. *that is to say,* e kutila; ni mukuti. *what do you say,* amuti shani?
saying, nsoselo (n).
scabies, lupele (m).
scaffold, cintamba (fi).
scale, (balance), cipimo (fi); (– of fisha, etc.), inongwa (ma).
scandal, ishiku (ma).
scandalize, – shikula (shikwile)·
scapula, ikôpe (ma).
scar, cibala (fi).
scarce, –cepa (cepele). (cf. rare).
scare (frighten),· tìnya (tînishe); (startle), –fulumuna (fulumwine). *scare* (keep birds away from sown land), –amina (amìne).
scatter, –salanganya (salangenye). v. stat. –salangana (salangene). *scatter seeds,* –tandanye mbuto (tandenye).
scent, senti (ba–); cena (fy). – *of animal,* bwema.
scholar, we sukulu (be).
school, isukulu (ma).
scissors, shisala (ba–); mikashi.
scoff, –wêla (wêlele).
scold, cf. rebuke.
scorpion, kamini (tu).
scoundrel, mubîfi (ba); mpulumushi.
scrape, –pala (palile); –kola (kolele).
scratch, –fwena (fwenene); cf. also claw. v.t. –kôla (kôlele) of thorns, etc.
scream, –kûta (kûtile).
screen, –cinga (cingile)·
screw 1. n. lusunga (n). 2. v.t. –nyongo lusunga

(nyongele).

scrub, –pukusa (pukwise); –kolopa (kolwêpe).

sea, bemba (ba–).

seal, 1. n. namba (n); **2. v.t.** –bikapo namba (bikilepo). or –kambatikako nshimbi (kambatikeko).

search, –fwaya (fwaile).

season, 1. n. cipande ca mwaka (fi). *rainy* –, mainsa. *windy* –, mwêla. *cold* –, mpepo. *dry or hot season.* lusuba.

season, 2. v.t. –lungo mucele (lungile).

seat, cipuna (fi).

secret, nkâma (n). *keep a secret,* –kupika kanwa (kupike); –ba ne nkâma. *reveal a secret.* –sosa fya nkâma (sosele); –tumbulo mulandu (tumbwîle).

secretly, mu mbali; mu bumfisolo.

section, citente (fi).

secure, 1. adj. cf. quiet. **2.** v.t. cf. obtain.

securily, bwino.

seducer, katunka (ba–).

see, –mona (mwene). v. rec. –monana (monene). *glad to see somebody,* –ekelo muntu (sekele), *see distinctly,* –mwensekesha (mwensekeshe).

seed, mbuto (m); luseke (n).

seek, –fwaya (fwaile).

seem, –ba nga; moneka nga (moneke). *it seems,* caba nga or camoneka nga.

seer, wa ngulu (ba)

seize, –ikata na maka (ikete); –bûla na maka (bûlile).

seldom, miku imo imo fye;

limo limo fye. *seldom if ever,* nalimo nangu umo.

select, –sala (salile).

self, ...ine. cf. T. II, & T. III.

sell, –pôsa (pôsele); –shitisha (shitishe).

seminary, seminalio (ba–).

send, –tuma (tumine). *send ahead.* –tangisha (tangishe). *– away* or *off,* –tamfya (tamfishe).

sense, common –, mâno. *talk with* –, –landa na mâno (landile). *have no –,* –pelwa mâno (pelelwe).

sensible, cf. reasonable.

sensitive, –tefya (tefeshe).

separate, v.t. –lekanya (lekenye); –patula (patwile). **v.i.** lekana (lekene). – *fighting ones,* –lamununa (lamunwine).

September, Lusuba lunono.

sepulcre, cf. tomb·

serious, 1. adj. ...kulu ...kalamba: *a – matter,* mulandu ukulu or ukalamba. **2. v.i.** –tekanya (tekenye); –nasho kupusauka (nashishe). ῶ

sermon, mafundisho. *give a –,* –pêla mafundisho (pêle).

serpent, nsoka (n).

serpentine, cinshoko (fi).

serval cat, mbale (m).

servant, mutumishi (ba) mubomfi (ba).

serve, –tumika (tumîke).

serviette. citambala ca pe têbulo (fi).

set, –bîka (bîkile). *set aside,* –têka (têkele). *– for future use,* –sunga (sungile). *set free,* cf. redeem.

settle, –ikala (ikele); cifulo, *settle a case,* –putulo mulandu (putwile).

seven, cine lubali·

several, ...mo ...mo: *several men.* bantu bamo bamo.

severe, ...kali; –kalipa.

severity, bukali.

sew, –bila (bilile).

shade, cintelelwe (fi). *go into* –, –ûba (ûbile). *procure* –, –cinga (cingile).

shadow, cinshingwa (fi).

shake, v.t. –sukunsha (sukwinshe); –tensha (tenseshe); v.i. –sukunta (sukuntile); –tenta (tentele). – *down* (fruits), –kungula (kungwîle). – *head in denial,* –kunto mutwe (kuntile). – *hands,* –funka (funkile). – *off* (dust) –kunta (kuntile).

shallow, –selauka (selawîke).

shame, nsoni. *put to shame,* –sebânya (sebênye).

shameless, –bulwe nsoni.

shape, 1. n. musango (mi). 2. v.t. –bumba (bumbile).

share, 1. n· cipande (fi). 2. v.t. –akana (akene). *give one's share* (in a collection), –sangula (sangwile). *give no full* –, senga (cengele).

sharp, –twa (twîle).

sharpen (iron), –nôna (nônene); (wood), –songola (songwele).

shave, –beyo mwefu (bêle). – *the whole head,* –beyo lukuso.

she, cf. T. II.

shed, n. itanga (ma).

shed tears, –tibinte filamba (tibintile).

sheep, mpanga. *female sheep,* mpanga ikota. *male sheep,* sukusuku (ba–).

sheepfold, icinka (ma).

sheer, cf. absolute or simple.

shelf (over fireplace), lwino (nyino).

shell, 1. n. cipâpa (fi); *shell of tortoise,* cipanga (fi) 2. v.t. –tongola (tongwele). *shell beans,* –puma cilemba (pumine).

shelter, 1. n. nsaka (n). *a rough* –, nsakwe (n). *build a rough* –, –sake nsakwe (sakile).

shelter, 2· v.t. –uba (ubile); –cinga (cingile).

shepherd, kacema (ba–).

shield, nkwêla (n).

shift, cf. move.

shilling, lupiya (mpiya).

shine (sun), –balika (balîke). (glitter), –bêka (bêkele).

ship, bwato (mato); shitima (ba–).

shirt, ilaya (ma).

shiver, –tutuma (tutwîme).

shoe, lusapato (n).

shop, ishôpo (ma).

shoot from stump of tree, cimpûsa (fi); musambo (mi).

shore, lulamba.

short, ...ipi; –ipipa (ipîpe); –cepa (cepele).

short-cut, take a –, –cilinganya (cilingenye).

shorten, –cefya (cefeshe); –ipifya (ipifishe).

shortness, bwipi.

shorts, pair of –, kaputula (ba–).

should, –fwile; kuti: *he should do it.* afwile ukucite ci or kuti acite ci.

shoulder, kubeya (mabeya). *shrug the shoulder,* –tensha makôpe (tenseshe).

shoulderblade, ikôpe (ma).

shout for help, nkûta (n).

shout (of derision), kawêle (tu).

shout of welcome, kapundu (tu). *utter – of welcome,* –aulo tupundu (awile).

shout, v.i. –punda (pundile). *shout after somebody,* –bilikisha (bilikishe).

shovel, fosholo (ba–).

show, 1. n. bulangisho. v.t. –langa (langile). *show the way,* –tungulule nshila (tungulwîle). – *how to do,* –langa (langile); –sambilisha (sambilishe).

shrink, –tunkana (tunkene).

shun, –taluka (talwîke).

shut, –isala (isele). v. appl. –isalila (isalîle): *shut the door,* isalêniko cibi.

shy, –ba ne nsoni.

shyly, nsoni nsoni.

shyness, nsoni.

sick, –lwala (lwele). v. caus. –lwalika (lwalike). *feel sick,* –seluka (selwike); –selauka (selawike).

sick feeling, musêlu.

sick person, mulwle (ba).

sickle, cikwakwa (fi).

sickly, –lwalilila (lwalilile).

sikness, bulwêle (ma).

side, lubali (m); ishilya. *on the side of.* lubali lwa. *on this –,* kuno ishilya. *on the other –,* peshilya *on what –.* lubali kwi? *on both sides,* kubili kubili.

sieve, sefa (ba–); lunyungo (n).

sift, –nyunga (nyungile); –sensa (sensele).

sigh, –teta (tetele).

sight, menso; lwinso. *keep in sight,* –linda ku menso (lindile). *be in –,* –ba pa menso. *know by –,* –ishiba ku menso (ishibe). *at first –,* pa kubala; pa menso. *be sharp-sighted,* –ba no lwinso.

sign. 1. n. cishibilo (fi); 2. v.t. –bîkapo cishibilo (bîkilepo). *sign of the cross,* cilembo ca musalaba. *uneffaceable sign,* cishibilo icishifwaluka.

sign, 3. v.t. (write one's name), –lembako ishina (lembeleko).

signature, ishina (ma).

signify, –tila (tile): *it signifies,* catila acîti.

signpost, cipampa (fi).

silence, tondolo. *keep silence,* interj. congo; lekêni congo!

silent, –talala (talele).

silently, tondolo; shilili.

silk, shiliki.

silliness, buwelewele; butumpe.

silly, –tumpa (tumpile).

similar, –palana (palene).

simple, cf. easy or foolish.

simpleton, ciwelewele (fi); cipuba (fi); cipumbu (fi).

simply, fye.

sin, 1. n. isambi (ma). 2. –bîfya (bîfishe); –cite sambi (citile).

since, ukufuma; apo (with verb): *since this morning,* ukufuma lucêlo or apo bucelele. *since, (all the time),* nshita yonse iyo.

sincere, wa cishinka; wa cine cine. *Yours sincerely,* nine wênu wa cine cine.

sinew, lushipa (n).

sing (of man), –imba (imbile). (of bird), –lila (lilile).

singe, –baba (babile).

singer, muomba (ba). *poor –,* wa cileya (ba).

singing, dissonant –, cileya.

single, ...mo fye: *one – man,* muntu umo fye.

sink, –bunda (bundile). *sink in,* –kofola (kofwele) (when man); –tika (tikile) (e.g. a car).

sinner, mubîfi (ba); wa masambi (ba).

sip, –fipa (fipile); cimfula (cimfwile).

sir, interj. mukwai. *yes sir,* ee mukwai.

sisal, bukonge (n).

sister, cf. T. V. *sister-in-law,* bukwe (ba–). *elder sister,* mukalamba! *younger –,* mwaice.

sister, mama (ba–).

sisterhood, bumâma.

sit, –ikala (ikêle); also sit down.

site, ncende (n).

sitting room, nsaka (n).

situated, bêla (bèlele): *the Zaire is – in the West,* câlo ca Zaire cabêla ku masamba.

situtunga (antelope), nsobe (n).

six, mutanda.

size, cipimo (fi).

skeleton, misakalala.

skid, –sholoka (sholweke).

skill, bufundi; bucibinda.

skim (take cream off), –ambulula (ambulwîle); –yengula (yengwile).

skin, 1. n. (human), nkanda (n); (of animal), mpapa (m); (of fruit), cipâpa (fi).

skin disease (kinds of –): lubu; cisongo; fundwe-fundwe; lufine; nsunda.

skin, 2. v.t. –funde nama

(fundile).

skirt, cifunga (fi).

skull, cipanga (fi).

sky, mùlu; lwelele.

slander, 1. n. lwambo 2. v.t. –amba (ambile).

slap, 1. n. lupi (ndupi). 2. v.t. –tobo lupi (tobele); –umo lupi (umine). –koshamo lupi (koseshemo).

slash grass, –kumpe cani (kumpile).

slate, seleti (ma–) (for writing on); itamina (ma) (for roofing). *slate pencil,* côko wa seleti (ba–).

slaughter, –cinja (cinjile).

slave, musha (ba).

slave trade, bunonshi bwa mu bantu. *make slave –,* –nonkela mu bantu (nonkele).

slavery, busha.

slay, –koma (komene); –ipaya (ipeye).

sleep, 1. n. tulo. 2. v.i. –lâla (lèle); –sendama (sendeme). *put to sleep,* –sendamika (sendamike). *– in the open,* –lâla panse or pa lwalala. *– on the ground,* –lâla panshi. *sleep soundly,* –lâlisha (lâlishe). *– on the road.* –lâla pa nshila. *– without eating,* –lâla ne nsala. *– like an antbear,* –lâla tûlo twa nengo.

sleeping place, bùlo (mâlo). *sleeping sickness,* bulwele bwa kushipula.

sleepy, –shipula (shipwile).

slice, 1. n. kapande (tu). 2. v.t. –putaula (putawile).

slide down. –telemuka (telemwike); –pulumuka (pulumwike); –solomoka (so-

lomweke).
slightly, panôno.
slip, v.t. (lose footing), –sholoka (sholweke); (escape), –pusumuka (pusumwike): *the plate escaped my fingers*, mbale yapusumuka ku minwe yandi.
slippery, –telela (telele): *the path is* -, nshila naitelela.
slope, 1. n. matelo (mi) 2. v.i. –suluka (sulwike).
slow, –shingashinga (shingashingile) – *in walking*, –fina môlu (finine).
slowly, bucebuce; panôno panôno.
slumber, –shipula (shipwile).
smack, cf. slap.
small, ...nôno; ...nîni; ...ipi; –ipipa (ipîpe). *very* -, ...nôno nôno; ...nîni nîni. *what a –egg*, ilini ubuce!
smallness, buce; bwipi etc.
smallpox, kampasa.
smash, –tobâ (tobele). v. stat. –tobeka (tobeke). – *to pieces*, –sansaula (sansawile). v. stat. –sansauka (sansawike).
smear, –shinga (shingile); –shingula (shingwile).
smell, 1. n. bununko. 2. v.t. –nunsha (nunshishe); v.i. –nunka (nunkile). *smell good*, –nunke cisuma; – *badly*, –nunko bubi.
smell of animal, bwema; *smell of fish*, luce.
smelting furnace, ilungu (ma).
smile, –censa (censele).
smoke, 1. n. cushi (fy). 2. v.i. –pêpa (pêpele). *smoke meat*, –kange nama

(kangile). – *out*, –fukilisha (fukilishe).
smoker, kapêpa (ba-). *heavy smoker*, –ba no bulembo.
smoking, habit of –, bulembo.
smooth, –telela (telele); engula (engwile).
snag, cf. obstacle or difficulty.
snail, nkola (n).
snake, nsoka (n).
snap off, v.t. –kontola (kontwele); v. stat. –kontoka (kontweke).
snare, citevo (fi). *snare for birds*, lukose (n); (for animals), citembo (fi); cilindo (fi). – *made of a rope with a noose*, mukolobwe (mi).
snatch, –sompola (sompwele); –fûba (fûbile).
sneak away, –ongoloka (ongolwêke).
sneeze, v.i. –tesemuna (tesemwine).
sniff, –nunsha (nunshishe).
snore, –fôma (fômene).
snout, kanwa (tunwa).
snuff, 1. n. fwâka. 2. v.i. –pêpa ku myona (pêpele).
snuffbox, ntekwe (n).
so, ifyo; ifi. *it is not so*, ifyo tefyo. *is it not so*, *interj.* of surprise, ala! cine cine! *quite so*, ifyo fine; naendi! *so and so*, kampanda (ba-); ntwanikane (ba-); ntwêno (ba-). *so that*, pakuti.
soak, (make wet), –bomfya (bomfeshe) v. stat. –bomba (bombele). (put under water) –abika (abike).
soap, isopo (ma).

society, kabungwe (tu).
sober, become –, –kololoka (kololweke).
sod, cishinde (fi).
soft, (not stiff), –naŋana (naŋene); (not hard), –naka (nakile); (over-ripe), –bonsa (bonsele). *soft in touch*, –telela (telele).
soften, –nasha (nashishe).
soil, 1. n. mushili. 2. v.t. –lamfya (lamfishe). *virgin soil*, mushili wampuma. *virgin soil erosion*, kusendwa kwa mushili ku mfula.
solder, –lundikanya (lundikenye); – kumbinkanya (kumbinkenye).
soldier, mushilika (ba); mushikale (ba). *enlist as a soldier*, –ingilo bushilika (ingile). *job of a –*, bushilika.
sole, cinyantilo (fi).
solicit, –pimpila (pimpile).
solid, –kosa (kosele).
some, ...mo ...mo. *some books*, fitabo fimo fimo.
somebody, muntu: *somebody told me*, muntu anjebele; cf. also: so and so.
something, cintu. *something else*, cimbi. *– extraordinary*, cimbi cimbi; also: something quite different.
somewhat, panôno.
son, mwana mwaume (bâna baume).
son-in-law, cf. T. V.
song, lwimbo (nyimbo). *intone a song*, –bûlo lwimbo (bûlile). *make a new song*, –shiko lwimbo (shikile). *sing a song badly*, –lusho lwimbo (lushishe).
soon, pa nshita inôno; –swa

(swîle). *he is coming –*, alebwela pa nshita inôno or alaswa abwele. *very soon*, nombaline.
soothsayer, wa ngulu (ba).
soprano, ishiwi lya pa mûlu.
sorcerer, muloshi (ba); ndoshi (n).
sorcery, buloshi; bwanga.
sore, 1. n. cilonda (fi). 2. adj. cf. hurt.
sorghum, sonkwe (ba–). *white sorghum*, masaka.
sorrow, bulanda.
sorry, –languluka (langulwike); –lêtelo bulanda or –ba no bulanda: *I am sorry about...*, nalanguluka ukuti or ndi no bulanda ukuti or candetelo bulanda ukuti.
sorry, interj. yaba!; yangu!
sort (manner), musango (mi).
sort out, –sala (salile); –sobolola (sobolwele).
soul, mutima (mi); mweo (my). *soul of a departed*, mupashi (mi).
sound, 1. n. cf. noise. 2. adj. cf. healthy.
soup, supu; muto.
sour, –sasa (sashile).
source, ntulo (n).
sourness of stomach, cimisha.
south, kapinda ka ku kulyo.
sow, –tanda (tandile).
space, ncende (n). *space out*, v.t. –talushanya (talushenye).
spanner, shipanala (ba–).
spare, (set aside), –tengela (tengele); (set aside for future use), –sunga (sungile).
spark, lusase (n).

sparrow, kancelelya (tu).
speak, –sosa (sosele); –landa (landile). – *clearly,* –sosesha (soseshe). – *ill of,* –amba (ambile). *speak louder.* –ikatishe shiwi (ikatishe).
spear, ifumo (ma).
species, bwina.
specify (explain clearly), –londolola bwino (londolwêle).
specimen, cilangililo (fi).
spectacles, makalashi. *wear* –. –fwala makalashi (fwele).
speech, mashiwi.
speed, 1. n. lubilo. 2. v.i. cf. hurry up. *speed up,* interj. lubilo!
spell 1. n. (charm), bwanga. *cast a* – –lowa (lowele) –soko bwanga (sokele); –pando bwanga (pandile). *remove a* –. –looloka (loolweke). v. stat. –looloka (loolweke). *dry* – *in rainy season.* cilala.
spell, 2. v.t. –lumbule filembo (lumbwile).
spend, –pôsa (pôsele): *how much money did you spend,* wapôsele ndalama shinga?
spider, tandabube (ba–). (kind of –), lembalemba (ba–). *spider's web,* bwile; tandabube: lembalemba.
spill, –itila (itile). v. stat. –itika (itike); –sempaula (sempawile).
spin thread, –pyato bushishi (pyatile); – *round,* –shinguluka (shingulwike).
spinach, musâlu (mi).
spine, longololo lwa numa.
spire, lupungu lwa njelwa

(m).
spirit, mweo (myeo); mupashi (mi). *evil* –, cibanda (fi); ciwa (fiwa); ngulu (n). *evoke spirits,* –buka (bukile). *worship spirits,* –pepe mipashi (pepele); –pupo lupupo (pupile). *spirit's medium,* wa ngulu (ba).
spit, –fwisa mate (fwishile). *spit at,* –saka mate (sakile).
spite, in –, nelyo; nangu.
spitting snake, kafi (ba–).
spittle, mate.
splash, –sabaula (sabawile).
spleen, lamba (ba–).
splint, n. kapekesa (tu).
splinter, –pandaula (pandawile).
split, –lepula (lepwile), cf. also splinter.
spoil, –onaula (onawile). v. stat. –onaika (onaike); (a child) –lemo mwana.
spook, mulungulwa (mi).
spoon, supuni (ba–).
spoor, makasa. *follow a spoor,* –lonsha makasa (lonseshe).
spot, 1. n. (place), ncende; (– of colour), ibâla (ma). 2. v.t. –balâlika (balâlike).
spotted, be –, –balâla (balêle).
spouse, muka (ba–); mwina (bêna). (with poss.) mwina mwandi mwina mobe.
sprain, –minya (minishe); –byutula (byutwile).
spray, –kana (kanine).
spread, –ansa (anshile); (scatter), –salanganya (salangenye). *spread out to dry,* –anika (anike). – a disease. –ambukisho bulwele (ambukishe).

– *news*, –lundulula mashiwi (lundulwile).

sprinkle, (water) –kana menshi (kene) (flour, salt) –pupila (pupite).

sprout, –mena (menene); –pûka (pûkile).

spy, 1. n. nengu (n). 2. v.t. –lengela (lengele).

square, cibwanse (fi).

squat, –peta makunda (petele).

squeeze, –kama (kamine); –tina (tinine). – *through*, –peka (pekele). – (jam), –fenenkesha (fenenkeshe). *be squeezed*, –fyama (fyeme); –fyantika (fyantîke).

squint, –uluka menso (ulwîke); –shongoka menso (shongweke).

stab, –lasa (lashile).

stable, itanga (ma).

stage on journey, ndo (n).

stagnant, cikalishi.

stain (spot), imata (ma).

staircase, mutanto (mi).

stammer, –bulubusa (bulubushile).

stamp, 1. n. (rubber –), nshimbi. (postal –), shitampa (ma–). 2. v.t. –bîkapo shitampa; nshimbi.

stand up, –ima (imine). *stand still*, –iminina (iminine). *be at a standstill*, –lâla (lêle). – *in line*, –lantama (tantême). *stand by*, –afwa (afwile).

star, lutanda (n). *morning star*, mulanga.

stare, –tumbula menso (tumbwile); –tontomesha menso (tontomeshe).

start, –tampa (tampile); –amba (ambile); –tendeka (tendeke). – *again*, –bûka (bûkile): *school starts*

again, isukulu lyabûka. – *early*, –bangilila (bangilile); –celela (celele). – *out on journey*, –ima (imine).

startle, –fulumuna (fulumwine). v. stat. –fulumuka (fulumwike).

starve, v.i. –fwa ku nsala (fwîle).

station, citeshoni (fi).

statue, nsalamu (n).

stature, cimo.

stay, cf. remain. *stay quiet*, –ikala (ikele).

steak, mutante.

steal, –iba (ibile).

steam, cushi (fy)

steamer, shitima (ba–).

steep, –lundumana (lundumene); –sansuka (sanswike).

steer, –tekenya (tekenye).

steinbuck, katili (tu).

stem, mukonso (mi).

step, 1. n. lutampulo (n). 2. v.i. –enda (endele). – *over*, –ciluka (cilwike). – *of a staircase*, itabo (ma).

sterile, –ba numba. *sterile woman*, numba.

sterility, bunumba.

sternum, nkombe.

stew, –ipika (ipike).

stick, 1. n. cimuti (fi). *walking stick*, nkonto (n). 2. v.t. –kambatika (kambatike); v.i. –kambatila (kambatile).

stick in, v.t. –soma (somene); –someka (someke).

stick on, as stickseed, –kungama (kungeme).

sticky, –limbuluka (limbulwike).

stiff, (clot), –tikama (tikeme); (rigid), –talama

(taleme).

still, 1. v.i. cf. quiet. 2. adv.
na nomba; na lino; *be –,*
(adv.), –ci–: *I am – here,*
ncili kuno.

sting, 1. n. lubola (m).
2. v.t. –suma (sumine).

stingy, cf. mean.

stink, –nunko bubi (nunkile).

stir, –kumba (kumbile). –
up mud, –fundaula (fundawile). – *up a quarrel* –kokesho lubuli (kokeshe).

stomach, cifu (fi). *stomach
trouble, suffer from –,*
lwala kameme (lwele).

stone, n. ibwe (ma). *small
stone.* kabwe (tu). *– of a
fruit,* mukôli (mi).

stool, cipuna (fi). *pass
stool,* –nya (nyêle); –sûka
(sûkile).

stoop, –babatala (babatele).

stop, –leka (lekele). *stop,*
interj. leka (lekêni)! ala!
– work for the day, v.t.
–inusha (inwishe); v.i.
–inuka (inwike). *stop* (of
rain), –kalika (kalîke).

stopper, nciliko (n).

store, ishitôlo (ma). *store
grain,* –tutila mu butala
(tutîle).

stork, (kind of), cipansankola (fi), 'locust bird'
marabou stork. mukanga
(mi); cipampa (ba-).

storm, cibulukutu (fi).

stormy, –bundama (bundeme).

story, mulumbe (mi).

stout, –tuluka (tulwike).

stoutness, bûtulushi.

stove, citofu (ba-).

straight, –lungama (lungeme); –tambalala (tamba-
lele); –ololoka (ololweke):

the road is –, umusebo
waololoka, or walungama.

straightaway, apo pene.

straighten (put in line),
–lungamika (lungamike);
(make flat), –olola (olo-
lwele).

straightforward, wa cishinka; –lungika.

straightforwardness, cilungi.

strain, –cemeka (cemeke);
–sansa (sanshile).

strainer, ncemeko (n); lu-
sansa (n).

strange, 1. (queer), –belebensa (belebensele);~ 2.
(different), –ba ...mbi
...mbi or –ibêla (ibêlele):
*he is a bit strange nowa-
days,* ali umbi umbi or
aibêla mu nshita ya no-
mba. 3. (astonishing),
–sunguka (sungwike). *it is
strange,* –ca kusunguka.

stranger, mweni (beni);
mwina fyalo (bena –). *be
strangers to one another,*
–lubana (lubene).

strangle, –kafula (kafwile);
–pwilisho mweo (pwili-
she).

straw, câni (fy).

strawberries, matunda.

stream, mumana (mi).
perennial –, mumana uu-
pita pe. *seasonal –,* mu-
mana-mainsa. *upstream,*
ku mulu wa mumana.
downstream. kwisamba lya
mumana.

street, musebo (mi).

strength, maka *put on all
your strength,* interj. na
maka yonse; pa maka;
makamaka.

strengthen, –kosha (koseshe).

stress a word. –shimpe shiwi (shimpile).

stretch, (flatten), –olola (olwele); (unfold), –petulula (petulwile). – *out arms.* –tambalika maboko (tambalike). – *out and fix,* –tanika (tanike). *stretch* (rubber, etc.), –limbulula (limbulwile); –nyunsulula (nyunsulwile).

strict, cf. severe or correct.

strike, cf. hit. *strike a match.* –fwalula macishi (fwalwile).

string, 1. n. mwando (my); lutambo (n); (– of a hide), lushinga (n). 2. v.t. –tunga (tungile).

strip off (clothes), –fûla (fûlile); (leaves), –pululula (pululwile); (necklace, shell, bark); –fotola or sotola.

strive, (mentally), –panda mâno (pandile); (physically), –bomba na maka (bombele); –tukuta (tukwite).

stroke, 1. n. (blow), lupumo (m). 2. v.t. –tentemba (tentembe).

strong, –ba na maka; –kosa (koscle). (of wind), –luma (lumine). (of drinks), –kalipa (kalipe).

struggle, cf. strive.

strychnine, sumu.

stubborn, –koso mutwe (kosele). – *person,* cintomfwa (ba–).

student, musambilila (ba).

stump (of a tree), cishiki (fi); ishinte (ma); (of amputated limbi), makunkutu.

stunted, –tusa (tushile).

stupid, –tumpa (tumpile).

stupidity, bupumbu; butumpe; buwelewele; bupuba.

sty, (on eyelid), kasokopyo (ba–).

subdue, –nasha (nashishe); –cimfya (cimfishe).

submission, bupete.

submissive, –petama (peteme); –nakilila (nakilile); –fûka (fûkile).

substitute, –lêta cimbi ca musango umo wine.

subtract, –fumya (fumishe).

succeed, 1. (finish off), –pwishisha (pwishishe); 2. (be successor), –pyana (pyene).

successor, mpyani (m).

such, ifyo; ...musango uyu; ...kuti: *I was in such a hurry,* nalipamfiwe fyo; *such a man.* muntu wa musango uyu or muntu wa kuti.

suck, –onka (onkele). *give –.* –onsha (onseshe). *honey,* –fyompo bûci (fyompele). – *a fruit,* –fipa (fipile).

suckle, –onsha (onseshe).

suddenly, apo pêne; bwangu bwangu.

sue, –pindo muntu (pindi le).

suffer, –cûla (cûlile). v. caus. –cûsha (cûshishe). – *from,* –lwala (lwele).

suffering, bucûshi (ma).

sufficient, –linga (lingile); –fula (fulile); –kumana (kumene). *it is –,* cafula; calinga; cakumana.

sufficiently, cilingile.

sugar, shûka. *sugar – cane,* cisankonde (fi).

suggest, –eba (ebele).

suicide, commit –, –iipayo mwine (iipeye). (– by

hanging), –ikulika (iku-like).

suit, 1. n. (set of man's clothes), suti (ba–), 2. v.i. (fit), –linga (lingile) *do not* –, –pata (patile): *the shoes do not* –, nsapato shapata.

sulk, v.i. –shuluka (shulwike); also be sulky.

sullen, cf. sulk or gloomy.

sum up, –longanya (longenye).

summon, –ita (itile). – *to court.* –kûta ku kôti (kûtile).

sun, kasuba. *sunrise,* kasuba katula. –*set.* kasuba kawa.

Sunday, Nshiku ya Mulungu.

superior, 1. n. mukubwa (ba–). 2. v.i. –cila (cilile).

supervise, –angalila (angalile).

supperation (of ears), mulemba.

supply, 1. n. fingi: filingile: *we have a good* –, twakwata fingi or filingile. 2. v.t. –fwaila (fwaile): *can you* – *me with,* kuti mwamfwaila.

support, 1. n. (help), cafwilisho. 2. v.t. afwa (afwile).

suppose, –bulunga (bulungile); nabulunga. *supposing that,* nga cakuti, nga cakutila.

sure, (know for –), –ishiba ca cine (ishibe); (make sure), –shininkisha (shininkishe).

surely, cine cine.

surface, ca kunse; ca pa mûlu: ... panshi: – *soil,* mushili wa pa mûlu. – *mail,* mêlu wa panshi.

surpass, v.t. –cisha (cishishe); –sûsa (sûshile).

surplus, pâpi (ba–), **cacilukako** (fy); cashala (fy).

surprise, –sungusha (sungwishe). *take by* –, –pumikisha (pumikishe).

surprised, be –, –sunguka (sungwike).

surrender, –cimba (cimbile).

surround, –shinga (shingile); –ofya (ofeshe).

surveyor, mangimêla (ba–).

suspect, –tunganya (tungenye).

suspend, –binda ku (bindile).

suspenders, makwelelo.

suspicion, mutunganya.

suspicious, –ba no mutunganya; cf. also suspect.

swallow, 1. n. kamimbi (tu). 2. v.t. –mina (minine).

swamp, wanga; nika.

swarm, 1. n. ifungu (ma); ibumba (ma). 2. v.i. –sokola (sokwele).

sway, –sunsha (sunshishe).

swear, –lapa (lapile).

sweat, 1. n. libe (mabe). 2. v.i. –piba mabe (pibile).

sweep, –pyanga (pyangile).

sweet, –lowa (lowele); –lowelela (lowelele).

swell, –fimba (fimbile). v. caus. –fimfya (fimfishe). v. rev. –fimbuluka (fimbulwike). *swell up,* –tumba (tumbile).

swelling, cipumba (fi). – *in the groin,* mutantamfula.

swim, –owa (owele).

swing, cf. sway.

swollen, –fimba (fimbile).

sword, lupanga (m).

syphilis, tuswende.

table 194 **teach**

— T —

table, itêbulo (ma). *lay the table,* –anse têbulo (anshile); –tantike têbulo (tantike). *clear the table,* –tantule têbulo (tantwile); –fumye mbale pe têbulo (fumishe); –teule fipe pe têbulo (tewile).
taboo, mwiko (mi).
tabooed. –saka (sakile).
tadpole, tombolilo (ba–).
tail, mucila (mi). *wag the tail,* –minyo mucila (minishe). *tail of a snake,* busòlo (ma). *tail of a fowl or bird,* lusuka (n); *of fish,* cipêpe.
tailor, kabila (ba–).
take, –bûla (bûlile). *take away,* fumya (fumishe); cf. also remove. *– a rest,* (tûshishe). *– a seat,* ikala (ikele). *– by force,* –tapa (tapile). *– care,* –tekanya (tekenye). *– care of,* –sunga (sungile). *– fire,* v.i. –àka (àkile). *– from,* –poka (pokele). *– off,* cf. take away. *– off a lid,* –kupukula (kupukwile). *– out of a container,* –tapula (tapwile). *– out of water,* –abula (abwile). *take to pieces,* –pangulula (pangulwile). *– with both hands,* –pokelela (pokelele).
tale, mulumbe. *tell a tale,* –umo mulumbe (umine).
tale bearer, wa lusebo (ba); mukwâkwa (ba); sèse (ba–).
tale bearing, lusebo.
talk, 1. n. ilyashi. 2. v.i. –landa (landile); –sosa (sosele). *– against,* –seba (sebele). *– correctly,* –lungika (lungike). *talk incorrectly,* –benda (bendele). *– evasively* (refusing), –leshalesha (leshaleseshe). *– indistinctly,* –sosela mu masaya (sosele). *– ill of,* –amba (ambile). *– quickly,* –longofya (longofeshe).
tall, ...tali; *be tall,* –lêpa (lêpele).
tallness, butali.
tame, v.t. –belesha (beleshe); –nasha (nashishe); v.i. –belela (belele).
tangle, v.t. –lukanya (lukenye); v.i. –lukana (lukene); cf. also confuse.
tank, tanki (ma–).
tape, cipimo (fi). *tape worm,* nsokanda (n).
tapioca, kalundwe.
tarantula, ikalashi (ma).
tarry, cf. remain, or late.
task, mulimo (mi); ncito (n).
taste, 1. n. cinunkilo. 2. v.t. –sonda (sondele); v.i. –nunkila (nunkile).
tasteless, fyantalala.
tasty, –nunkila (nunkile); –lowa (lowele); –lowelela (lowelele).
tatter, ciboshi (fi); lusâmu (n).
tattoo, 1. n. (on temples), nakonde (ba–); (on chest and abdomen), lupoloto (mpoloto). 2. v.t. –shila nakonde or lupoloto (shilile).
tax, musonko (mi). *levy taxes.* –sonkesha bantu (sonkeshe). *pay –,* –sonka (sonkele). *person exempted from –,* mulâla (ba).
tea, ti.
teach, –funda (fundile);

–sambilisha (sambilishe).
teacher, kafundisha (ba–).
job of a –, bukafundisha.
teaching, ifunde (ma).
tear, 1. n. cilamba (fi). *shed tears,* –tibinte filamba (tibintile). 2. v.t. –lepula (lepwile). v. stat. –lepuka (lepwike). – *with beak,* –sompa (sompele).
tease, –konya (koneshe).
teasing, musange.
tell, –eba (ebele): *tell me,* unjebe. – *a story* –shimika (shimike).
temper, 1. n. bad –, cau. 2. v.t. (moderate), –nasha (nashishe). *lose* –, –sakâtuka (sakâtwike).
tempt, –pimpila (pimpile); –tunka (tunkile); –esha (eseshe).
temptation, ntunko (n); kupimpilwa. *yield to* –, –konkelela mu fibi (konkelele).
ten, num. ikumi (ma).
tender, –naka (nakile); ... teku: – *meat,* inama yanaka. *a – shoot,* musambo uteku.
tenderness, cikûku.
tent, tenti (ma–).
tentpole, mulongoti (mi).
tepid, adv. cifulefule: *bring – water,* leta menshi ya cifulefule.
test, cf. tempt; measure.
testament, cishilano (fi); mulao (mi).
testify, –ba kambone.
testimony, bunte.
thank, –sosa santi; –pika santi; –tôtela (tôtele). *thank you!* santi mukwai; natôtela mukwai; eya mukwai! cf. T VII.
that, 1. pr. cf. T. III, and

T. IV. 2. cj. ukuti; pakuti; so that; in order that. – *is to say,* ni mukuti; e kutila. – *is it,* interj. e papo; te papo. – *is why,* cj. e ico.
thatch *a roof,* –fimbo mutenge (fimbile). *remove thatch.* –fimbulo mutenge (fimbwile).
thee, ku cf. T. II.
theft, bupûpu.
their, 1. ... abo with nouns of class 'mu/ba': *the cats and their tails.* bacona ne micila yabo. 2. **with the** other classes it is transcribed by 'of them', followed by the suffix 'ko': *the leopards and their tails,* mbwili ne micila yashiko.
them, cf. T. II.
then, elyo; kabinge; ninshi; e pa (followed by inf.): *then he left,* e pa kuya.
there, eko; uko; apo; *just there,* uko kwine; apo pêne.
therefore, e ico; êco; icalenga; kanshi.
therein (in that respect), mu mulandu uyu; (in that place), emo.
thereupon, same as then.
there yonder, kulya; palya.
these, cf. T. III.
they, cf. T. II.
thick, ... kulu.
thicket, iteshi (ma); lububa. – *of high grass,* cisonso (fi).
thickness, bufumo.
thief, mupûpu (ba).
thigh, itanta (ma).
thin, –onda (ondele); anguka (angwike): *a – body,* mubili uwaonda. – *cloth,*

nsalu yaanguka.
thine, ... obe.
thing, cintu (fi). *thing, (the name of which one cannot remember),* cintweno (fi).
think, –tontonkanya (tondonkenye). *one would think that,* kuti wati (bati); kwati.
thirst, cilaka.
thirsty, –ba ne cilaka. *very thirsty,* –fwe cilaka (fwile).
this, cf. T. III. *as for this,* cf. T. III. *under 'however'.*
thorn, mûnga (my). *remove a thorn,* –bangulo mûnga (bangwile).
thoroughly, bwino bwino.
those, cf. T. III.
thou, iwe; we, cf. T. II.
though, nelyo; nangu; nangula.
thought, muntontonkanya (mi).
thousand, sausandi (ba–); alufu (ba–).
thrash, –kanda (kandile); –lapula (lapwile); –uma nka (umine).
thread, bushishi (n); butonge (n).
threaten, –tînya (tînishe); –pangila (pangile).
three, ... tatu.
thresh, –twa (twile).
throat, cikolomino (fi); mukoshi (mi).
through, prep. mu: *pass – the garden,* pita mu malimino.
throw, –pôsa (pôsele); *also* throw away. – *down,* –wisha (wishishe); –pôsa panshi.
thumb, cikumo (fi).
thunder, 1. n. cibulukutu; nkuba. 2. v.i. –bulukuta

(bulukwite).
Thursday, pali Cine or muli Cine; *also* on Thursday.
thus, ifyo; fino.
thy, ... obe.
thyself, we mwine.
tick, lukufu (n). *grass tick,* konto (ba–). *tick-bird,* nkôba (n).
ticket, itikiti (ma).
tickle, –tekunya (tekwinye).
tidiness, busaka.
tidy, –fûtuka (fûtwike): *this house is –* mu ŋanda ii namufûtuka.
tie, –kaka (kakile). – *a knot,* –fundike cifundo –fundike cifundo (fundike). – *strings together,* –fundikanye myando (fundikenye). – *lath on roof,* –kangala (kangele). – *poles of a wall together,* –banga (bangile).
tile, 1. (for roof), tailoshi (ma); 2. (for floor), cisele (fi).
till, mpaka na: *till the end,* mpaka no kupwa. *up till now,* ukufika na nomba.
tilt, –sendeka (sendeke); –sulula (sulwile).
time, 1. nshita. *another –,* limbi. *at what –?* mu nshita nshi? *from – to –,* mu nshita mu nshita. *in no –,* kale na kale. *it is a long time,* kale fye. *in old times,* kale na kale. *it is a long – since,* nshita yalêpa apo. *have no –.* nshita yabula. *what – is it?* nsa yafika shani?
time, 2. (occasion) muku (mi).
the first –, umuku wa ntanshi or wa ŋa kubala. *how many times,* miku

inga? *many times,* miku ingi. *innumerable times,* miku te ya kupenda. *sometimes,* limo limo; miku imo imo. *each –,* lyonse.

times, Math. –mikula (mikwile): *2 x 3 is 6,* fibili mikula na fitatu fyaba mutanda.

timidity, mwenso.

tin can, cikopo (fi); itepe (ma) (of 4 gals).

tiny, 1. adv. adj. ubuce: *what a – egg,* ilini ubuce. 2. adj. ...nononôno.

tip, 1. n. (end), mpela (m). 2. v.t. –pêlo bupe (pêle).

tiptoe, walk on –, –endela pa tukondo (endele).

tire, –nasha (nashishe).

tired, –naka (nakile). *– of something,* –tendwa (tendelwe).

tithe, mutûlo (mi).

to, prep, ku or kuli.

tobacco, fwâka: *good –,* fwâka musuma.

to-day, lelo: *just –,* lêlo line *not –,* lêlo telyo. *– again,* na lêlo. *as for –,* lêlo lyena.

toe, cikondo (fi).

together, pamo; kumo; cima.

tomato, matimati; tomatoshi (ba–).

tomb, cilindi (fi); luputa (m).

to-morrow, mailo. *just to-morrow,* mailo line. *not –,* mailo telyo. *– again,* na mailo. *as for –,* mailo lyena. *day after –,* bulya bushiku.

tongue, lulimi (ndimi). *wicked tongue,* nkakashi (n).

tongs, (a pair of –), lumano (mano).

to-night, lelo cungulo.

tool, cibombelo (fi). *set tool to handle,* –kwika (kwikile). *remove tool from handle,* –kwikula (kwikwile). *tool fall out of handle,* –sokoka (sokweke).

tooth, lino (mêno). *start teething,* –mena mêno (menene).

toothache muca.

tooth-brush, muswaki (mi).

top, mûlu. *on top,* pa mûlu.

torch, tôki (ba–); lusaniko (n).

torrent, mulamba (mi).

tortoise, fulwe (ba–).

total, conse pamo. *what is the total,* conse pamo ni shani?

totem, mukowa (mi). *person of the same totem,* muntu, followed by poss. pr. *person of an opposite totem,* munungwe (ba–).

totter, v.i. –talatanta (talatantile).

touch, –kumya (kumishe).

tough, –kosa (kosele): *the meat is tough,* nama yakosa.

tour, lwendo (nyendo); bulendo.

towards, ku or kuli.

towel, citambala (fi).

tower, lupungu lwa njelwa (m).

town, musumba (mi).

townsman, mwina musumba (bêna).

toy, ca kwangasha (fya).

trace, 1. ishinda (ma); makasa. 2. v.t. –lengula makasa (lengwile).

track, 1. n. cf. trace. 2. v.t. *track game,* –lonshe nama (londele).

trade, bukwebo (ma); bu-nonshi.

tradesman, musulwishi (ba); musulushi (ba); wa makwebo (ba).

tradition, cishilano (fi).

train, shitima lya panshi (ba–).

transfer, v.t. –sesha (seseshe).

transgress, –pulamo (pulilemo).

translate, –alula (alwile).

transplant, –limba (limbile).

trap, citeyo (fi); (for rats), ciliba (fi); (for moles), cikwa (fi); (for fish), môno (myono). *set a trap,* –tea (têle). *set a fish-trap,* –têko mono (têkele). *remove a fishtrap,* –fubo môno (fubile).

travel, –tandala (tandele); –enda (endele).

traveller, mulendo (ba).

treachery, busangu.

tread, –nyanta (nyantile).

treason, busangu.

treasure, cuma (fy).

treat as, –cita (citile): *you treat me as a friend,* wancita nga cibusa. *treat well,* –tentemba (tentembe). – *badly,* –cûsha (cûshishe). *treat one another fraternally,* –citana bumunyina bumunyina.

treaty, cumfwano (fy).

tree, muti (mi). *names of trees,* cf. T. IX *sprouting trees after having been lopped,* cifumbule (fi). *stump of tree,* cishiki (fi). *shoots or stumps of tree,* cimpusa (fi). *treeless place,* cipya (fi).

tremble, –tutuma (tutwime).

trench, ngalande (n).

trench round a village, mpembwe (m). *trench for foundations,* mufula (mi).

tribe, mutundu (mi; mushobo (mi); luko (nduko).

tribute, mulambo (mi); mutûlo (mi). *pay tribute,* –leko mulambo (lekele).

trickery, malêle.

trickle down, –konkoloka (konkolweke); –pôloloka (pôlolweke).

trifle, ca fye (fya fye).

trigger of a gun, buta bwa mfuti (mata ya –).

trim, –angwila (angwile).

trip, lwendo (nyendo); bulendo.

trot along –sunsunta (sunsuntile).

trouble, 1. n. bwafya; mpasase. 2. v.t. cf. annoy. *bring into trouble,* –letelela (letelele).

troublesome, cf. annoy.

trough, mulimba (mi).

trousers, itoloshi (ma).

trowel, mwiko (mîko); mupeni (mi).

true, …ine …ine. *it is true,* cine cine; ca cine.

truly, wa cine (ba); wa pe (ba): *I remain Yours truly,* nine wenu wa pe or wa cine.

trumpet, ipenga (ma). *blow the trumpet,* –lishe penga (lishishe).

trunk, mukonso (mi).

trust, –tetekela (tetekele); also –cetekela; –sûbila (sûbile).

trustful, –ba ne citetekelo; cf. also trust.

trustworthy, wa cishinka (ba).

truth, cumi; bufuma cumi;

ca cine; cishinka. *say the truth*, -lungika pa kulanda (lungike); -sosa ca cine (sosele).

truthful, -ba no bufuma cûmi.

try, -esha (eseshe). – *hard*, -tukuta (tukwite).

tsetsefly, kashembele (tu).

tuberculosis, ntanda-bwanga.

Tuesday, muli Cibili or pali Cibili; also *on Tuesday*.

tumour, mumena (ba-).

tunnel, cilongoma (fi); (made by rats, etc.), bwendo.

turkey, kalukuluku (ba-); nkokolembe (n).

turn, v.t. -pilibula (pilibwile); v.i. -pilibuka (pilibwike). *turn against*, cf. hate & hostile – *bad* (morally), -sanguka (sangwike); (become sour), -sasa (sashile): *egg turns bad*. lini lyasuka. – *down* (fold downwards), -peta panshi (petele); cf. reduce or refuse. – *in* (fold inwards), -peta mukati. – *off*, e.g. water tap, -cilika (cilike). – *on*, e.g. water tap, -cilula (cilwile). – *out*, cf. expel. *turn inside out*, -fukula (fukwile). – *over*, cf. tilt. – *round*, cf. turn or look around. – *upside down*, cf. tilt. *take in turns*, -pokana (pokene). *in turns*, adv. kombokombo: *it is (my) turn*, nomba (nine).

turtle, cf. tortoise.

turtle dove, cipêle (fi).

twice, miku ibili.

twig, musambo (mi); dry twig or branch, lusansu (n).

twine, butonge (n).

twinkle (of stars), -shibantukila (shibantukile); (with the eyes), -shibashiba (shibashibe).

twins, mpundu (ba-). *bear twins*, -pasa bampundu (pashile).

twist, -nyonga (nyongele). – *a rope*, -pyato mwando (pyatile). – *thread*, -luko bushishi (lukile).

two, ... bili: *two men*, abantu babili.

type (kind), musango (mi): *what type is he?* uyu aba shani? or uyu aba musango shani?

tyre (metal –), mupeto (mi); (rubber –), mupila (mi).

— U —

udder, ibêle (ma).

ugly, ... bi; -bipa (bipile).

ulcer, cipute (fi).

umbrella, mwamfuli (my).

unable, -filwa (fililwe); tekuti or teti: *I am unable*, nafilwa. *I am – to do it*, nafilwo kuciteci or tekuti (teti) nciteci.

unacquainted, -lubana (lubêne).

uncertain, -twishika (twishike).

unclean, cf. dirty.

uncleanliness, busafya.

uncombed, -fulubana (fulubêne).

unconscious, -lufya mâno (lufishe); -fwa cipûpu (fwîle).

uncork, –cilula (cilwile).

uncooked, ... bishi.

uncover, (blanket, etc.), fimbula (fimbwile); (take off lid), –kupukula (kupukwile).

unction, extreme –, cisubo ca balwêle.

undecided, –kutumana (kutumene).

under, mwisamba; pesamba: *under the tree,* mwisamba lya muti.

undersized, –tusa (tushile).

understand, –tesha (teseshe); –umfwa (umfwile: *do you –,* bushe mwatesha; bushe mwaumfwa. *come to an understanding,* cf. agreement. *fail to come to an –,* cf. agreement. *be beyond one's understanding,* –pesha mâno (peseshe): *it is beyond my –,* campesha mâno.

underwear, cifunga (fi).

undress, –fûla (fûlile).

unearth, –shula (shulile); –shukula (shukwile).

unemployed, –kupauka (kupawike).

unexpected, on an – day, bushiku bushilile kantu.

unexpectedly, cf. unexpected. *come –,* –pumikisha (pumikishe).

unfasten, cf. untie or loosen.

unfix (unglue), –kakatula (kakatwile). v. stat. –kakatuka (kakatuke). cf. also loosen.

unfold, –petulula (petulwîle).

unfortunate, –shama (sheme). *– person,* mulanda (ba).

ungrateful, –pontela (pontele). *– person,* munsha-

nya (ba).

unhook, –kobola (bokwele).

unhurt, ... tuntulu.

unit over ten. mpusho. e.g. *eleven,* ikumi limo ne mpusho imo.

unjust, –ba no lufyengo.

unless, kano.

unlock, –fungula (fungwile).

unlucky, –shama (sheme). *– person,* mupîna (ba).

unmanageable, –belebensa (belebensele).

unmarried person, mushimbe. *– state.* bushimbe.

unnoticed, pass –, –lubika (lubîke).

unoccupied, cf. unemployed.

unpack, –longolola (longolwele): *help to –,* mungafweko ukulongolole fipe.

unrecognizable, –lubana (lubene).

unripe, ... bishi.

unroll, –pombolola (pombolwele).

unsalted, fyantalala.

unseasoned, cf. unsalted.

unsew, –bilulula (bilulwile).

unstitch, cf. unsew.

unstuck, be –, –kambatuka (kambatwike).

untidy, cf. dirty. *untidy person,* musanku.

untidiness, (on a person) busanku; (elsewhere) busafya.

untie, –kakula (kakwîle).

until, mpaka na; nga; ukufika na ku: *until death,* mpaka no kufwa: *until he returns,* nga abwêla. *until the rainy season,* ukufika na ku mainsa.

up, is expressed with the verb it stands with, e.g.

go up, –nina (ninine).

upon, cf. up.

upright, –ololoka (ololweke).

uproar, mpasase (m).

uproot, –limbula (limbwile); –shula (shulile).

upset, (physically), –bundama (bundeme); (of stomach), –seluka; (mentally), –pamfya (pamfishe).

upstairs, pa mulu.

urge, –cincisha (cincishe); –pamfya (pamfishe).

urgently, cf. very much.

urine, misu.

urinate, –sunda (sundile).

us, tu, cf. T. II.

use, 1. n. mulimo: *what is the – of this?* mulimo wa ici mulimo nshi? 2. v.t. –bomfva (bomfeshe): *how do you – it?* mulecibomfya shani?

useful, –bomba (bombele); –afwa (afwile); –ba bwino: *this is –.* ici cilebomba or ici cileafwa or ici cili bwino.

useless thing, cinangwa (fi). canangwa (fy); ca fye (fya fye). *be useless*, –ba cinangwa or canangwa or ca fye. It can also be translated by the neg. of useful.

— V —

vaccinate, –lase nshindano (lashile).

vagabond, 1. n. mutalantanshi (ba) 2. v.i. –talatanta (talatantile).

vain, in –, cabe.

valley, nika (n).

valuable, . . . mutengo.

value, mutengo (mi): *what is the –?* umutengo ni shani?

vanish, –uluka (ulwike).

vapour, cushi (fy).

vary, v.t. –alula (alwile); –cilanya (cilenye); v.i. –aluka (alwike); –ibela (ibelele).

vassal, muleshi (ba).

vegetable, musálu (mi).

vein, mushipa wa mulopa (mi).

venerable, –cindama (cindême).

venereal disease, tuswende.

vengeance, cilandushi.

venom, busungu.

verandah, lukûngu (n).

verdict, cipingulo (fi).

verify, –shininkisha (shininkishe).

vertigo, lunshingwa.

very, adv. 1. . . . ine: *he is the – man I want,* uyu wine eo mfwaya. 2. sâna. *very good,* cisuma sâna; cawama sâna. 3. se, used with –kaba. *it is – hot,* cakaba se. 4. tutu. used with –bûta. *it is – white,* cabûta tutu. 5. pa, used with –isula. *it is – full,* caisula pa 6. pêne, used with apo, apa, palya, cf. apo pêne, apa pêne & palya pêne.

vex, –panika (panike).

vice, mubêle ubi (mi).

vigil, cibelushi.

village, mushi (mi). *– in construction,* misokolo. *build a –.* –sokolo mushi (sokwele). *deserted village,* cibolya (fi).

vine, mwangashi (my).

vinegar, shiki.

violate. cf. **transgress.** *violate a law.* –onaule cebo (onawile).

virgin. virjine (ba–); nacisungu (ba–).

virtue. mubêle usuma (mi).

visible. –moneka (moneke).

visit. –pempula (pempwile); –tandala ku bantu (tandele).

visitor. mweni (bêni).

view. 1. n. be in –, –ba pa menso: –moneka (moneke). 2. v.t. cf. **inspect.**

vocation. bwite.

vulture. ikubi (ma); mpungu (m).

— W —

wade. –tubula (tubwîle). *wade across water.* –abuka panshi (abwike).

wag the tail. –minyo mucila (minishe).

wages. malipilo.

wagtail. katyetye (tu).

wail. –lôsha (lôseshe).

wailing. malilo.

waist. musana (mi).

wait. –linda (lindile); –pemba (pembele); also wait for: *wait a bit,* linda or pembela panono. *keep waiting,* –lindika (lindike); –pembesha (pembeshe).

wake up. v.t. –bûsha (bûshishe); v.i. –bûka (bûkile); v.t. –shibûsha (shibwishe); v.i. –shibûka (shibwike).

walk. –enda (endele). *walk quickly,* –endesha (endeshe). *walk about,* –tandala (tandele). *walk on,* –nya-nta (nyantile). *go for a walk,* same as *walk about.*

wall. cibumba (fi).

wander. –talatanta (talatantile).

wanderer. mutalatanshi (ba).

want. –fwaya (fwaile): *what do you want?* mulefwaya nshi or cinshi mulefwaya? *be in want,* –kabila (kabile); *(I am in want of money),* nakabila indalama. *be wanted,* –fwaikwa (fwaikwe): *what is –ed is,* icafwaikwa ni. *be wanting* (missing), –shala (shele).

war. nkondo (n). *make war on,* –lwisha (lwishishe). *civil war,* nkondo ya bukaya.

warm. –kaba (kabile): *warm water,* menshi yakaba. *very warm,* –kaba sana; –kabisha (kabishe); kaba se. *warm oneself,* –onta (ontele).

warn. –soka (sokele). *– through winking with eyes,* –kapisha ku menso (kapishe).

warrior. cita (fi).

wart. lusundu (n).

warthog. munjili (ba–).

wash oneself. –samba (sambile); –owa (owele). *wash clothing,* –capa (capile).

wasp. (kind of –), ilonda (ma).

wastage. bonaushi.

waste. –pôsaika (pôsaike).

watch. 1. n. nsa (n). 2. v.t. –linda (lindile). *– over,* –angalila (angalile).

watchman. shimalonda (ba–). mulinda fipe (ba–).

water, menshi. *deep water,* itenga (ma). *running –* (in river), mulonga (mi). *stagnant –,* menshi ya cika- lishi.

water, v.t. (with a furrow), –tapilila (tapilile); (with a hose), –kontelela (konte- lele). *put under water to soak,* –abika (abike). *take out of water after soaking,* abula (abwile).

waterbuck, cuswe (fy).

water closet, cimbusu (fi). *go to the –,* –ya ku cimbu- su; –ya kunse.

waterfall, cipôma (fi).

water-hole, cishima (fi).

watering place, kwifwe; pe fwe.

wave, itamba (ma).

waver, –shingashinga (shi- ngashingile).

wax, nyali (n); ipula (ma). *sealing wax,* namba.

way, cf. path or manner. *way of doing,* micitile. *that is not the –,* te musa- ngo iyo! *– of sitting,* mika- lile. *– of talking,* mila- ndile. *– of working,* mibo- mbele. *get out of the way,* –sela (selele); –taluka (talwike). *take a round- about way,* –shoka (sho- kele).

we, tu, cf. T. II.

weak, can be transcribed by the neg. of strong: *he is –,* takosa iyo. *weak* (feeble), –bonsa (bonse- le).

weakness in legs, cite (fi).

wealth, cûma; bukankâla.

wealthy, –ba ne fyuma –ba no bukankâla. *wealthy person,* wa fyuma (ba); mukankâla (ba); musa-

mbashi (ba).

wean, –sumuna (sumwìne).

weapon, canso (fy).

wear, –fwala (fwele).

weariness, citendwe.

weasel, kapandwe (tu).

weather, hot –, kukaba; cold –, mpepo; cloudy –, cikutika.

weave, (with wool), –pikula (pikwile); (with thread or rope), –luka (lukile); (with reeds etc.), –pika (pikile).

wed, v.i. –upa (upile) when man; –upwa (upilwe) when woman. v.t. –ufya (ufishe).

wedding, bwinga. *wedding present,* mpango. *give the –,* –leke mpango (lekele).

Wednesday, muli or pali Citatu.

weed, –sekwila (sekwile), mankumba.

week, mulungu (mi).

weekly, cîla mulungu: mi- lungu yonse.

weep, –lila (lilile) filamba. *weep bitterly,* –lilisha (lilishe). *– for no reason,* –tefya (tefeshe).

weevil, lupese (m).

weight, cipimo (fi).

weir, bwamba (mâmba).

welcome, –sekelela (seke- lele); –sengela (sengele); –tangâta (tangâte). *utter cries of welcome,* –aulo tupundu (awile).

well, 1. n. cishima (fi). 2. adv. bwino. 3. interj. *well done!* cisuma; cawa- ma.

wench, iule (maule).

west, masamba. *to the west,* ku masamba.

wet, v.t. –bomfya (bomfeshe); v.i. –bomba (bombele).

what, 1. inter. pr. cinshi? nshi? shani?: *what have you done?* cinshi mwacita? or mwacita nshi? or mwacita shani- 2. pers. pr. cf. T. II. *what about,* nga: *what about them,* nga aba ni shani? *what for,* ...nshi?: *I want a hoe, what for?* ndefwayo lukasu, lwa nshi?

wheat, ŋanu.

wheel, mupeto (mi).

wheelbarrow, ntontoka (n); ngolofwani (n).

when, 1. inter. pr. lilali? mu nshita nshi? 2. cj. ilyo; lilya; cilya; lintu. 3. (with participle), pa. *when eating,* pa kulya.

whence, kwi?

whenever, apo: *come whenever you like,* isa apo uletemenwa.

where, 1. inter. pr. kwi?: *where are you?* muli kwi? pi? (on which part): *where did you wound the duiker?* mwalashile mpombo pi? 2. adv. uko: *go back where you came from,* bwêlela uko ufumine.

whereas, apo: *I do this – you do that,* ine ndeciteci apo imwe mulecite fyo.

wherein, umo; umwa; muntu: *put it – you like,* bîka umo utemenwe. *I have nothing – to put it,* nshikwete umwa kubika. *here is the house – we live,* ii ni ŋanda muntu twaikala.

whether, nga: *I do not*

know – *you like it,* nshishibe nga mwacitemwa.

whether or. nga atemwa.

which, 1. inter. pr. nshi? *which tree?* muti nshi? 2. rel. pr. cf. T. IV *in which,* same as wherein.

while; whilst, mu nshita.

whimper, –tefya (tefeshe).

whip, cikôti (n).

whirl, –libila (libile).

whirlwind, kankungwe (ba–).

whisker, mwefu (my). – *of cat, dog,* etc., linwana (ma).

whisper, –sosa mu kapôpô (sosele); –tôtôsha (tôtôseshe).

whistle, 1. n. kapyelele (tu); pintu (ba–). 2. v.t. –lisha kapyelele; –lisha pintu (lishishe).

whistling, munsôli (mi). *be –.* –lisho munsôli.

white, –bûta (bûtile). *very white,* –bûta tutu; –bûta sâna; –bûtisha (bûtishe).

whitewash, –shingula (shingwile); –kupaula (kupawile).

whitish, –butuluka (butulwîke).

who, 1. inter. pr. ani (bâni?): *who is this man?* uyu nani? 2. rel. pr. cf T. IV.

whoever; whosoever, onse (bonse): – *wants to come,* onse utemwo kwisa.

whole, ... tuntulu.

wholly, adv. conse; cituntulu; cf. also entirely.

whom, 1. inter pr. it is transcribed by the rel. pr. together with the inter. pr.: *whom do you want?*

uo mulefwava nani? 2. rel. pr. same as 'who'.

whose. 1. inter. pr. –a kwâni, pl. –a bâni (if it refers to a noun of class 'mu/ba' *whose work is this?* ncito ya kwâni/ya bâni? –a nshi (if it refers to a noun of all other clases): *whose traces are these?* makasa ya nama nshi? (lit. the traces of which animal are these?). 2. rel. pr. it may be omitted: *the child whose father died,* mwaice wishi afwile. It can also be expressed by means of: (a) the rel. object: mwaice uo wishi afwile; (b) the poss. pr.: mwaice wishi afwile; cf. his, her, its, their. (c) with the prep. 'of': *the child whose name is* Mutale, mwaice we shina lya Mutale.

why? cinshi? nshi? mulandu nshi? *that is why,* e uko; e cilya; e ico.

wick, lutambo (n); pl. mire used.

wide, –lepa (lepele); –senama (seneme) (with a wide opening).

widen, –kusha (kushishe); –senamika (senamike).

widow, widower, mushimbe (ba); muka mfwilwa (ba–).

widowhood, bushimbe.

width, bukulu; bufumo.

wife, mukashi (ba). *first – of a polygamist,* mukolo (ba–). *additional wife,* mwinga (ba–). *wife of,* muka (ba–): *the wife of* Mutale, muka Mutale.

wild, ...kali. *be wild,* –kalipa (kalipe).

wilfully, ku mufulo.

will, 1. n. kutemwa. 2. aux. verb, –ka: *he will do it,* akacicita. *last will,* mulao (mi).

wilt, –bonsa (bonsele); –fota (fotele).

wind, n. mwela. *strong wind,* cîkûku. *break wind,* –nya cisushi (nyêle). *breaking of wind,* cisushi (fi).

wind round, v.t. –pomba (pombele). – *up,* –sumba (sumbile).

winding (of road or river), cinshoko (fi).

windpipe, cikolomino (fi).

window, iwindo (ma).

wine, ndifai (n).

wing, ipindo (ma).

wink, –kapisha (kapishe).

winnow, –ela (elele); –sensebula (sensebwile).

wipe, –pukuta (pukwite). *wipe out,* –fûta (fûtile).

wire, lusale (n).

wireless, waileshi (m–).

wise, ...mâno: *he is wise,* wa mâno.

wisdom, mâno.

wisely, mâno mâno.

wish, –fwaya (fwaile).

witch, muloshi (ba).

witchcraft, buloshi; bwanga. *practice –,* –panda bwanga (pandile).

witchdoctor, shinanga (ba–).

with, na.

withdraw, –funtuka (funtwike).

wither, –bonsa (bonsele).

withhold, –tana (tanine).

within, mu or pa; muli or pali.

without, apashili; **apabula.**
without reason, **apabulo**
mulandu.
witness, 1. n. kambone (ba-).
cilola (ba-). 2. v.t. –ba
kambone. *bearing of* –
bukambone.
woman, mwanakashi (ba).
womanhood, bwanakashi.
womb, ifumo (ma).
wonder, 1. n. cisungusho
(fi); cipesha màno (fi).
2. v.i. –sunguka (sungwi-
ke); –papa (papile).
wonderful, ca kusunguka
(fya).
wood (forest), mutengo
(mi).
woodpecker, tondwe (ba-).
word, ishiwi (ma).
work, 1. mulimo (mi); ncito
(n). 2. v.i. –bomba (bo-
mbele). *half a day's* –
ipenga. *compulsory – for
a chief,* mulâsa (mi).
cease a day's –, –inuka
(inwike). *relieve from* –,
–inusha (inwishe). *look
for* –, –fwayo mulimo
(fwaile). *it works out,*
cabomba. *it does not* –
out, cakâna. *enlist for* –
v.i. –*ingile ncito* (ingile)
or –lembwe ncito (lembe-
lwe); v.t. –lembe ncito
(lembele). *run away from
work,* –tâba ku ncito
(tâbile). *leave the work,*
–leke ncito (lekele). *work
for food,* –pula (pulile).
– for something, –kwila
(kwilile). *– in vain,* –*icu*-
sha. *look in vain for* –,
–ambakala (ambakele).
piece –, cikongwani (fi).
world, calo (fyalo); isonde.
on this world, muno calo;

pano isonde.
worm, mwambo (my).
intestinal – nsokanda.
glow-worm, kabeshamulilo
(tu).
worn out, –kota (kotele).
– by sickness, –fumuka
(fumwike).
worry, 1 n. isakamika (ma).
2. v.i. –sakamana (saka-
mêne). v. caus. –sakamika
(sakamike).
worship, v.t. –pepa (pepele).
worshipper, kapepa (ba–).
worth, –fwa (fwile). *it is
worth while,* cifwile.
worthy, cf. worth.
wound, 1. n. cilonda (fi).
2. v.t. –lasa (lashile).
– caused by a spear etc.,
cilaso (fi).
wrap, –pomba (pombele).
wrath, cipyu.
wrestle, –cena (cenene).
wrinkles, nkanshi.
wrist, nkolokoso (n).
write, –lemba (lembele).
wrong, 1. n. lufyengo; cibi
(fi). 2. v.t. –fyenga (fyengele): *he wronged me,*
amfyenga. v.i. –luba (lu-
bile): *he is wrong,* aluba.
do wrong, –bifya (bifi-
she) –lufyanya (lufye-
nye). *do wrong with
others,* –ulungana (ulu-
ngêne).

— Y —

yam, mûmbu (my).
yawn, 1. n. mwau (my).
2. v.i. –aulo mwau (awile).
yard, cf. step. *one yard of
cloth,* ipande (ma). *court
yard,* lubansa (mansa).
year, mwaka (my).

yearly, cîla mwaka; myaka yonse.

yearn, –kumbwa (kumbilwe).

yeast, nsashiko.

yell, –pumba (pundile).

yes, ee; è; endita; mukwai.

yesterday, mailo. *day before* –, bulya bushiku.

yet, not –, na nomba.

yield, v.i. –cimba (cimbile); –tontoloka (tontolweke); v. caus. –tontolola (tontolwele).

yonder, kulya; palya.

young man, mulumendo (ba).

you, imwe; mwe, cf. T. II.

younger brother or sister, mwaice (ba), followed by poss. pr: *my* –, mwaice wandi.

your, ... enu.

yourself, imwe bene.

youth (boy), mulumendo (ba); (girl), mukashana (ba).

youth (of boy), bulumendo; (of girl), bukashana.

— Z —

zealous, –cincila ku milimo (cincile).

zebra, colwa (ba-).

zinc, mutofwe.

APPENDIX

Table I. THE PREFIXES & THE PREPOSITION 'OF'

class	number	noun pre-prefix (initial vowel)	noun class-prefix	verb	adj. pre-prefix (initial vowel)	adj. class-prefix	prep. 'of' - A
1	s.	u	mu	a	u	mu—	wa
	pl.	a	ba	ba	a	ba—	ba
2	s.			a	u	mu	wa
	pl.		ba	ba	a	ba	ba
3	s.	u	mu	u		u	wa
	pl.	i	mi	i		i	ya
4	s.	i	n/m	i		i	ya
5		u	lu	lu	u	lu	lwa
	pl.	i	n/m	shi	i	shi	sha
6	s.	i	ci	ci	i	ci	ca
	pl.	i	fi	fi	i	fi	fya
7	s.	(i)	i	li	i	li	lya
		i	li	li	i	li	lya
8		u	lu	lu	u	lu	lwa
9		u	ku	ku	u	ku	kwa
10		u	bu	bu	u	bu	bwa
	pl.	a	ma	ya	a	ya	ya
11	s.	a	ka	ka	a	ka	ka
	pl.	u	tu	tu	u	tu	twa
12	s.	u	bu	bu	u	bu	bwa
13	s.	u	ku	ku	u	ku	kwa
14	s.		ku	ku		ku	kwa
			mu	mu		mu	mwa
			pa	pa		pa	pa

- The prefix of the noun is called nominal prefix.
- The prefix of the verb is the verbal prefix.
- The harmony between the prefixes in a sentence is called the concord.
- The prefixes of all words in a sentence which require the concord with the noun are called concord prefixes.

(i) The "L" of most of the words of this class is dropped, but the concord remains "li".

EXAMPLES

Umuntu ali umusuma, the man is good.
abantu bali abasuma, the men are good.

cona ali umusuma, the cat is nice.
bacona bali abasuma, the cats are nice.

umuti uli usuma, the tree is nice.
imiti ili isuma, the trees are nice.

insalu/imbuto ili isuma, the cloth/seed is good.
insalu imbuto/inkasu shili ishisuma, the cloth/seeds/hoes
are nice.

icitabo cili icisuma, the book is nice.
ifitabo fili ifisuma, books are nice.

isembe lili ilisuma, the axe is nice.
ilini lili ilisuma, the egg is good.
ulubansa luli ulusuma, the yard is nice.
ukutwi kuli ukusuma, the ear is nice.
ubutanda buli ubusuma, the mat is nice.
amasembe/amani, etc. yali ayasuma, the axes/eggs, etc.
are nice.

akalulu kali akasuma, the hare is nice.
utululu tuli utusuma, hares are nice.

ubutani buli bubi, stinginess is bad.

ukubomba kuli ukusuma, work is good.

kuntu kuli kusuma, here it is nice.
muntu muli musuma, in here it is nice.
pantu pali pasuma, on this place here it is nice.

Rules guiding the pre-prefix or initial vowel

1. Most nouns, adjectives and the infinitives of all verbs can have a pre-prefix, except nouns of class 2.

2. Nouns which have no pre-prefix are: names, nouns denoting relationship, profession or trade, foreign nouns.

3. Adjectives which have no pre-prefix are: numerals and quasi-numerals. e.g. *cimo*, one thing, *umo*, one man, etc. or one tree etc.

4. Adjectives lose the pre-prefix if they follow immediately after a noun.

5. Nouns and adjectives lose the pre-prefix :
   (a) in the vocative, e.g. we mfumu isuma, o good chief.
   (b) after the 1st & 2nd person singular and plural of the verb -*li*, be; e.g. *uli musuma*, you are good; *tuli basuma, we are good.*
   (c) after a demonstrative, e.g. *ifi fitabo*, these books.
   (d) after the preposition '*of*' in all classes, except class 7; e.g. *masako ya fyuni*, the feathers of the bird; but, *ishina lye sukulu*, the name of the school.
   (f) in the copulative form, e.g. *ici cinshi? citabo,* what is this? a book. In class 4 it is replaced by "ni" e.g. *ni mbwili*, it is a leopard. Class 7 follows the general rule e.g. *lisukulu*, it is a school.

The Possessive form -a

1. The possessive is in English expressed by the preposition '*of*' or the Saxon genetive, e.g. the name of the chief or the chief's name. In Bemba it is formed by the vowel A and the concord prefix of the preceding noun, e.g. *ishina lya mfumu*, the name of the chief. The possessive differs therefore according to the classes of nouns.

   Note: In class '*mu/ba*' the concord prefix is U and not MU, e.g. *mwana wa mfumu*, the child of the chief.

2. The possessive never fuses with a following vowel except with the 'l' of class 7 nouns when the "L" is dropped, e.g. *ishina lye sukulu*, the name of the school.

The possessive may have an initial vowel. This initial vowel fuses with preceding vowels.

The possessive must have an initial vowel if it is used (a) substantively, e.g. *sosa ifya cine*, say the truth; (b) to express emphasis, e.g. *lete fipe ifya mfumu*, bring the loads, the ones of the chief.
The possessive is used to make nouns and adjectives, e.g. *wa ncito*, worker; *insalu yabûta*, white cloth.

If the possessive is followed by a noun indicating a place, this noun is put into class 14, e.g. *inama ya mumpanga*, an animal of the bush.

The possessive is omitted (a) after nouns which express the possessive: *shiCileshe*, the father of Cileshe; *naMulenga*, the mother of Mulenga; *shifyala Lesa*, the father-in-law of Lesa, etc. (b) after the following words: *muka*, husband/wife; *mwine*, owner; *mwina*, citizen; *mwana*, child (in singular only); *bampundu*, twins; *mukamfwilwa*, widow/widower; *mwishikulu*, grandchild; *mwipwa*, nephew/niece.

The particle '*kwa*' is added to the possessive in the following cases (singular only):

(a) before names, e.g. *bana ba kwa Paolo*, the children of Paul.

(b) before nouns of class 2, which have no prefix, e.g. *mfuti ya kwa bwana*, the gun of the master; e.g. *citabo ca kwa kafundisha*, the teacher's book. e.g. *ishina lya kwa nabwinga*, the name of the bride.

Table II. THE PERSONAL PRONOUNS.

1. Separable pronouns, used for emphasis, calling people, pointing out people, etc.

person	positive/it is me		negative/it is not me
1 I, me	ine	nine	ine tene
2 Thou, thee	iwe	niwe	iwe tewe
3 he, him/she her/it	uyu	ni uyu	uyu teo
1 we, us	ifwe	ni fwe	ifwe tefwe
2 you	nimwe	ni mwe	imwe temwe
3 they, them	aba	ni aba	aba tebo

personal pronouns in connection with:

it is	alone	it is really/same
nine	ine neka	nine wine
niwe	iwe weka	niwe wine
ni uyu	uyu eka	uyu wine or eo
nifwe	ifwe fweka	nifwe bêne
nimwe	imwe mweka	nimwe bêne
ni aba	aba beka	aba bêne or ebo

self	na = and; also; too	na = with
ne mwine	na ine	na ine or nani
we mwine	na iwe	na iwe or nobe
umwine	na uyo or no'yu or nao	noyu or nankwe
fwe bêne	na ifwe	na ifwe or nefwe
mwe bêne	na imwe	na imwe or nenu or nemwe
abêne	nabo	nabo

Notes: 1. The following abbreviations take place before nouns, relative pronouns and the pronoun 'mwine': ne for ine; we for iwe; fwe for ifwe and mwe for imwe.

2. There is no proper pers. pronoun for the 3rd person; the demonstratives are used instead, for all classes. cf. T. III.

2. Inseparable pronouns, used in conjunction with a verb

(a) when subject:

person	positive	negative
1 I	n/m —	nshi —
2 thou	u —	tau —
3 he/she/it/	a —	ta —
1 we	tu —	tatu —
2 you	mu —	tamu —
3 they	ba —	taba —

(b) when object:

person	in positive & negative sentences
1 me	— n/m —
2 thee	— ku —
3 him/her/it	— mu —
1 us	— tu —
2 you	— mu —
3 them	— ba —

Note: The pronouns of the 3rd person (singular & plural), both when subject or object, change with the different classes. The various kinds have been laid down in TABLE I, for subject under 'verb'; for object under 'adj.', (class-prefix only!).

Table III. THE DEMONSTRATIVES

class		"this here"	"this"	"that"	"that yonder"
1 – 2	s.	uno	uyu	uyo	ulya
	pl.	bano	aba	abo	balya
3	s.	umo	uyu	uyo	ulya
	pl.	ino	ii	iyo	ilya
4	s.	ino	ii	iyo	ilya
5		luno	ulu	ulo	lulya
	pl.	shino	ishi	isho	shilya
6	s.	cino	ici	ico	cilya
	pl.	fino	ifi	ifyo	filya
7	s.	lino	ili	ilyo	lilya
8		luno	ulu	ulo	lulya
9		kuno	uku	uko	kulya
10		buno	ubu	ubo	bulya
	pl.	yano	aya	ayo	yalya
11	s.	kano	aka	ako	kalya
	pl.	tuno	utu	uto	tulya
12	s.	buno	ubu	ubo	bulya
13	s.	kuno	uku	uko	kulya
14	s.	kuno	uku	uko	kulya
		umu	umu	umo	mulya
		pano	apa	apo	palya

e.g. *uno mulungu,* this week (we are in).
uyu mulungu, next week (in front).
ulya mulungu, the week before last.
the week after the next.

Demonstratives in connection with

"not"	"same" "self"	"however"
teo	wine	ena (wena)
tebo	bene	bena
teo	wine	wena
teyo	ine	yena
teyo	ine	yena
telo	lwine	lwena
tesho	shine	shena
teco	cine	cena
tefyo	fine	fyena
telyo	line	lyena
telo	lwine	lwena
teko	kwine	kwena
tebo	bwine	bwena
teyo	yene	yena
teko	kene	kena
teto	twine	twena
tebo	bwine	bwena
teko	kwine	kwena
teko	kwine	kwena
temo	mwine	mwena
tepo	pene	pena

Note: The negative can also be expressed with neg. particle *"te"*, + demonstrative, + neg. particle *"iyo"*, e.g. *te uyu iyo; te cilya iyo;* etc.

Table IV. THE RELATIVES

1. when subject

class	person	singular		plural	
1	1	ne u — I who		fwe ba — we who	
	2	we thy thou who		mwe ba — yu who	
	3	uu — he/she who, which		aba — they who, which	
2	3	uu —		aba —	
3	3	uu —	which	ii —	which
4	3	ii —	which		
5		ulu —	which	ishi —	which
6	3	ici —	which	ifi —	which
7	3	ili —			
8		ulu —	which		
9		uku —	which	aya —	which
10		ubu —			
11	3	aka —	which	utu —	which
12	3	ubu —	which		
13	3	uku —	which		
14	3	uku —			
		umu —	which		
		apa —			

Note: The negative particle is SHI for all persons and all tenses, e.g. *ushisumina,* the one who does not believe; *nkalamo ishafwile,* the lion which did not die.

2. when object

Class	person	singular	plural
1	1	ne o, I whom	mwe bo, you whom
	2	we o, thou whom	mwe bó, you whom
	3	uo, whom, which	abo, whom, which.
2		uo, which, whom	abo, which, whom
3	3	uo, which	iyo, which
4	3	iyo } which	
5		ulo	isho, which
6	3	ico, which	ifyo, which
7	3	ilyo	
8		ulo	ayo which
9		uko } which	
10		ubo	
11	3	ako, which	uto, which
12	3	ubo, which	
13	3	uko, which	
14	3	uko	
		ubo } which	
		apo	

Note: The relative, when object, may be omitted when the
noun to which it refers is expressed, e.g. *citabo waleta
cili kwi?* where is the book which you brought?

3. The Relative "...ntu".

...ntu, being; the one which, is used like an adjective,
both as subject and as object, e.g. *bakolwe bantu bace-
njela,* monkeys are clever beings. *ŋanda intu wakulile
isuma,* the house, the one you built, is nice.

Table V. TERMS OF FAMILY RELATIONSHIP

	singular	plural
	Father	
1	tata, my father	shifwe, our father
2	wiso, thy father	shinwe, your father
3	wishi, his/her father	shibo, their father
	Mother	
1	mayo, my mother	nyinefwe, our mother
2	noko, thy mother	nyinenwe, your mother
3	nyina, his/her mother	nyinabo, their mother
	Father-in-law or son-in-law	
1	tatafyala	shifyalefwe
2	sofyala	shifyalenwe
3	shifyala	shifyalebo
	Mother-in-law or daughter-in-law	
1	mamafyala	nafyalefwe
2	nokofyala	nafyalenwe
3	nafyala	nafyalebo
	Grandfather	
1	shikulu	shikulwifwe
2	sokulu	shikulwinwe
3	shikulu	shikulwibo
	Grandmother	
1	mama	nakulwifwe
2	nokokulu	nakulwinwe
3	nakulu	nakulwibo
	Son or Daughter	
1	mwana wandi	mwana wesu
2	mwana obe or mwano	mwana wenu
3	mwana wakwe or mwane	mwana wabo
	Brothers or Sisters	
1	munyinane	munyinefwe
2	munyinobe or munonko	munyinenwe
3	munyina	munyinabo
	Brothers only	
1	ndume nandi	ndume nensu
2	ndume nobe	ndume nenu
3	ndume nankwe	ndume nabo

singular	I plural
Sisters only	
1 nkashi nandi	nkashi nensu
2 nkashi nobe	nkashi nenu
3 nkashi nankwe	nkashi nabo
Brother re- Sister	
1 nkashi yandi	nkashi yesu
2 nkashi yobe	nkashi yenu
3 nkashi yakwe	nkashi yabo
Sister re- Brother	
1 ndume yandi	ndume yesu
2 ndume yobe	ndume yenu
3 ndume yakwe	ndume yabo
Paternal uncle	
1 tata mwaice	shifwe mwaice
2 wiso mwaice	shinwe mwaice
3 wishi mwaice	shibo mwaice
Maternal uncle	
1 yama	nalumefwe
2 nokolume	nalumenwe
3 nalume	nalumebo
Paternal aunt	
1 mayosenge	nasengefwe
2 nokosenge	nasengenwe
3 nasenge	nasengebo
maternal aunt	
1 mayo mwaice	nyinefwe mwaice
2 noko mwaice	nyinenwe mwaice
3 nyina mwaice	nyinabo mwaice
Husband	
1 mulume wandi	mulume wesu
2 mulume obe or bâlo	mulume wenu
3 mulume wakwe	mulume wabo
Husband/wife	
1 mwina mwandi	mwina wesu
2 mwina mobe	mwina wenu
3 mwina mwakwe	mwina wabo
Friend; Companion; Comrade; Colleague	
1 munandi	munensu
2 munobe/mubiyo	munenu
3 munankwe/mubiye	munabo

Table VI. THE NUMERALS

The Cardinal Numbers		root
1	cimo	– mo
2	fibili	– bili
3	fitatu	– tatu
4	fine	– ne
5	fisano	– sano
6	mutanda	
7	cine lubali	
8	cine konse konse	
9	pabula	
10	ikumi limo	– kumi
		s - i -
12	ikumi limo na fibili	pl. ma -
	etc.	
20	makumi yabili	
21	makumi yabili na cimo	
	etc.	
30	makumi yatatu	
40	makumi yane	
50	makuhi yasano	
60	makumi mutanda	
70	makumi cine lubali	
80	makumi cine konse konse	
90	makumi pabula	
100	mwanda umo	
101	mwanda umo na cimo	
200	myanda ibili	
300	myanda itatu	
	etc.	
1000	sausandi; alufu	
2000	basausandi babili;	
	or baalufu babili	

Note: The numbers 1 to 5 (Cardinal numbers) are adjectives and their prefixes change according to the noun with which they stand, e.g. one man, *umuntu umo;* two trees, *imiti ibili,* etc.

The Ordinal Numbers

    the 1st   *icalenga cimo*
    „ 2nd   „   *fibili*
    „ 3rd,   „   *fitatu*
    „ 4th,   „   *fine*
    „ 5th,   „   *fisano*
    „ 6th,   „   *mutanda*
        etc.
    „ 10th, *icalenga ikumi limo*
    „ 11th,   „   *ikumi limo na cimo*
        etc., etc.

Note: 1. in above examples the noun 'cintu', thing is taken as understood.

2. the first can also be expressed by: ...*ntanshi* or ...*pa kubala*. the last is ...*pa kulekelesha*.

'once'; 'twice', etc. are translated by the noun *'muku'*, e.g. once, *muku umo;* twice, *miku ibili;* etc., etc.

firstly   **pa kubala; ca bumo**
secondly,   pabili; ca bubili
thirdly,   patatu; ca butatu
fourthly,   pane; ca bune
fifthly,   pasano; ca busano
sixthly   pali mutanda; ca mutanda.
        etc., etc.
lastly   pa kulekelesha.

Table VII. COURTESY AND GREETINGS

1. Some terms of addressing somebody are:
   - *mukwai*, sir/madam. It is used for everybody in singular and plural.

   - *bwana (ba-)*, master, Mr.

   - *mama (ba-)*, lady, Mrs.

   - *missisi (ba-)*, same as *mama*.

   - *mune (bane)*, my friend. It is used between equals who are known to one another, both men and women.

   - *tata, mayo, shikulu, nakulu*, are also used as forms of courtesy, *tata, mayo* may be addressed to married men and women; *shikulu, nakulu* to old men and women.

   - *kanabesa* or *mulopwe*, my Lord, Lady. Both are terms of great respect.

2. Terms to express "thank you": (see: thank you)
   - *eya mukwai* or *endita mukwai*, yes sir/madam.
   - *mwacita* or *mwawamya*, you have done well.

3. Terms to express regret for an offence which has been committed involuntarily:
   - *yangu* or *owe* or *nshishibe*, sorry; I beg your pardon.

4. **Greetings:**

   - Verbs, which are used as greetings, are put in a special Imperative, derived from the 2nd person plural of the a — tense, e.g. *mwapola* (in singular), *mwapoleni* (in plural).

   - There are also some nouns used as greetings like *milimo*, plural of *mulimo*, work and *mutende*, health.

   - A list of the more common greetings is given on the following page.

GREETINGS AND RESPONSES.

Note: The response is given after each greeting and is indicated by: R.

Mwashibukeni, good morning (lit. you have awakened).
R. *endi* or *endita mukwai,* yes, sir/madam.

mwapoleni, how are you, how do you do (lit. are you well).
R. *mwapoleni.*

mutende, same as mwapoleni.
R. *mutende.* If ill one replies: *ala, nindwâla, no,* I am ill,

kulici? what is the news?
R. *kwatalala,* all is well.

mwaiseni, welcome (lit. you have come).
R. *endita mukwai.*

mwalyeni bwino, are you eating well!
R. *kulila mulelya,* provided you eat well.

mwabombeni, are you working!
R. *endita mukwai.*

milimo, same as *mwabombeni.*
R. *endita mukwai.*
mwalimeni, same as *mwabombeni.*
R. *endita mukwai.*

bambeni, or *mabingo* or *cibamfi,* greeting to a returning hunter
R. *endita mukwai,* if he has been successful.
R. *ala ya mpanga,* if he has not.

bweleniko or *cibweshi,* you are back.
R. *endita mukwai.*

mwasalipeni or *mwasakuleni,* greeting to one who killed a dangerous animal as lion, snake, etc.
R. *endita mukwai.*

mwapusukeni, greeting to one who escaped a danger.
R. *endita mukwai.*

twapakata mukwai, greeting to a chief, when leaving.
R. *endita.*

kafikenipo, reach safely, good-bye, farewell.
R. *shalenipo,* stay well, good-bye.

Table VIII. NAMES OF SNAKES

Bemba	English	Scientific name
cilambanshila (fi)	night-adder	Cuasus rhombeatus
kafi (ba-)	spitting cobra	Naja nigricollis
kanshimonamitenge (tu)		
ibalabala (ma)	boomslang	Dispholidus typus
ifwafwa (ma)	puff-adder	Bitis arietans
nalukunilumo (ba)	twig-snake	Theolotornis kirtlandi
itiya (ma)		
iyongolo (ma)		
luminuminu (minuminu)	blind snake	T. gracilis
lusato (n)	python	Python sebae
mâmba	forest cobra	Naja melanoleuca
mâmbalushi	water cobra	
mbôma	gaboon viper	bitis gabonica
mbulushi	blind snake or two-headed snake	Typhlops shlegelii & Typhlops punctatus.
mpîni (m)		
mulalu (mi)	hissing sand-snake	Psammophis sibilans
mwendalwali (mi)	file-snake	Mehelya capensis
namabula (ba-)		Philothamnus
namutukuta (ba-)	egg-eating snake	Dasypeltis scabra
muswema (mi)		
ndele (n)	1. house-snake	Boaedon fuliginosus
	2. white-lipped snake	Crotaphoueltis hotamboeia
ngoshe (ba-)	common cobra	Dendroaspis polylepis
nondo (n)		
ntukamatumba (n)	grey-beaked snake	Scaphiophis albopunctatus

Particulars
Poisonous, stout, 6.5. cm. long.
poisonous, large black necked snake.

very poisonous.
poisonous, tree snake.
very poisonous, long, sluggish.

poisonous, tree snake, resembling twig.
kind of viper, long, found in "mishitu".
poisonous, long.
harmless, pinkish-white, long & narrow.

very poisonous, large, darkbrown.
very poisonous, long, black.
very poisonous, sluggish.
harmless, head and tail similar.

poisonous kind of viper, big, but short.
poisonous, over 1.5 m. long.

harmless, rough scales like a file.

harmless, green.
harmless, eats eggs, resembles a viper.
poisonous, long.
harmless, small, blackish.

mildly venomous, also small, blackish.

very dangerous, tree snake, olive brown.

kind of water snake.
harmless, sharp beak.

Table IX. NAMES OF TREES

1. Timber trees

Bemba	Scientific names	Used for
kaimbi (ba-)	Erythrophleum	all Carpentry.
mululu (mi)		" " , canoes
mofu (myofu)	Entandrophragma delevoyi Guerke	all carpentry.
mulombwa (mi)	Pterocarpus angolensis D. Wild	" " , canoes
mupapa (mi)	Afzelia quanzensis Welw.	" "
mupundu (mi)	Parinarium mobola Oliv.	bridges, carpentry.
saninga (ba-)	Faurea Speciosa Welw.	" " , rafter.
mubanga (mi)	Afromosia angolensis	rafters.
cipamba (fi)	Monotes oblongifolius Hutch.	
lwamba (ba-)	Syzygium	"
mucenja (mi)	Diospyros	"
mukuwe (mi)	Hirtella bangweolensis	"
museshi (mi)	Marquesia macroura Gilg.	" , ladders.
mwengele (my)	Xylopiya	mortars, drums.
musase (mi)	Albizzia sericocephala Benth.	frames.
mutobo (mi)	Barlinia craibiana Bak. f.	
mulunguti (mi)	Erythrina abyssinica Lam.	handles.
ndale (n)	Swartzia madagacahensis	
kalongwe (tu)	Dalbergia nitidula Welw.	"
mutondo (mi)	Brachystegia allenii Burt Davy	"
mpasa (m)		"
ciya (ba-)		"
miombo (mi)	Brachystegia longifolia	bark rope.
ngalati (n)	" taxifolia Harws.	"
mushike (mi)	" microphylla Harms.	"
muputu (mi)	" speciformis Benth.	"

		drums.
mufutu (mi)	Virex	"
mutiti (mi)	Erythina excelsa	"
musaye (mi)	Strychnoe pungens	"

2. Fruit Trees

Bemba	Scientific names	fruit
mupundu (mi)	Parinarium mobola Oliv.	lupundu (m).
musuku (mi)	Uapaca	lisuku (ma).
mufungo (mi)	Anisphyllea pomifera	lufungo (m).
mukunyu (mi)	Ficus graphalocarpa (Miq) Steudd.	likunyu (ma).
musafwa (mi)	Syzygium	lisafwa (ma).
mukome (mi)	Strychnos	likome (ma).
mulebe (mi)	Strophanthus	lulebe (ma).
muteke (mi)	Landollphia parvifolia K. Schum.	liteke (ma).
musongole (mi)	Strychnos cocculoides Bak.	cisongole (fi).
musokolobe wafita (mi)		lusokolobe (n).
musokolobe wabuta (mi)	Uapaca nitida Muell. Arg.	lusokolobe (n).
muminu (mi)	"	kaminu (tu).
mukole (mi)	"	likole (ma).
mungolomya (mi)		lingolomya (ma).

Table X. NAMES OF BIRDS

Bemba	English	Scientific
cembe (ba-)	fish eagle	Haliaetus vocifer
cikwekwe (fi)		Coracias sp.
cipampa (ba-)	marabou stork	Leptoptilos crumeniferus
cipele (fi)	turtle dove	Treron Australis
cipingila (fi)	quail	Frankolinus sp.
cipululu (fi)	owl	Bubo Africanus
cipungu (fi)	bateleur eagle	Terathopius ecaudatus
cisokopela (fi)	weaver	Ploceus sp.
coso (fy)	duck (wild)	
ikanga (ma)	guinea fowl	Numidia Meleagris
ikubi (ma)	vulture	Neophron monachus
kakandamatipa (tu)	snipe	Capella sp.
kakolenkole (tu)	crowned plover	Stephanibyx coronatus
kakoshi (tu)	chanting go-hawk	Melierax metabates
kakoshi kanika	pale harrier	
kamimbi (tu)	swallow	Hirundo sp.
kapeshi (tu)	frankolin	Frankolinus sp.
kapumpe (ba-)	eagle	Hieraaetus spilogaster
katutwa (tu)	dove (small kind)	Turtur sp.
katyetye (tu)	wagtail	Motadilla aguimp.
kuwe (ba-)	go-away bird	Crinifer concolor.
lukona (n)	hornbill	Tockus sp.
lukoshi (n)	hawk (small kind)	
lumbasa (ba-)	nightjar	Macrodipteryx vexilarius
mbata (m)	spurwing goose	Plectropterus gambensia
milumbe	bee-eater	Merops sp.

milumbelumbe	speckled coly	Colius striatus
mucence (ba-)	parrot	passer sp.
mukanga (mi)	pelican	pelicanus sp.
mukufi (mi)	roller	Coracias sp.
mukuta (mi)	cougal	Centropus sp.
muleya (ba-)	long-tailed widow bird	
mulowa (mi)	king-fisher	
mutengwe (mi)	Drongo	Dicrurus adsimilis
mwakatala (my)	ostrich	Struthio camelus
mwankole (ba-)	Pied Raven	Corvultur albicollis
namungwa (ba-)	long-legged Koahaan	Lissotis melanogaster
ngôli (n)	crested crane	Balrearica regulorum
nkôba (n)	heron; tickbird	Ardeola Ibis
nkondonkondo (n)	green pigeon	Treron Australia
nkwale (n)	red-necked Frankolin	Frankolinus Afer
nseba (n)	wax bill	
nsolo (n)	honey bird	Indicator
lûni (ŋûni)	honey bird	Indicator
pungwa (ba-)	falcon	Falco sp.
sosa (ba-)	sunbird	
titi (ba-)	small warbler	
tondwe (ba-)	woodpecker.	

Also of interest from Hippocrene . . .

**AFRIKAANS-ENGLISH/
ENGLISH-AFRIKAANS PRACTICAL
DICTIONARY**
430 pages • 4 ¹/² x 6 ¹/² • 14,000 entries •
0-7818-0052-8 NA • $11.95pb • (134)

**AMHARIC-ENGLISH/ENGLISH-AMHARIC
DICTIONARY**
629 pages • 5 ¹/² x 9 • over 20,000 entries •
0-7818-0115-X • NA • $40.00hc • (75)

**THE HANDBOOK OF EGYPTIAN
HIEROGLYPHS, Revised Edition**
184 pages • 5 ¹/² x 8 ¹/² • 0-7818-0625-9 • W •
$16.95pb • (741)

EGYPTIAN HIEROGLYPHS
96 pages 6 x 9 0-7818-0629-1 W $11.95pb (736)

Fulani (Western Africa)

**FULANI-ENGLISH PRACTICAL
DICTIONARY**
264 pages • 5 x 7 ¹/⁴ • 0-7818-0404-3 • W • $14.95pb
• (38)

Hausa *(Niger, Nigeria)*

HAUSA-ENGLISH/ENGLISH-HAUSA PRACTICAL DICTIONARY

431 pages • 5 x 7 • 18,000 entries • 0-7818-0426-4 • W • $16.95pb • (499)

Lingala *(Zaire)*

LINGALA-ENGLISH/ENGLISH-LINGALA DICTIONARY AND PHRASEBOOK

120 pages • 3 ³/⁴ x 7 • 0-7818-0456-6 • W • $11.95pb • (296)

Pulaar *(Senegal, Mauritania)*

PULAAR-ENGLISH/ENGLISH-PULAAR STANDARD DICTIONARY

450 pages • 5 ¹/² x 8 ¹/⁴ • 30,000 entries • 0-7818-0479-5 • W • $19.95pb • (600)

Pushtu *[Pashtu]*

THE MODERN PUSHTU INSTRUCTOR

Script and romanized form
343 pages • 4 x 8 • 0-7818-0204-0 USA • $22.95 • (174)

Sesotho ([Sotho] Lesotho and Southern Africa)

POPULAR NORTHERN SOTHO DICTIONARY: SOTHO-ENGLISH/ ENGLISH-SOTHO
335 pages • 4 3/8 x 5 3/8 • 25,000 entries • 0-627015-867 NA • $14.95pb • (64)

Swahili

SWAHILI PHRASEBOOK
184 pages • 4 x 5 3/8 • 0-87052-970-6 • W • $8.95pb • (73)

BEGINNER'S SWAHILI
200 pages • 5 1/2 x 8 1/2 • 0-7818-0335-7 • W • $9.95pb • (52)
2 Cassettes: • 0-7818-0336-5 • W • $12.95 • (55)

Twi (Ghana)

TWI BASIC COURSE
225 pages • 6 1/2 x 8 1/2 • 0-7818-0394-2 • W • $16.95pb • (65)

TWI-ENGLISH/ ENGLISH-TWI CONCISE DICTIONARY
250 pages • 4 x 6 • 0-7818-0264-4 • W • $12.95pb • (290)